CONSTRUCTING A LEGACY

CONSTRUCTING A LEGACY

THE WEITZ COMPANY AND THE FAMILY WHO BUILT IT

WILLIAM B. FRIEDRICKS

Business Publications Corporation Inc.

Constructing A Legacy:
The Weitz Company and the Family Who Built It is published by
Business Publications Corporation Inc., an Iowa corporation.

ISBN-13: 978-0-9965213-0-7
Library of Congress Control Number: 2015916916
Business Publications Corporation, Des Moines, Iowa

Business Publications Corporation Inc.
The Depot at Fourth
100 4th Street
Des Moines, Iowa 50309
(515) 288-3336

For John and Holly Burns

CONTENTS

Illustrations appear following pages 80 and 155.

ACKNOWLEDGMENTS

There has never been a full-fledged history written about the Weitz Company. Yet it is one of Iowa's oldest firms, founded before the Civil War, which grew to be among the largest general contractors in the nation. Over the years, several Weitzes have written accounts of their ancestors or the business, but their works did not circulate beyond the family. In 1969, Rudy Weitz, then the head of the company, gave a speech in which he suggested that a history of the Weitz Company was needed. The firm, he said, had to that point "endured for 115 years [and] has a lot to report—some good and some bad. Its story should really be told objectively by someone not a principal in the organization." Forty-six years have passed since Rudy's recommendation, and 160 years after the company's founding, its story has finally been told.

I began talking with Fred and Steve Weitz about such a book in 2012, and early the following year, they agreed that I should write it. I was given editorial freedom throughout the project and have done my best to tell the story honestly and fairly.

Members of the Weitz family helped as my research progressed. Fred Weitz was generous with his time, answered countless questions, and opened a number of doors for me. The writings of Greta Weitz Brown and Ann Weitz were good introductions to the family and the company. Steve Weitz, Charles Godfrey Jr., and Bob Weitz provided me with a variety of material.

People at the Weitz Company, Life Care Services (LCS), and Essex Meadows were helpful as well. Special thanks to former

CEO and chairman Glenn DeStigter, Dave Strutt, Tricia McClain, LuAnne Davey, Rhonda Clark-Leyda, and Kevin Foelske at the Weitz Company; Jennifer Beal, Joan Hinners, and Tina Bagenstos at LCS; and Lisa Grieve and Marcia Wing at Essex Meadows.

As he has done before, John Zeller graciously shared research notes, Traci Larsen and Linda Birocci located property records, Becki Plunkett and Shari Stelling assisted me at the State Historical Library and Archives of Iowa, and Burke Shiffler and Marci Behm were especially helpful at the Des Moines Public Library. Susan Berg tracked down an important photo for me. Linda Sinclair transcribed interviews, while others at Simpson College were supportive, including Steve Griffith, Nick Proctor, Becca Livingstone, Judy Walden, Daryl Sasser, and Brian Browning, who unexpectedly passed away this summer. I also am grateful to all who sat for interviews, visited with me by telephone, or gave me access to their personal papers. A list of these individuals is included at the end of the book.

It was again a pleasure working with the staff at Business Publications Corporation. Ashley Holter efficiently managed the project, Adam Feller capably handled the book's layout and design, and Renee Johnson cleaned up my prose and saved me from careless mistakes.

The encouragement of my parents has been a constant over the years; I'm only sorry my mother didn't live long enough to see this book. Once again, my daughters Sarah and Emily endured many stories about another research project. My wife, Jackie, was, as always, devoted and understanding, poring over several rough drafts and offering smart criticism, often punctuated with her good sense of humor. She undoubtedly sharpened the manuscript.

Finally, I'd like to dedicate this book to John and Holly Burns. Their friendship has been steadfast and their support unwavering. Here's to you, John and Holly.

INTRODUCTION

In 1985, Frederick "Fred" Weitz, then chairman and president of the Weitz Company, looked back over his firm's 130-year history. It was Des Moines's oldest company continuously owned and managed by the same family and the oldest construction enterprise west of the Mississippi River. He had every reason to be proud of its longevity, but much like the generations of Weitz men who led it before him, Fred focused on the present and future, noting only, "I suppose when you get right down to it, if there's a reason why we've been successful in growing, it must be because we're doing the job."[1]

On one level, Fred was right: the company succeeded because its leaders, managers, and employees did their jobs. They built quality structures and met or exceeded customer expectations. But there was obviously more to it than that. A number of successful businesses were operating in Des Moines when Karl "Charles" Weitz arrived in the mid-nineteenth century and set up shop. But today, the Weitz Company is the second oldest in the city, founded just six years after the establishment of the *Iowa Star*, a predecessor to the city's present newspaper, the *Des Moines Register*.[2]

How did the Weitz Company endure while the rest of these firms, save one, fell by the wayside? According to the *Des Moines Register*, the city's "oldest companies are a testament to the founders and families that created and sustained them." Clearly, the Weitz family was a key reason for the company's success. Beginning with Charles, the clan created a strong familial stake in the company and then, over the generations, identified and developed family members with a passion and talent for running the firm. Through war and peace, good times and bad, the company remained family owned, building and rebuilding Des Moines and adapting to the changing marketplace. It also grew, branching out well beyond its home base to become one of the nation's fifty largest contractors by the mid-1990s.[3]

Engineering News-Record, the standard source for the construction business, added, "The secret to longevity for…contractors is finding the right mix of hubris and humble pie, creating a culture of adaptable entrepreneurs that can change with the times and preserve the company for future generations without letting greed get out of control." Charles Weitz and his descendants did just that; they took risks and innovated, they had vision but made pragmatic adjustments as necessary, and they enjoyed some good luck. All of these elements proved important to establishing and building the firm.[4]

The story began in 1849. Charles Weitz, a German carpenter who had been conscripted into the Hessian army two years earlier, was shot and injured on the battlefield. After recovering, he decided against returning to the fight. Instead, he gambled that he could make a better life for himself in the United States. The following year he deserted, evaded capture, and crossed the Atlantic, initially settling in Ohio. Several years later, when he read that Iowa's capital was being relocated to Des Moines, Charles realized that the move would create opportunities. Gambling again, he headed to Des Moines in 1855. When he could not find a job, he hung out his own shingle and founded the company.

Charles became involved in the town's building sector early. This factor, combined with the connections and contacts he made within Des Moines's sizable German community, brought him clients. After several initial jobs, such as the remodeling of a drugstore, word of his quality craftsmanship spread, and Charles won more and more work. Within months, he was employing seven carpenters. And he had guessed right: the move of the state capital to Des Moines brought growth, and Charles and his business were well positioned to grow as well. Small carpentry jobs gave way to larger ones, and soon Charles was erecting homes, commercial buildings, mercantile shops, schools, and churches. By the 1870s, he had changed his signage and letterhead to reflect these larger projects, and "Charles Weitz: Carpenter and Builder" became "Charles Weitz: Practical Builder and Contractor."

Still, competition was stiff among Des Moines contractors, and Charles was not involved in all the important buildings being erected in the city. For example, he had nothing to do with the state capitol or the new city hall, which went up in the 1880s. But his business was growing, and he readied the next generation to succeed him. While sons Charlie, Fred, and Edward learned the business and moved up in the company, Charles became involved in other endeavors including local banking and city government. Yet construction remained his primary concern, and by the 1890s, the firm was focused almost entirely on commercial work, putting up, for example, the downtown Younkers department store. Unfortunately, this original portion of the Des Moines landmark was completely destroyed by a 2014 fire.

Shortly before his sons took over the construction business, Charles had the foresight to establish a companion firm called Century Lumber. The company filled a niche, supplying Weitz and other contractors with building materials. But the family patriarch also understood that the Weitz firm could not be run by committee, and he saw the lumber business as a means to fend off possible conflicts between his three sons. Thus, when Charles retired and gave the construction operation to his sons in 1903, they were equal partners in the enterprise, but Fred served as managing partner and ran the business. The brothers also shared ownership of Century Lumber, with Charles and later Edward overseeing that venture. The scheme worked; the brothers consulted each other but concentrated on their particular jobs, and both businesses thrived.

Fred continued to lead "Charles Weitz' Sons," as the company became known, down the path his father had established even as the projects grew larger and more complex. The firm continued working at the Iowa State Fairgrounds—where in 1902, it had constructed the Livestock Pavilion—by erecting the iconic Agriculture Building two years later. Downtown, Fred enjoyed success where his father had failed, winning the job to build Des Moines's new city hall in 1909. Other prominent projects followed with Weitz' Sons erecting the Hotel Fort Des Moines and Drake University's field house and stadium.

More importantly, however, Fred saw opportunities in federal contracts and began actively seeking such work. In 1905, the firm was awarded the first of several jobs for the United States Army at Fort Des Moines and, ten years later, got a big boost when Fred won his initial contract to build a US post office. Post office work proved critical for the company, which built dozens of them across the country over the next couple of decades.

This background and the respect the family and firm had garnered in the community and among fellow contractors meant Weitz' Sons led the way in successfully lobbying federal officials to convert Camp Dodge—a small Iowa National Guard post north of Des Moines—into one of several national cantonments during

World War I. The company also won the job and led a consortium of Iowa contractors in the rapid expansion of the vast installation.

After the war and through the 1920s, Fred's sons Rudolph "Rudy" and Heinrich finished their education and joined the firm to be primed to follow in their father's footsteps. Eldest son Rudy took the lead, and by the mid-1930s he was heading the firm.

Renamed the Weitz Company, the business struggled through the dark days of the Great Depression. Jobs were scarce. Fortunately, several post office contracts helped keep it afloat. Business picked up late in the decade, but it took another war and more work for the federal government before the company was back on solid footing. The first such job was constructing the Des Moines Ordnance Plant, an expansive complex in Des Moines's northern suburb of Ankeny. Other military and defense-related contracts followed.

Now in good shape, the firm flourished during the war and in the succeeding economic boom. Rudy's connections and the company's solid reputation brought plenty of work. In greater Des Moines, for example, the company converted the Des Moines Ordnance Plant to a John Deere factory, constructed a major addition to the Register and Tribune Building, and built numerous structures for local school districts as well as regional colleges and universities.

But Rudy was not one to stand by and merely ride the wave of prosperity. He pushed the company into new areas, employing the latest building techniques and materials that cut construction time, and because of the continuing housing shortage, erected apartment buildings and managed them.

While not losing sight of his firm's core construction business, Rudy continued pursuing other prospects. In the late 1950s, he bought Midwest Concrete Industries, a fabricator of architectural precast concrete panels, and expanded the operation into a large regional supplier of these building components. Several years later, Rudy learned of the lack of modern bulk grain storage facilities in developing nations and bought Jones-Hettelsater, a Kansas City firm specializing in such construction. He then traveled the globe selling the services of this new subsidiary and landed a number of contracts, including a large design and build project in what is now Bangladesh. Neither of these ventures lived up to expectations, however, and both were ultimately sold in the 1970s.

Meanwhile, Fred Weitz, Rudy's oldest son, had joined the family firm. While looking for jobs in the early 1960s, he and his father were introduced to the relatively new concept of continuing care retirement communities. Fred saw potential here and, with Rudy's blessing, gradually moved the company into the business of building senior living complexes. This interest later evolved into a subsidiary called Life Care Services (LCS), which developed, built, managed, and eventually owned retirement communities. It soon became an engine of growth and expansion for the company.

By the time Rudy died in 1974, Fred had already taken over the helm. Much like his predecessors, he remained committed to his home market, and over the next twenty years, the company built a number of the city's well-known structures, including the Civic Center of Greater Des Moines, Capital Square, the State Historical Building, and Prairie Meadows Race Track. But Fred was also intent on growing the firm. Critical to this vision was his ability to hire and retain talented employees.

Over the years, the Weitz Company had been successful in this area, but it had also lost capable staff to rivals. To avoid this and keep key executives, Fred broke with family tradition and offered top managers a financial stake in the company through a stock purchase plan. The strategy worked, and the expansion began. Fred added a nonunion shop to attract new work and established branch offices in Arizona, Florida, and Massachusetts, where the company had been building retirement communities. Shortly thereafter, the Weitz Company moved into the Denver, Colorado, market with the purchase of Al Cohen Construction.

The resulting growth was significant: Fred took a state and regional company with annual revenues of $24 million in 1975 and built it into the forty-fifth largest contractor in the country in 1995 with revenues of $303 million. This expansion was carefully planned, and when the down economy of the late 1980s and early 1990s forced seven thousand US contractors out of business, the Weitz Company trimmed it sails and pushed forward.[5]

However, the Weitz story was not always one of steady success. The company experienced its share of problems and endured false starts, setbacks, and dead ends. Costly lawsuits were brought against them, contracts sometimes went to rivals, and business ventures did not always pan out. There were disagreements and personality clashes among the Weitzes, and during the Great Depression, the company was forced into receivership and reorganization. But through all of these issues, the family persevered and kept its business going and growing.

Fred believed the family had been lucky to produce company leaders for over four generations, but his ambition went beyond simply prolonging family ownership. He wanted to develop a larger and stronger business than the one he had inherited. From his experience at the Harvard Business School, he knew that this required a meritocracy, where the company's most capable managers could rise to the top but also required sharing ownership with them. Ultimately the Weitz family sold their shares in the company to the employees, and the operation was broken up and sold, with the transfer of the two major units—the construction group, still called the Weitz Company, and Life Care Services—taking place in 1995. Although this was what Fred had wanted, the sale ended an era, bringing to a close 140 years of family ownership of the firm.

As he had hoped, LCS remained in employee hands and went forward successfully. But the Weitz Company did not. After a decade of rapid growth, it ran into serious trouble, dragged down by the deep recession that began in 2007. These difficulties prompted its sale. In 2012, it was purchased by Orascom Construction Industries, a multinational giant then based in Egypt. The Weitz Company remained headquartered in Des Moines, but it was now part of an overseas corporation. Local ownership and control of the firm came to a close, ending another era for the historic Iowa enterprise.

CONSTRUCTING A LEGACY
THE WEITZ COMPANY AND THE FAMILY WHO BUILT IT

Chapter One

OLD WORLD TO NEW

By 1840, fourteen-year-old Karl Weitz already had his future laid out. He planned on being a carpenter and began the process by apprenticing with a local craftsman. After several years of training, he became a journeyman, hoping to earn enough to establish his own shop. But events intervened. Economic, social, and political turmoil shook Central Europe, shattering the traditional world Weitz had hoped to enter. From 1840 to 1860, more than four million people abandoned the old world in favor of the new and came to the United States. Nearly three-quarters of these immigrants were from Ireland or the German states. One of them was Karl Weitz, who joined the exodus to America in 1850. Once he arrived, he followed the path laid out by earlier German immigrants, initially settling in Ohio and later, in 1855, blazing his own trail to Fort Des Moines, Iowa.[1]

Karl Weitz was born to Heinrich and Anna Elizabetha Weitz on May 4, 1826. He was the youngest of the family's four children. The Weitzes had a modest stocking weaving operation in Schotten, a small town thirty miles northeast of Frankfurt in the then Grand Duchy of Hesse. His brothers and sisters, Katharina, Johannes, and Christian, all worked in the business, but as Karl was growing up, the family firm faced increasingly difficult times. Following the Napoleonic Wars, Central Europe had been inundated with cheap textiles from the mechanized mills in England, and the Weitz business was likely undercut by the inexpensive English goods. Later, with the *Zollverein*, or German Customs Union, established in 1834, internal tariffs throughout the member German states were eliminated, and a high tariff wall protected the zone from goods imported into the region. While this all but ended competition from foreign nations, it also increased the rivalry between companies within the union, and the Weitzes now confronted competition from larger and more efficient textile manufacturers within the zone.

By the time Karl completed his elementary education, it was clear that a position at the family firm was not a possibility, nor was continuing his education. Indeed, only 1 percent of young males at the time were able to do so. Tuition was high, and very few families could afford to support their adolescent sons in school instead of having them earn an income. Instead, Karl and his parents decided he should learn a trade, and at fourteen, he became an apprentice to a local carpenter in Schotten. Here he learned all aspects of the business.[2]

After four years with an artisan, Karl completed his training. Equipped with his own set of tools, he went out on his own as a journeyman. The path to becoming a master craftsman now mandated that he travel the countryside, perfecting his skills by working for other carpenters. This required the purchase of a *Wanderbuch*, or journey book, which served both as an official government-issued travel book and resume. Like a passport, it contained vital information about the holder—at eighteen years old, the blond-haired, blue-eyed Karl had an "emerging beard" and was six foot six, exceptionally tall for the time—authorizing him to move from town to town. Local officials stamped the book when the bearer entered or left the region. When a suitable opportunity arose, Karl would turn his *Wanderbuch* over to the master craftsman who would keep it until the job was completed. The artisan might comment in the *Wanderbuch* about the quality of the journeyman's work or his comportment, and then return the book, sending Karl off to look for another job.[3]

Karl purchased his *Wanderbuch* in early 1844 and prepared for his travels, but his timing could hardly have been worse as it corresponded with major upheavals in Central Europe. Population growth had outpaced job opportunities, and real wages had fallen by 20 percent since the mid-1820s. Crop failures in the 1840s made matters worse, and the continent fell into a deep recession. Meanwhile, industrialization pushed forward, upending the traditional world. Increasingly independent artisans saw the value of their skills decline as mechanization changed the way products were made. Cabinetmakers, for instance, who once made entire pieces of furniture from start to finish, might now be hired by factory owners to complete a cabinet that had been roughed out by unskilled labor aided by machinery. This decrease of independence and status for craftsmen blurred the once distinct lines between masters and journeymen.[4]

Over the first several decades of the nineteenth century, fewer and fewer journeymen were able to earn enough to become independent master craftsmen. The resulting oversupply of journeymen would make it more difficult for Karl to find work. And when he did find a job, his wages were probably in the piece-rate form, with the larger, better-capitalized masters now able to extract longer hours from their workers. Nonetheless, Karl left Schotten in early February 1844, heading south and west. He initially stopped in Darmstadt, a town outside of Frankfurt, on his way toward Heidelberg.

But two weeks into his journey, he ran into trouble in Mannheim, when an official discovered Karl was traveling without any money. This was a violation of vagrancy laws of the time. He noted the problem in the young man's *Wanderbuch* and ordered the penniless journeyman out of the city. The reprimand evidently had an impact, for there were no other negative comments made in his *Wanderbuch*.[5]

Karl then moved south to Karlsruhe, the capital of Baden on the Rhine River. Here he found work and stayed for several weeks before continuing along the river toward Switzerland. The move made sense; the Rhine was a major commercial artery, which grew in importance after steamboats first plied its waters in the 1830s, and the prospects for work would be better along the hustle and bustle of the waterway. Over the next fifteen months, Karl worked his way south, largely taking jobs in villages along the river, until he reached Lorrach, a German town near the Swiss and French border.[6]

In mid-1845, it appeared that his training and travels would be cut short when he received notice of military conscription to begin the following year. However, when Karl sent his *Wanderbuch* in for annual review in early 1846, it was renewed for another year, and he was able to postpone his entry into the army until 1847. By then he was in Switzerland, having crossed into Basel in the summer of 1845. Through the spring of 1846 he worked in several Swiss towns, including Neuchatel and Geneva, and then turned north to head back home. He found jobs in the town of Darmstadt that summer and in Heidelberg and then Speyer through January 1847, when he returned to Schotten to take up his required duties in the army. Unfortunately, his time in the military coincided with a period of unrest and revolution that swept across Europe at midcentury.[7]

Several poor potato harvests, changes wrought by industrialization, and the economic slump led to increasing frustration. Peasants and a growing urban proletariat focused on improving their living and working conditions, while those in the new middle class sought greater political freedom and representative government. The situation first boiled over in Paris when demonstrations broke out in February 1848. Crowds clashed with police and erected barricades. When the army was called out, it refused to fight, and King Louis Philippe abdicated. This victory of liberal forces in France led to a republic and encouraged similar action across the continent.[8]

At the time, there were thirty-nine sovereign German states, loosely tied together by the German Confederation. Karl had been drafted into the army of Hesse-Darmstadt and was assigned to the fifth squadron of its light cavalry in the spring of 1847, a year before rebellions broke out in Central Europe. In March 1848, the King of Prussia responded to rioting in Berlin by promising a constitution and backing national unification. Smaller German states had answered growing discontent by appointing liberal ministers as well.[9]

Buoyed by these moves, German nationalists called a "pre-parliament" to discuss plans for a German National Assembly with the hopes of creating a constitutionally governed, unified German nation. Meanwhile, rulers in Bavaria, Hohenzollern-Sigmaringen, Nassau, Saxe-Meiningen, and Württemberg faced uprisings, but it was Baden that briefly became the center of revolution. There in April, lawyer Friedrich Hecker and politician and journalist Gustav Struve—both unhappy when the pre-parliament failed to take up plans for radical reform—declared a republic in Baden and rallied a small group of supporters in the town of Constance. Their hope of stirring a mass uprising did not materialize, however, and soldiers from Baden and neighboring Hesse-Darmstadt, including Karl's unit, quelled the rebellion in eight days. Both rebel leaders ended up in Switzerland. Hecker soon immigrated to the United States, becoming one of the so-called Forty-Eighters—radical republican reformers who fled Germany for America when the revolutions failed. Struve tried leading another revolt in Baden that September. It was again put down by government forces, and Struve was arrested. Karl's unit apparently did not see action in this altercation.[10]

But the next year he did. A third and much larger insurrection broke out in Baden the following May 1849. This time, thousands of rebels, including many disaffected journeymen and artisans, had the support of many of Baden's soldiers who had mutinied. The Grand Duke of Baden fled and asked for Prussian intervention to restore order. It sent an army, assisted by troops from several other states including Hesse-Darmstadt. Even though rebel forces were outnumbered by at least three to one, the fighting dragged on for a couple of months. Karl may very well have sympathized with some of the journeymen and craftsmen rebels he was sent to subdue, but he left no record of this. It is known, however, that he was injured in the fighting, probably that June 1849, when Karl and the Hessian light cavalry were forced to retreat through Käfertal Forest, just outside Mannheim. Karl was shot in the upper left leg and hospitalized at Darmstadt. His recovery, he noted, took one hundred days.[11]

The rebellion in Baden was finally suppressed a month after Karl's injury, marking the end of insurgences in Germany. By 1850, it was clear that the revolutions begun in 1848 had failed and the old order was being restored. Meanwhile, during his three-month convalescence, Karl had a lot of time on his hands, and he may have begun reevaluating his situation and that of his homeland. His future in Germany appeared uncertain, and perhaps it was then that he started considering immigrating to the United States. This thinking could have been prompted by one or more of the many emigrant guidebooks touting the benefits of moving to America that were circulating extensively throughout the German territories by the 1840s.[12] These travel guides praised the United States for its widely available land, good soil, healthful climate, low taxes, and plentiful jobs, accolades that were reinforced by a large number of glowing letters sent home from friends and relatives who had already made the move.

A minister captured the feelings of many Germans at midcentury: "The name of America has now become as familiar to every peasant and laborer, yea to every child in the street, as that of the nearest neighboring country, whilst to thousands and hundreds of thousands, it is a goal of their warmest wishes and boldest hopes."[13]

By the fall, Karl had recuperated enough to return to his unit, although with a slight limp that remained with him the rest of his life. He was with the cavalry for several months before receiving leave to go home at the beginning of March 1850. While there, he noted simply, "I decided—because of the many, in my opinion, unjust demands—not to obey the government and to trade my homeland with a different one." Planning such a trip would have been complex, and although he came to the final decision while visiting his family, Karl undoubtedly had been ruminating over relocating in the United States for some time.[14]

More and more Germans, in fact, were moving to America, and the growing numbers may have influenced Karl to do so as well. Early-nineteenth-century emigration had come mainly from the southwestern German states such as Baden, Bavaria, and

Württemberg, but slowed in the 1820s, only to pick up again with the mounting economic and social changes of the 1830s and 1840s. Nearly six hundred thousand Germans immigrated to America over these two decades. No longer just from the southwestern kingdoms and duchies, the exodus now spread north and east into Franconia, Hanover, Hesse-Darmstadt, Hesse-Kassel, Oldenburg, and Westphalia as well.[15]

A number of factors pushed these emigrants out of Central Europe. Some, like the Forty-Eighters, left for political reasons, and others departed to escape military duty, but the majority made the journey for better economic prospects. Historian Roger Daniels explained that it was the "economics of prosperity, not of poverty, that impelled most of them." He was referring to the many people who saw the forces of industrialization and urbanization ending their traditional way of life. Rather than deal with declining opportunities or trying a new line of work, they saw migration as "a rational alternative." And unlike most of the poor, unskilled Irish emigrants who were pushed out of their homeland by the infamous Potato Famine, many of these Germans were skilled workers.[16]

Karl fit right within this group of emigrants. Although dodging further military service was also an issue for him, the difficult economy he witnessed during his journeyman years and worry about his future must have been uppermost in his mind. In fact, this interest in improving one's fortune was weighing on his older brother too. Industrialization had battered many smaller businesses such as the Weitzes' weaving operation, which closed in 1850, probably a victim of larger, mechanized competition. His brother Christian, therefore, would have been looking for other opportunities as well, and while it is not clear who came up with the idea first, the brothers decided to travel to the United States together.[17]

The two set out in early March, but the journey was complicated. Because Karl had deserted the army, he could not obtain the necessary government-issued emigration documents, which required, among other things, proof that he had satisfactorily fulfilled his military duty. Thus the Weitz brothers were traveling illegally, and while Karl noted that "there was severe persecution and checking by Swiss and Darmstadt police and gendarme," the two evaded capture. But that was one of the only comments he made about the trip, and it is not clear the route he and his brother traveled. At the time, most German emigrants went to Holland, crossed the channel to Hull, England, and then went to Liverpool by rail, where they boarded ships for America. Although this was the most popular and competitively priced route, the Weitz brothers probably made their way to England through the French port of Le Havre, which was often used by those traveling illegally because its officials were much more lax about passport regulations than those at Dutch or German harbors.[18]

From the continent, Karl and Christian went to London, where they embarked for America. They arrived in New York City at the end of March 1850. The brothers spent only eight days in the city; maybe that was their intention all along or maybe they found the metropolis of a half million people overwhelming. Regardless, they continued their journey west, probably by train and probably following advice gleaned from guidebooks or word from earlier German settlers. They passed through the cities of Buffalo and Cleveland, each with sizable German settlements, as they made their way toward what historical geographers sometimes call the German triangle, the region between the cities of Milwaukee, Saint Louis, and Cincinnati.

But the Weitzes did not travel that far south or west. Instead, Karl and Christian stopped in Ashland, Ohio, about sixty-five miles southwest of Cleveland.[19]

Ohio had a large German population by the mid-nineteenth century, and this must have been a lure for Karl and his brother. As many others before them, the two would have appreciated staying among those from the same culture and who spoke the same language. Interestingly, at least one source challenged this idea, explaining that Karl had become fluent in both French and English during his journeyman years in the mid-1840s, which would have made settling among Germans less necessary. The account seems improbable, however. English was rarely spoken in the areas Karl had traveled, and although he may have picked up some French along the Rhine River or in Switzerland, it was not likely he mastered either language.[20]

It is unclear exactly why the brothers first settled in Ashland, although there are some clues to its appeal. Incorporated just six years before their arrival, Ashland was a small county seat of 1,300 people, located in the middle of a broad settlement belt where Germans made up between 50 and 75 percent of the population. Its relative small size, coupled with its large German population and the economic activity generated by its local government services, would have made Ashland a logical place for Karl and Christian to reside.[21]

Here the two gradually adjusted to their new country. Karl worked as a finish carpenter, probably with or for other German immigrants, while Christian may have worked with his brother in carpentry or taken jobs at local farms or factories. Karl still wrote in German, but he was likely picking up English and was certainly interested in assimilating, as suggested by his application for naturalization. He applied for citizenship at the courthouse in Ashland sometime in 1851. At the time, becoming a citizen was a straightforward, two-step process. It required that the applicant appear before a local court of record, declare his intention to become a citizen, and renounce allegiance to his former country. Then after several years of residence, the applicant had to reappear before a court to swear he had been a good citizen. An oath of allegiance was administered following the sworn statement, and United States citizenship was granted. Karl completed the process in 1855. Indicative of the Americanization process, his naturalization papers referred to him as Charles—the English version of Karl—Weitz.[22]

But that was a few years down the road. Sometime after initially applying for citizenship in 1851, Karl and his brother moved eighty miles southwest to Columbus, the state's capital. With a population of eighteen thousand, the much-larger city would have offered many more opportunities. Karl found a variety of carpentry work and built several homes in Columbus, sometimes working alone and later as part of the small construction firm of Raden and Whikhoe. Sometime in 1853, that business broke up, and Karl partnered with a man named Riarden. Payment in kind sometimes substituted for payment in wages, and it appears that much of his work was done for other Germans, including, for example, people with such surnames as Kuchendorfer, Bachman, Schmidt, and Mecktown.[23]

Much of this work, and in fact much of Karl's life in Columbus, undoubtedly revolved around the area south of downtown, originally referred to as "das alte Süd Ende," or the Old South End, but now called the German Village. The several hundred acres were first platted in the early nineteenth century, and most of the lots were purchased by the large number of German immigrants coming into the city. By the time Karl arrived in Columbus, he and other German immigrants would have felt right at home in the Old South End. Here, "people spoke German in the stores, schools, and churches; their homes were solid yet unpretentious. After work, bakers, stonecutters, storekeepers, carpenters, tanners, bricklayers, and brewery workers relaxed in nearby biergartens. Most belonged to gymnastic and singing societies. This simple yet distinctive working-class neighborhood was a little bit of Germany."[24]

Although there is no record of where Karl lived in Columbus, one can reasonably assume that he resided and socialized among other Germans in the Old South End. This was most likely where he met Helena Kinnel, the woman who later became his wife. Helena was born in 1834 in Bavaria, and her parents brought the family to the United States the following year, eventually settling in Columbus. While little is known about how Karl and Helena became acquainted or how long they courted, they married in the summer of 1854. Interestingly, the wedding seemed to reflect Karl's desire to maintain his German culture while at the same time embrace his new land. The two were married in the German English Evangelical Lutheran Church situated near Third and Mound Streets, which at the time conducted its Sunday services solely in German, so it can be safely assumed that the wedding ceremony was in German as well. But in an apparent nod to their adopted country, the two married on the fourth of July, 1854.[25]

While Karl's time in the United States had been spent almost entirely in Ohio, his next move was serendipitous and would take him off this beaten Germanic path. In January 1855, the Iowa legislature passed a law relocating the seat of state government from Iowa City to Fort Des Moines (the name would be shortened to Des Moines in January 1857). A newspaper account of the move caught Karl's eye. After living in both a county seat and a state capital, he knew that there were economic advantages to working in a city where government services were based. Des Moines would require a lot of construction, and carpenters, Karl probably thought, would be in great demand. According to one source, he exclaimed upon seeing the news, "That is the place for me. The new capital city shall be my future home. I will go to Iowa and grow up with the country." Once Karl and his wife, Helena, decided to make the move, Christian, who was living with them at the time, chose to join them on the trip to Des Moines.[26]

The threesome headed west, taking a train to Cincinnati at the end of March 1855. They then boarded a steamboat and traveled down the Ohio River to the Mississippi, where they turned upstream until they reached Keokuk, Iowa. There they disembarked, and with no railroads yet crossing into the state, they took a mule-drawn wagon for the last 175 miles to Fort Des Moines, arriving on April 5 in a town that Karl described as "a settlement of 1,500 souls." Although he could not have known it at the time, his years of wandering were over. He would, as he had optimistically suggested, build and develop his business as the city and state grew over the coming decades.[27]

Chapter Two

BUILDING A BUSINESS

Whether it was an entrepreneurial flair or wanderlust left over from his youth, Charles Weitz, as he now called himself, saw what he thought were opportunities in Des Moines and moved there in 1855 to seize them. But when he arrived in town, his enthusiasm must have been dampened. That same year, writer Tacitus Hussey came to Des Moines as well and described the small village as a "dirty, smoky little place."

Still, there were positive prospects. As Iowa moved toward statehood in 1846, Des Moines, the largest settlement in newly formed Polk County, was named the county seat. That put it in line with the last two places Charles had called home in Ohio. Des Moines received another boost in 1853, when the federal government established a land office there and began selling newly opened Iowa land for $1.25 per acre. The office generated a lot of activity, bringing thousands of buyers through the community, while the city's central location eventually earned it the prized designation of state capital.[1]

Regardless of Hussey's jibe, Charles had arrived at a good time, for Des Moines was just moving beyond the frontier stage. Incorporated only four years earlier, in 1851, the town's origins dated back to the founding of Fort Des Moines at the confluence of the Des Moines and Raccoon Rivers in 1843. Two US Army companies—one of dragoons and one of infantry— were based at the outpost to maintain peace on the frontier. Although the fort was never intended to be permanent, a small community developed around it, and when it was abandoned in early 1846, settlers moved into the vacant buildings. That December, Iowa achieved statehood, and Des Moines's population stood at 127 people.[2]

By the mid-1850s, Des Moines had grown more than ten times. A main business district consisting largely of small shops, stores, and offices had been established along Second Street south of Court Avenue. The center of activity was at the juncture with Market Street just north and west of "The Point," where the Des Moines and Raccoon Rivers met. Larger structures included two boarding hotels, the Everett House, located a couple of blocks north and west near Third and Walnut Streets, and the Demoine House, which sat at the corner of Walnut and Front Streets. These were all wood frame structures; one of the few brick buildings in town was the county courthouse, situated to the west at Cherry and Fifth Streets.[3]

A building boom ensued with the announcement that the state capital was moving to the city, and Des Moines's emerging elite began erecting a number of larger structures. These included the community's first brick business and retail center, a three-story building located at "The Point," completed in early 1855. More impressive and important was the first brick business block also erected that year. Called the Exchange Block, it was built on the corner of Third and Walnut Streets. Soon housing two banks, the US Land Office, a dry goods store, a grocery store, a pharmacy, law offices, the justice of the peace, a saloon, as well as fraternal halls for the Masons and Odd Fellows, the Exchange Block was the finest business facility in town and nudged the center of the growing commercial district toward the north and west.[4]

This increasing activity brought a growing number of immigrants to Des Moines. At the time, writer H. B. Turrill noted, "Men of all classes...men of all professions...from the keen Connecticut clock-peddler, to the broad-faced German, just from 'Der Faderland,' are incessantly crowding toward Iowa." Then, focusing on Des Moines, he continued, "Carpenters, stone-cutters, brick-layers, painters, plasterers, and such other mechanics as are required in erecting and completing buildings are in good demand" and would be compensated well.[5]

This optimistic tone notwithstanding, Charles had trouble finding work once he and his wife arrived in Des Moines in April 1855. After making arrangements to board with a Mr. Esterling, who agreed that Charles could do odd jobs around the house in exchange for their rent, he surely headed down to the business district in search of employment. But he was not successful; no one was hiring. Others found the job market difficult as well. A month later in May, for instance, sixteen-year-old Frederick Marion Hubbell—who became one of Des Moines's leading business figures and by century's end was the state's richest person—walked these same streets struggling to find a job, until with his last inquiry, he landed a position as an office boy at the federal land office.[6]

Out of options, Charles went into business for himself. From his time in Ashland and then Columbus, he had learned the significance of building relationships, especially within the German community, for finding jobs and creating opportunities. He also understood that flexibility was important, and by now he could do all types of carpentry work, from framing homes to finish work and cabinetry. Charles took these lessons to heart in Des Moines, first among the town's Germans and then more broadly with others in its business and civic circles. Connections made in these early years led to friendships, but also to clients, associates, and, importantly, repeat customers, helping Charles build his business and spread the word about his quality craftsmanship.

Initially Charles moved easily among the town's large numbers of Germans, which local historian Paul Ashby estimated made up roughly 60 percent of the population. Several days after arriving, Charles met Francis Grimmel and bought a lot at Eighth and Pleasant Streets from him for $450. A successful physician and one of the largest landowners in town, Grimmel had immigrated to the United States from the German kingdom of Hanover in 1833. He first settled in Maryland before being drawn to the large German settlements in Ohio in 1839. Seven years later, he moved to Des Moines, and like other early settlers, he and his family initially moved into the abandoned fort. Specifically they took up residence in the guard house, where Grimmel established a drugstore, before acquiring a number of acres and building a home northwest of the downtown area. It was in this section, soon known as Grimmel's Addition, that Charles bought his lot. The doctor allowed him to pay for the land by doing carpentry work, and with the money he had saved, Charles hired his brother Christian and a Joseph Lanz to help him build the structure.[7]

His carpentry work impressed both Esterling and Grimmel, and they soon began recommending Charles to friends and acquaintances. This word of mouth, coupled with continuing growth and prosperity in the community, won Charles business, which usually consisted of small carpentry jobs, until merchant Charles Good hired him to do substantial work on his drugstore at Second and Market Streets. Besides putting in new windows, Charles did extensive work inside, repairing and facing the stairs, and redoing the counter, shelving, and drawers in a rich black walnut. Good and his customers were apparently happy with the craftsmanship, for jobs picked up for Charles, and by the fall of 1855, he had seven journeymen and laborers working for him. That December, business had grown to the point that he needed a dedicated work space, so he purchased a lot and building at 119 Third Street, between Court Avenue and Vine Street, and set up a shop for "Charles Weitz, Builder and Carpenter."[8]

Not surprisingly, many of Charles's other initial clients were fellow Germans, including, for example, people named Felsen, Kufner, Holkamp, and Kessler, as well as businesses Warner & Co. and the Stutsman Co. One early exception was James C. Savery, owner of the Everett House. Charles had done some work at the hotel owner's home in 1855, and the following year, when Savery and a group of investors began building a grand hotel that would bear his name at Walnut and Fourth Streets, Charles installed the building's basement windows. Still, he continued finding eager customers among the city's Germans, doing carpentry work and "put[ting] up a building 16 by 32 feet from out to out" for Mr. Maierhoff and a house for Mr. Kepner.[9]

Charles actively worked to expand his client base. One significant effort was being awarded the Catholic church contract. Because of the town's brief history, many churches were still in their infancy and just beginning to erect their first buildings. A parish had been established in 1854, and the church acquired land on the southeast corner of Locust and Sixth Streets. Father George A. Plathe was sent to the new Saint Ambrose parish and led the effort to build a sanctuary. By 1856, he had the money in hand, and that spring he hired Charles for the job. Although only a small frame facility, it was another public display of Charles's quality workmanship.[10]

While his work was starting to speak for itself, Charles also quietly networked within the small community. Francis Grimmel must have played a role here, as he had evidently befriended Charles from the outset and looked out for him since his arrival in Des Moines. It was most likely Grimmel who helped connect Charles with the town's nascent English Lutheran Church. Grimmel was a leading proponent of the denomination and held an organizational meeting at his home in 1854. The small group first met in the public school building at Locust and Ninth Streets and struggled over the years until the church was formally established in 1865. Two years later, a building was erected at Grand and Seventh Streets. The name was changed to Saint John's Lutheran Church in 1881, and the congregation moved to its present location at Sixth Street and Keo Way in 1890.[11]

Ties with the Lutheran church suggested that Charles was also involved in its efforts to establish a denominational college in Des Moines. Though the group ultimately failed to raise adequate funds and the property was eventually turned over to the local Baptists, who established Des Moines College at the site, work on this project put Charles in contact with a number of the town's prominent figures. Others involved in the effort included attorney and land dealer Phineas Casady, pioneer banker Francis R. West, and Presbyterian minister Thompson Bird, who had also served as the town's first mayor.[12]

Interestingly, a German Evangelical Lutheran Church was established in Des Moines in 1859, but Charles and Grimmel remained connected with the group that would eventually establish the English Lutheran Church, probably because the German church forbade membership in secret societies or fraternal organizations. And Charles had already joined one of these secret societies;

in October 1856, he was initiated into Des Moines's Independent Order of Odd Fellows (IOOF). Here he met and socialized with other members of the business elite, including merchant and banker Benjamin F. Allen.[13]

Connections and early success notwithstanding, other events had a more immediate impact on Charles and the rest of the city's business community. First was the decision to situate the capitol on the east side of the Des Moines River "within two miles from the juncture of the Des Moines and Raccoon rivers." Governor James Grimes appointed a five-member commission in 1856 and charged it with selecting a specific site for the building. Those on the west side of the river in Fort Des Moines, including Francis Grimmel, Francis West, banker Hoyt Sherman, coal dealer Wesley Redhead, and R. L. Tidrick lobbied hard and donated ground. Together, they offered twenty acres to the state as well as additional land at favorable rates. Charles supported their efforts but had no land to donate to the cause.[14]

Meanwhile, leaders on the east side of the river—which at the time was a separate community and not part of Fort Des Moines—proposed a donation of ten acres to the state and the lease of a $35,000 building on the ground for use as the capitol for $1 per year. When the east siders won the capitol, a number of Fort Des Moines businessmen, including Charles, cried foul and suggested that fraud and bribery had carried the day. The decision stood, however, and the rivalry between the two communities remained until January 1857, when the town of Fort Des Moines gave way to the city of Des Moines, bringing the west and east side communities together. Writer H. B. Turrill estimated that the new city limits were seven times larger than the original town, whose population now stood at about 3,500.[15]

Ordinarily, such expansion and the addition of a state capital would have led to economic growth and prosperity, but the failure of the Ohio Life Insurance and Trust Company in the summer of 1857 sparked a national financial panic. Amid the larger problems, including a growing surplus of American manufactured goods and shrinking European markets for US grain, concerned banks began calling in loans and tightening credit. These factors, combined with mounting fear, led to a deep depression; prices fell, factories closed, construction slowed, businesses went under, and unemployment soared.

The downturn reached Des Moines by the fall of 1857, ending a boom the town had enjoyed since 1854. According to journalist Will Porter, "A check was at once placed on all speculation in lots and land," while historian John Larson noted more broadly that "by the end of 1857, business was at a standstill in Iowa." As credit dried up and prices plummeted, many planned projects in Des Moines were shelved and those underway were halted. Such was the case with the Savery House; Charles had put basement windows in the new hotel in 1856, but when depression set in, hotel investors found themselves short of cash, and construction stopped. The partially completed hotel finally opened for business in 1862 but was not finished until three years later.[16]

Charles managed to struggle through the first years of the depression, which lasted into the early 1860s, by remaining flexible and seeking money-making prospects. Although he sometimes landed large contracts—erecting a storeroom and a store front for butcher John Gottschalk; commercial buildings for Rawson and Christy and woolen manufacturer W. W. Carpenter; and homes for George Sneer, a stepson of Grimmel, and stone mason John Roof—most of his work consisted of smaller carpentry tasks, such

23

as hanging doors, installing windows, or putting in shelves. One of these jobs acquainted him with Conrad Youngerman, a stonecutter who had hired Charles in 1859 to install casing and shelving. The two men discovered they shared a similar background and quickly became close friends and associates. Also born and raised in the Hessian region of Germany, Youngerman had completed his primary education and, like Charles, learned a trade—in his case, stonecutting—through apprenticing and then traveling about the country as a journeyman. Youngerman had immigrated to America in 1854 and worked briefly in New York before heading to Ohio. Three years later, he moved to Des Moines. In 1860, Youngerman went into the brickmaking business and become one of the city's major contractors. Soon he and Charles found themselves in the same clubs and associations. Their families socialized, and over the years the two builders would collaborate on a number of construction projects.[17]

Meanwhile Charles took on almost any carpentry opportunity he could find. Since steamboats plied the Des Moines River at the time, one of Charles's more interesting jobs was repairing a steamboat pilothouse, which included constructing a new steering wheel, adding a new door, and widening the structure's openings. As the construction slump lingered, Charles also got into the fencing business. Until the early 1850s, horses, cows, and hogs roamed freely about Des Moines, forcing residents to protect their homes and gardens by fencing in their lots. Fences and gates required frequent repair, and when not doing more skilled work, Charles began mending them, doing so for Francis Grimmel and lawyer Marcellus Crocker, as well as erecting new fences for a number of others.[18]

He also made money by taking in boarders. Christian lived with Charles and Helena immediately after their home was built and then sporadically over the next few years. When he was not there, a steady stream of boarders replaced him, starting with a man named Benjamin Moore during the last couple of months in 1855 and including one of Charles's workers, John Heller, who joined the family for twenty-seven weeks in 1856. Charles allowed Heller to pay his three-dollar weekly rent through work, and when the two settled their accounts, Heller owed his employer twenty-five cents.

In the fall of 1857 and through the summer of 1858, Charles and Helena became boarders themselves when Charles started to build a larger house at the same location. More space was needed; Helena had given birth to Eliese "Lizzie" Katherine, the couple's first child, in November 1856, and a second child, Karl "Charlie" Heinrich, was born in August 1859. Once the new home was completed, the Weitzes resumed taking in boarders; in the fall of 1859, for instance, Philip Kinnel, Charles's brother-in-law, stayed with the family for $2.50 a week; and the following year, a Mr. Loabe took a room in the house.[19]

Together, these tactics kept Charles and his company in business and provided a stable life for his young family. In the 1860 census, the thirty-four-year-old carpenter reported that he owned $4,000 worth of real estate and $200 of personal property, placing him among those who were comfortable but not wealthy. His holdings were comparable to F. M. Hubbell, then a young attorney and real estate investor who had $2,000 worth of real estate and $500 in personal property, or Lampson Sherman, a newspaper editor and later a one-time city mayor, who held $5,000 worth of real estate and $500 of personal property. Others who were more established were better off. A rung or two above Charles, for example, was Lampson's brother Hoyt Sherman, who had been involved in a number of early land deals in Des Moines, led construction projects, such as the prominent business block that bore his name, and founded a bank. He held $20,000 of real estate and $2,000 of personal property. At the top of the city's socioeconomic ladder in 1860 sat Benjamin F. Allen, the city's wealthiest person. He had established a mercantile business in town, bought and sold large tracts of land, and founded a highly successful bank. With real estate valued at $130,000 and $83,000 of personal property, Allen would soon build Terrace Hill, the city's grandest mansion, completed at a cost of $250,000 in 1869.[20]

Signs of an economic recovery were visible by 1860, but the turnaround was slowed by the outbreak of the Civil War the following spring. This meant several more tough years for Charles and others in Des Moines, and small jobs remained his bread and butter. Much of this work was for former customers, such as Gottschalk and Grimmel, but there were a number of new clients, including an A. Young, attorney John Dickman, insurance solicitor L. Foster, ice dealer Albert Grefe, and saloon owner and then brewer Gottlieb Münzenmeier. Larger jobs included extensive carpentry work on brickmason Frank Geneser's home and constructing another small storehouse for Gottschalk.[21]

Finally, in 1863, the economy began picking up. Despite the war that raged on for another year and a half, Des Moines's population was growing, up by more than 40 percent since 1860 and rising to 5,722 by 1865. Increasing demand pushed prices and wages higher, and with more currency in circulation, prosperity returned. Better times were signaled for Charles in the fall of 1863 when Conrad Beck hired him to construct a barbershop. In early 1864, whether with an eye to battling competition among Des Moines carpenters—whose numbers stood at 152 in 1866, making it the largest occupational group in the city—or to keep up with increasing business and expand operations, Charles partnered with a John Hermann. The two planned to split the work, and Hermann agreed to rent space at the Weitz shop for four dollars per month.[22]

Meanwhile, the Civil War's impact on Des Moines and Iowa went well beyond economic concerns. Shortly after the fighting began in April 1861, President Abraham Lincoln called for volunteers to join the Union forces and put down rebellion in the South. Instead of depending on conscription, he relied on each state to provide a specific number of soldiers. That spring, when Governor Samuel Kirkwood led the drive to meet Iowa's initial quota of one regiment—made up of ten companies, or approximately eight hundred to one thousand men—the effort was immediately oversubscribed. For three years, Iowans met their wartime quotas for recruits entirely with volunteers until the fall of 1864, when a one-time draft was required. In all, more than 76,000 Iowans saw military service during the war, more per capita than any other state. Of these, over 3,500 were killed or mortally wounded, 8,500 died of disease, and 515 died as prisoners of war.[23]

Iowa's general enthusiasm for the Union cause was reflected in Des Moines as well, and for the first few years of the war, more men volunteered for service than were needed. Just after the fighting started at Fort Sumter, for instance, city leaders held a meeting where one of Charles's former customers, Marcellus Crocker, an attorney and West Point graduate, spoke passionately about organizing a Polk County company to join an Iowa regiment that was currently being assembled. One hundred Polk County men enlisted, forming Company D of the Second Iowa Infantry Volunteers. Crocker was named the company's captain, and in May, the unit headed east to Keokuk and mustered into service. But the war took its toll, and like many other counties of the state,

Polk County resorted to conscription in the fall of 1864, drafting forty-nine men to meet its obligation.[24]

Although Charles was a Democrat—and the party included a vocal minority dubbed Copperheads or Peace Democrats who opposed the war—he backed the war effort, but at thirty-five years old and with a family to support, he did not initially volunteer for duty. However, according to one contemporary source, Charles agreed to a request "to drill several companies of [new] recruits." Whether or not true, this is in line with the activities of many German Americans, who largely sympathized with the Union cause.[25]

The *Iowa State Register* noted this loyalty, writing in 1863, "Ever since this war commenced, the Germans of the State as well as everywhere else have demonstrated their devotion to their adopted country by enlisting in the army and holding up the hands of the Administration." In fact, over the course of the conflict, roughly two hundred thousand German Americans would serve in the Union army, making up 10 percent of all its troops.[26]

In 1864, Charles evidently became more involved, when he and a number of fellow Germans in Des Moines responded to an appeal from the governor and created a company within the Iowa militia. Over the course of the war, rebel guerillas from Missouri occasionally raided towns along the border in southern Iowa. After several of these incursions that summer, Governor William Stone called on citizens in towns and counties across Iowa to form self-defense units under the auspices of the Iowa militia. In September, Charles and forty other Germans met and created such a company. Charles was elected as the group's captain, and Daniel Vieser, one of Charles's early employees, was selected as its first lieutenant. Many others in the company were Charles's friends, clients, or employees and included, for instance, Conrad

Youngerman, Conrad Beck, Frank Geneser, George Sneer, and John Hermann.[27]

Although it is unclear whether or not this unit ever saw actual duty, there was an incident in southern Iowa the following month that involved local militia members. In early October, Confederate guerrillas from Missouri crossed into Davis County in southern Iowa, terrorized the town of Bloomfield, and killed three people. Although only a band of a dozen armed men, rumors spread quickly that the group amounted to several hundred and that it was making its way north. Concerned officials in Des Moines actually called out members of its militia and "placed mounted patrols on all roads leading to the city," but the fear was greatly exaggerated, and guerillas never made it out of Davis County. Calm was soon restored in the capital city.[28]

That same year, the *Iowa State Register* commented on Des Moines's rapid growth, noting that despite "the erection of a hundred new buildings," demand for housing remained high and "every tenantable building in town is full." Expansion picked up over the last half of the decade, and over the next five years, the city more than doubled in size, reaching 12,055 in 1870. Besides merely growing, the city was changing as well. The Savery House at Fourth and Walnut Streets had become the gathering spot for most community functions, and it pushed the city center in a northwesterly direction, where there was a demand for new, larger buildings.

At the same time, Des Moines had begun moving beyond its isolated frontier stage. In 1862, the telegraph had finally reached the city, providing convenient and reliable access to national news. Four years later, residents had more to celebrate, when the Des Moines Valley Railroad became the first railway to enter the city. Until that time, Des Moines had relied on sporadic riverboat service and overland stage lines for its ties to the outside world. Much more significant was the arrival of the Chicago, Rock Island & Pacific Railroad in 1867, which connected the city directly to Chicago and the national rail network.[29]

Other improvements were taking place as well. Area boosters and elites undertook a number of infrastructural projects, which they hoped would attract business and move the city toward being the commercial as well as political center of the state. Such improvements included more and better bridges spanning the Des Moines and Raccoon Rivers as well as the first railroad bridge, constructed across the Des Moines River by the Rock Island in 1868. That same year saw the opening of the city's first streetcar line, a mile-long track that ran eastward along Court Avenue from the county courthouse on Fifth Street across the Des Moines River to what was called Capitol Hill. Shortly thereafter, investors including F. M. Hubbell and his partner Jefferson S. Polk, who were initially involved in the streetcar company, began building narrow-gauge rail lines out of Des Moines. Along with B. F. Allen and other investors, they also opened the city's first waterworks in 1871.[30]

These and other signs of progress sparked what the *Iowa State Register* called "the consciousness of advancement" and reflected a general return of prosperity over the last half of the 1860s. Charles did well in that period. Much of his business came from repeat customers or people he knew, making it clear that the connections he had forged were critical. The majority of his time was devoted to constructing private houses, but he also continued working on shops and commercial buildings as well as landing contracts with two local churches.[31]

Charles's new home construction increasingly consisted of larger, more commodious structures for friends and associates who were upgrading to houses befitting their improved economic standing. These included previous customers Raimond Seeburger, John Roof, George Sneer, and Charles Gamp, whose new residences ranged in cost from just over $1,000 to nearly $1,600. Charles built an even higher-end home for new customer E. W. Sparhawk at $3,100. Generally, though, most residences he built were more modest and in line with the three he had constructed for previous customers: a $510 two-room structure for Joseph Lehner, a one-story $750 home for J. C. Huttenlocher, and a $680 two-story for A. Young.[32]

Charles was doing well, despite his partnership with John Hermann, which was proving problematic. Work was not equitably distributed, and Charles ended up doing many more jobs than Hermann. The issue finally came to a head, probably during construction of the Seeburger house in the fall of 1865. The two dissolved the partnership, apparently amicably, with Charles taking over all accounts receivable, except for what was owed on the Seeburger job, which was to be split evenly.[33]

Meanwhile, the booming economy brought new businesses to Des Moines and pushed many current shop owners to update or expand their operations. At the same time, the growing community required more services and facilities. Charles was there to meet those construction needs, which kept him and his crews busy. In 1865, for example, he erected a new ice house for Albert Grefe, a warehouse for Manning & Miller's carpet business, and a shop for harness maker John Koenigsberger. The following year, Charles built an addition for Louis Kurtz, who had been trained as a tinsmith and opened Kurtz & Brother, a stove and tinware dealer. The business soon became a hardware store, and Charles constructed a building for Kurtz in 1868. Over the years the two became close friends and good customers for each other.[34]

Charles landed another substantial contract in 1868, when he was hired to construct a coal shed for the Des Moines Gas Company. He may have won the job because he was acquainted with banker B. F. Allen, who at the time served as the gas company's treasurer. Regardless of how he obtained the work, it proved important and led to a number of substantial contracts with the firm.[35]

His longstanding ties with other Lutherans in town and harness maker Koenigsberger, who also served as a trustee of the Lutheran Evangelical Society, led to a string of church building jobs. In 1865, Koenigsberger hired him to do $350 worth of carpentry for the new brick English Lutheran Church. Larger, more lucrative contracts from other denominations soon followed: Charles expanded the German Methodist Episcopal Church at Second and Locust Streets in 1866, and later did interior renovations in the sanctuary. In 1869, he erected a building for the Universalist Church at Sixth and Cherry Streets, and then, probably because of his relationships with Kurtz and Lehner, who each took out large subscriptions to pay for its construction, Charles was hired to build Saint Mary's German Catholic Church at Second and Crocker Streets.[36]

His connections, especially with other Germans in town, also played an important role in his life outside the world of business. Shortly after arriving in Des Moines, Charles had joined the local IOOF Lodge 25, where he forged a number of valuable business relationships during his ten years of membership. But because his closest friends and most important networks remained within the city's German community, Charles led the way in founding a German Odd Fellows organization, Jonathan Lodge No. 137 of the IOOF, in April 1865 and served as a trustee. Although completely integrated into American society, Charles remained committed to "fostering and preserving German thought, culture, and refinement," and thus the new organization conducted its meetings in German and highlighted members' German heritage with a number of social events. A little over a year after its creation, for instance, the lodge—which then had a membership of thirty-five and initially met weekly on Wednesday evening in the Cooper Building on Court Avenue—hosted a picnic featuring lemonade, ice cream, and German meats and cakes. Most noteworthy, according to the *Iowa State Register*, was "the music and waltzing and a variety of German plays, which made the time pass most agreeably."[37]

This interest in German culture combined with his growing family steered Charles toward a group that founded a German American school. Over the course of the 1860s, Charles and Helena had four more children: Emilie "Amelia" Helene born in 1862, Rosa Karoline in 1865, Frederick "Fred" Wilhelm in 1867, and Emma Marie in 1869. Nine years later, in 1878, twenty-two years after the couple's first child was born, Helena gave birth to Edward Kinnel, the Weitzes' last child. The seven children made for an active household, and while Charles was clearly busy with work, he found time for the family. Eliese Katherine, the eldest child, was his favorite, and he often took her on business trips. Charlie, Fred, and eventually Edward, meanwhile, spent time with their father learning the carpentry and building business, with the expectation that they would one day take over the company from their father.[38]

All the children were raised speaking German. Helena, in fact, remained much more connected to the German language and traditions than Charles, and although she had "lived only nine months of her life in Germany, she never really learned the ways of America." She probably never needed to do so, for she was raised in German sections of American towns, and once she married Charles, their friends were largely other Germans.[39]

Thus, it is not surprising that Charles was involved in a group intent on setting up a German school in town. In September 1868, he joined with other friends and associates at the office of architect Hugo Wildt to consider the idea. He was selected to chair the meeting, which concluded in the founding of the German American Independent School Association. A week later, a permanent board was established, headed by Charles's close friend Conrad Youngerman. The school initially opened in the former Baptist church building on Mulberry Street between Fifth and Sixth Streets, with instructor James Weighe teaching a general curriculum of reading, writing, spelling, arithmetic, geography, United States history, and moral philosophy. In addition to English, which was taught in the morning, instruction in the German language took place in the afternoon. Within months, teaching duties were taken over by Conrad Beck, and by the winter, enrollment stood at twenty-one.[40]

With applications for admission coming in as well, plans were developed for a new building. In January 1869, the association purchased a lot on Eighth Street between Mulberry and Cherry Streets, and in October, its new, two-story brick facility was dedicated. By then enrollment had risen to seventy-five pupils, and although no records exist, it is most likely that at least some Weitz children attended the school. Charles also spent a lot of time there, as it became the meeting place for the Jonathan Lodge.[41]

Charles also joined the German Turner Society, which was founded in early-nineteenth-century Germany. The Turners (the German word for gymnasts) were an athletic and political association that originally emphasized physical fitness and German nationalism. The Turners had supported democratic reforms during the failed revolutions of 1848, and, in fact, a number of former revolutionaries who emigrated from Germany to the United States were Turners. These and other German immigrants established Turner Societies, or *Turnvereins*, in the United States. A *Turnverein* was founded in Des Moines in September 1866, and ironically arranged to use Turner Hall, which was space in a building owned by Dr. M. P. Turner on Court Avenue, for its activities. A couple of years later, the Turners took out a lease on the hall, and Charles was hired to do some renovations, including putting in new floors. Initially he was not a member and apparently had no interest in joining. It may have been his age: he was forty-two at the time and probably considered the gymnastic-oriented group more fitting for younger men. Yet in 1872, when the local Turners hosted a regional festival and asked Charles and several others, including Conrad Youngerman, for help, the two friends provided assistance and were rewarded with honorary membership into the society.[42]

Networking and his especially close ties within Des Moines's German community had helped Charles build his business, but there were setbacks. Most notably, on Tuesday evening, August 13, 1867, a fire raged through the Weitz carpentry shop, destroying it and two adjacent buildings. Fortunately, the *Iowa State Register* reported, there was no wind that night and the damage was confined to those three structures. Still, the paper estimated total losses at $2,500, although in a business ledger, Charles listed his own loss at $2,000. This was significant damage; roughly equal to what he had been earning annually over the past couple of years. In 1865, his net earnings stood at $1,825, while the following year they reached $2,100. But Charles had a number of jobs to complete and he moved forward, immediately establishing a temporary shop before rebuilding his facility the following year. Business remained good, and the Weitz firm hardly missed a beat. Despite the fire, Charles finished 1867 with net earnings of $2,160, slightly higher than the previous year.[43]

The following March 1868, weather dealt Charles another blow, though not nearly as serious as the first, when hail broke twenty-six windowpanes in his home. The storm may have brought down some trees in his yard as well, for when he replaced the glass, he also purchased twenty shade trees. Ultimately, this proved a minor irritation, and as the decade was winding down, Charles could look back with satisfaction over his fifteen years in Des Moines. Despite growing competition—by 1869 there were 250 carpenters in town, one hundred more than there had been just three years earlier—he had built a successful, growing business, survived a deep economic downtown, and integrated into the community.[44]

The 1870 federal census put Charles's accomplishments in perspective. His net worth had tripled since the 1860 census, with his real estate holdings valued at $10,000 and a personal wealth of $3,000. Some had done much better. Businessmen F. M. Hubbell, whose net worth had been comparable with Charles's in 1860, had seen his wealth rise spectacularly, increasing more than twenty times over the period, while B. F. Allen's real estate and personal property soared to over $2 million. On the other hand, many other successful business and community figures, such as Lampson Sherman or his brother Hoyt, had seen their fortunes go up and down, but by 1870 they were worth, respectively, $8,500 and $14,000, or roughly where Charles stood on the socioeconomic ladder. Clearly he was not among the city's wealthy elites, but at a time when his skilled workers were making $2.50 per day, Charles had risen into what might be considered the upper middle class.[45]

This hard-won success and middle age brought about another change. The physical labor involved in carpentry and building wore on a man's body, and by the time Charles was in his forties, he must have been relieved that his growing business required him to move away from on-site work. Instead, more and more of his time was taken up with managerial tasks of bidding on jobs, supervising worksites, buying materials, and hiring, paying, and sometimes firing workers. This shift from working alongside his employees to full-time manager was gradual, but by the end of the 1860s, Charles rarely did any carpentry work himself. At the same time, he was slowly moving his company from its origins as a small carpentry shop toward a full-fledged building contractor, ready to tackle larger and more complex jobs. The shift was propitious, for Des Moines's population would increase fourfold over the next twenty years, and "Charles Weitz, Carpenter and Builder" was soon ready to meet the public and private construction needs of the burgeoning city.

Chapter Three

GROWING WITH THE CITY

In an unusual move in 1872, Charles wrote a letter to family members who had remained in Germany. While he took great interest in his German heritage and insisted that his children learn the language and culture of his homeland, he did not keep in touch with his brother and sister or their families in Schotten. And once in the United States, he never returned to Europe. Charles had made a good life in America, and his last memories of Germany—his difficult *Wanderbuch* years and then war—were best forgotten. Nevertheless, on a cold December day, he drafted a long response to a letter he had received from his German relatives nearly five years earlier, and he evidently wrote only because his good friend Conrad Youngerman was traveling to Germany and offered to hand deliver the note. Among the many bits of news, Charles offered the reasons he believed some immigrants had not prospered in America: "I know," he wrote, "that many hundreds of Germans have come to our western states who wish they had never seen them. However, it [their failure] is two-thirds their own fault and one-third trying their best without success....That I prefer business in Germany, that I certainly do not mean." Then he offered his formula for success: "When energy and iron will and ability to stick to it are there, success does usually come."[1]

Most likely, the statement reflected what Charles thought accounted for his own rise. His determination no doubt played a role, but other factors were important as well. He had guessed right about the impact the capital would have on Des Moines; he had gotten into the carpentry business just as the city was beginning to expand; and early on, he had cultivated connections in the city's business community. All the while, he had built a solid reputation as an honest businessman known for quality construction, and he had the very good fortune of being in the right place at the right time. When the city population took off, Charles was there to meet the need for additional homes, churches, office buildings, warehouses, and schools.

Even after a decade of growth, Des Moines's 1870 population stood at twelve thousand, a huge increase since Charles had arrived fifteen years earlier, but still smaller and in many ways less significant than Iowa's Mississippi River towns of Davenport, Dubuque, Burlington, and Keokuk. All that changed over the next ten years, however, when a number of Des Moines businessmen and promoters built or encouraged others to build railroads through the state's centrally located capital city. Some boosters, of course, had delusions of grandeur, with one crowing in 1884 that "Des Moines is destined to soon become the greatest commercial and manufacturing center west of Chicago [and] east of San Francisco." Hyperbole aside, Des Moines had become the transportation center of the state. Nine railroads entered the city by 1881; three years later, the number had risen to fourteen, with thirty-eight passenger trains rolling through Des Moines on a daily basis.[2]

Increasing railroad connections and a rapidly expanding population, which nearly doubled by 1880, remade Des Moines. Now with 22,400 residents, Des Moines was the state's largest city, and the subsequent economic expansion and building boom made it the most important commercial center as well. In this environment, Charles had plenty of work.

Initially his bread and butter remained residential structures or small commercial buildings, such as homes for John Thompson and Gottlieb Münzenmeier in 1871 or a packing house for grocers Grefe and Weaver in 1872. Although he focused on the construction business, he apparently had not forgotten the lean times of a decade earlier, and his utilitarian bent led him to pursue other moneymaking ventures whenever opportunities arose. This entrepreneurial streak would be picked up by future generations of Weitz family leaders of the company as well.[3]

Nevertheless, in the early 1870s, when the expanding rail lines and city growth increased the demand for coal, Charles became attracted to mining. Polk County sat atop one of the state's richest coal deposits. Des Moines's first commercial coal mining company had been founded a few years earlier in 1864 by bookseller and insurance man Wesley Redhead. Charles's operation was a sideline and rather small. Beginning in 1872, he leased land for two years and had his men begin by clearing timber, which was eventually sold as cordwood, and then mining coal that was exposed, usually along creek beds. When the lease expired, his men had exhausted the coal on the property, and Charles had made nearly $2,500 from the sale of coal and cordwood. In 1874, he signed a new four-year agreement to mine coal on a Mrs. Alston's land through 1878, but it appears that he got out of the business, probably because a number of bigger mining firms had entered the market.[4]

Besides dabbling in coal, Charles continued renting property, including available space at his shop, other commercial facilities, and several houses he owned. On balance, it was probably worthwhile for Charles to stay in the rental business, but like many others who let property, he sometimes struggled financially with people who fell behind in their payments or failed to pay altogether. In 1876, for example, a Mr. Barnett, who lived in one of Charles's two houses on Third Street, fell four months behind in his rent and owed $140. It is unclear whether Charles ever recovered this money. There were also instances involving much larger sums with clients who hired him to build a building but then struggled to pay when the structure was completed. This was the case when he finished Saint Mary's Catholic Church, a project that had dragged on because the church's fundraising lagged. Charles completed the building in 1875, even though he was still owed nearly $4,700. Eventually Charles took out a lien on the property and signed a contract with the church's building committee, which included two of his friends, Louis Kurtz and John Roof. The document specified that he would receive 10 percent interest on the amount owed until the balance was paid off. The account was finally settled in January 1879, when Father Nicholas Sassell paid Charles the remaining $1,000.[5]

Occasionally when clients had difficulty making payments, Charles became creative. After he completed the Grefe and Weaver packing house in 1872, for instance, the grocers apparently had cash flow problems and were slow in paying off their balance. Instead of waiting for the money, Charles arranged something of a barter system. His deal with Grefe and Weaver allowed his employees to charge their purchases at the store to the Weitz account until his bill equaled the amount the grocers owed him for the building.[6]

Luckily Charles did not need to rely on such inventive payment plans often. His building business was expanding and well situated to take advantage of the growing demand. In fact, according to the

1874 *Bushnell's City Directory*, his stature had increased, and for the first time, rather than listing Charles among the city's several hundred carpenters, it included him as one of eleven carpenter and building contractors. The list was not definitive, but it was an indication of how Charles was viewed at the time and also identified his major competitors. Some would soon fall by the wayside, but four of the eleven remained important rivals—William Christy, H. N. Woods, and Whiting & Keemer, whose partnership ended in 1879 with both men becoming independent contractors. Others of note soon entered the contracting business, including Thomas Allum, James Garrety, Samuel A. Robinson, C. W. Van Horn, John Woods, and Conrad Youngerman.[7]

From the late 1870s on, a lot of building took place throughout the city, and competition among contractors was stiff. At some point in the decade Charles made an effort to differentiate himself, noting on company letterhead his areas of expertise: "Charles Weitz: Practical Builder and Contractor," giving "Special Attention to Churches, School Houses, and Public Buildings, and First Class Residences." In an era when bidding contests could be close, setting oneself apart was important. Something is known about the bidding because "practical builder" Weitz often recorded all the bids on the jobs he solicited. Although sometimes a successful bid was quite a bit lower than the rest—in the spring of 1878, for example, Charles's winning $2,700 proposal for the Mattes house was $400 lower than the next-lowest bid and over $800 less than the highest—more often than not, the contests were considerably tighter. A year earlier, for instance, Christy won the Hubbard house job with a $3,400 bid, which was $95 less than Charles's, and the following summer, a bid of $6,840 won the Insurance Block job—$150 less than the next lowest bid. Charles's proposal fell in the middle of the pack at $7,200.[8]

The information was indicative of larger patterns and trends as well. For example, on jobs Charles did not win, his bids generally fell roughly in the middle. Sometimes the bidding suggested cooperation, particularly between Charles and Youngerman, who occasionally submitted joint bids, such as their 1880 proposal for the Van Meter house, and the two often did subcontracting work for each other. But more importantly, the records revealed that some of Charles's toughest competitors were Christy, whose rivalry spilled over into a lawsuit, and later Garrety. Charles's records also indicated that a contractor named John Woods seemed to be lowballing proposals and hence getting a disproportionate number of jobs.[9]

After one incident in 1879, when Woods's bid of $2,780 for the Kaufmann house was $565 below the next-lowest bid and more than $1,200 below the highest, Charles confided in his ledger: "John Woods took the contract and mortgaged his homestead for security to complete the shop—the Fools ain't all dead yet." He believed Woods would be out of business soon. Somehow, however, Woods survived as a contractor for nine more years before dropping out of the *Bushnell's Des Moines Directory* listings altogether in 1888.[10]

Given the city's continued growth, Charles's letterhead assurance of his expertise in schoolhouses was wise. Population growth fueled a commercial expansion and building boom, but it also meant that more schools were needed, and from the late 1870s through the 1880s, a sizeable amount of his time was devoted to constructing area schools. In 1879, he built the Hawthorne School at West Crocker and Seventeenth Streets, and in 1881 into 1882, he erected the Garfield School on Third Street. Charles followed these jobs with work on what he referred to as the "Franklin school," which must have been Rawson School on Franklin Avenue, located in the then Oakdale School District, just northwest of where Drake

University would be located. He also did many smaller jobs on area school buildings. District and community leaders were evidently happy with his work, and soon Charles landed a much bigger project, or at least he thought he had.[11]

Up to that point, high school classes in the city were held in the Lincoln School at Ninth and Mulberry, but by mid-decade, it was clear the building was too small. In 1888, plans were readied to build a new high school at Fifteenth and Center Streets. Des Moines architects William Foster and H. F. Liebbe were retained to design the building, and Charles won the job with a bid of $52,425. The same day, the district hired builder F. S. Whiting, one of Charles's longtime competitors and currently a school board director, to oversee the project, agreeing to pay him 2 percent of the construction costs for his services. But then, before a written contract with Charles had been drafted or executed, the school board came across a lower bid for construction of the high school that had somehow been misplaced. The board felt obligated to go with the lowest bid. Not surprisingly, Charles felt cheated and believed the board reneged on his contract.[12]

As a result, he brought two suits against the school district. First, he sought damages resulting from the revocation of the contract. This case initially went well. Polk County District Court ordered the district to pay such damages, but in 1890, the Iowa Supreme Court reversed the ruling, arguing that by statute, the district was required to take the lowest bid. Then, apparently because he blamed rival Whiting for the board's reversal, Charles brought another lawsuit against the district, claiming that as a taxpayer, he believed Whiting's two positions with the Des Moines schools— board director and construction supervisor—were contradictory and could create a conflict of interest. The district court did not see a problem, but the Iowa Supreme Court believed there was a potential conflict of interest and ordered Whiting to return any monies he had been paid in his supervisory position.[13]

A win on the latter case may have taken some of the sting out of the defeat, but it was of little consolation, and Charles was about to face very public charges and litigation in an entirely different matter. But the incident did reveal a side of Charles not often evident. Generally the remaining records and biographical entries depict him as reserved, analytical, focused, and composed. He was a man known for honesty who crunched numbers and liked working behind the scene and outside the headlines, but this episode with the Des Moines schools had gotten under his skin. Charles was evidently outraged and went after the school board and Whiting with uncharacteristic vehemence.[14]

Though the encounter angered him and bruised his ego, he was too well connected and respected for the loss of the contract to hurt his business. As he had from the beginning of his time in Des Moines, Charles continued expanding his network of business associates. He had taken another step in that direction early in the previous decade. In February 1871, Charles and several others, including furniture dealer Louis Harbach, merchant W. L. White, and Conrad Youngerman, founded the first Knights of Pythias organization in Des Moines by establishing Myrtle Lodge No. 9. By 1876, the fraternal order had fifty members, and much like his association with the Odd Fellows and then the Jonathan Lodge, Charles must have considered this group a good place to exchange information and negotiate deals.[15]

These networks he had established were clear in July 1879, when Charles and Helena celebrated their twenty-fifth wedding anniversary. They had planned a large "open celebration" at their

45

home but had to cancel the party, reported Des Moines's German language newspaper, the *Iowa Staats-Anzeiger*, because of a death in the family (the deceased was not identified but was likely someone out of town, possibly one of Helena's relatives in Columbus, Ohio). The paper went on to explain, "Almost all German people would have attended since no German family is more popular than the Weitz family." Nonetheless, twenty-five of the couple's closest friends still gathered at the Weitz house to recognize the occasion, including Des Moines mayor George Sneer.[16]

Business, of course, came from friends and associates as well as satisfied customers. It was probably a combination of these that led to Charles's work on the Des Moines Syrup Refinery, touted in 1880 as "the largest manufacturing institution ever started in the Capital of Iowa." Initially the company converted corn into corn starch and laundry starch, and later corn syrup and glucose. Eventually the owners hoped to distribute amber cane (sorghum) seed to farmers and use the cane to produce sugar and syrup as well. The firm was the brainchild of a Saint Louis man named Martin Miller, who along with D. O. Eshbaugh, a local insurance representative, promoted the project and convinced prominent Des Moines businessmen of its viability. Although not originally involved with the firm, Charles had close ties to two of its directors, Conrad Youngerman and banker George Hippee, for whom he had done a lot of work since 1865, and it is not surprising that he was hired in 1879 as one of the subcontractors for the syrup company's building. During construction, Charles bought three shares of its stock, paying only 10 percent, or $30, of its par value. When he completed his $6,600 worth of work on the structure, he accepted cash and company stock valued at $4,800 as payment, and it appears he wrote off the rest. Now with 347 shares, Charles was one of the firm's leading shareholders and named to the board of directors. But the refinery never lived up to its grand expectations and closed just two years later in 1882.[17]

Shortly before the much-heralded syrup venture failed, Des Moines landed a considerably bigger prize in 1879, which would soon become an important and enduring fixture in the capital city. That September, the Iowa State Fair opened in the newly prepared grounds in Brown's Park, a sixty-acre site west of downtown between Center Street and Grand Avenue, and Thirty-Eighth and Forty-Second Streets. The state fair had grown out of county fairs and was first held in Fairfield, a small town 110 miles southeast of Des Moines, in 1854. Over the next twenty-five years, the fair moved from site to site in the eastern portion of the state until 1879 when, because of the growing population in central and western Iowa coupled with Des Moines's now extensive railroad network, the capital city was selected to host the summer event. Although other cities continued to vie for the fair and there were no initial plans to locate it permanently in Des Moines, the capital's central location gave it an edge over its rivals.[18]

In 1884, the Iowa State Agricultural Society, the fair's governing board, asked the state legislature for $100,000 to purchase a permanent fairground. Instead, the legislature appropriated $50,000 on the condition the society raise the other $50,000. Within months, the Des Moines business community responded with the necessary funds, and in the spring of 1885, the society purchased a fairgrounds site—266 acres two miles east of the state capitol, bounded by University and Dean Avenues and extending from East Thirtieth to East Thirty-Sixth Streets.[19]

Construction began in early 1886, and by the time the fair opened at its permanent location that September, sixty-seven buildings had been erected. Charles was evidently not involved in this rush of construction, but the following year, he landed a job at the fairgrounds. Earlier in 1884, McCormick Harvesting Machine Company set up a small branch in Des Moines, moving into an older facility on Court Avenue, and in 1887, it hired Charles to replace the floors and do some remodeling. Later that year, the implement manufacturer retained him to construct an exhibition hall at the fairgrounds, where McCormick planned to demonstrate its latest equipment. The company was actually slower than others to invest in fair space. A year earlier, shortly after the permanent fairground on the east side of Des Moines was established, five firms, including McCormick's rivals Moline Plow Company and Minnesota Harvester Works, announced plans to construct facilities in order to promote their latest equipment.[20]

Des Moines's acquisition of the Iowa State Fair seemed symbolic, acknowledgment that it was fast becoming the dominant city in the state. And its growth continued to outpace its rivals along the Mississippi. Aggressively promoted by the board of trade, its booster organization founded in 1871, Des Moines's population more than doubled over the 1880s, reinforcing its mounting primacy across Iowa. It was growing three times faster than any other city in the state, boasted the *Iowa State Register*, and in 1885, for example, Des Moines "expended more money on improvements than Burlington, Keokuk, Davenport, Dubuque, and Council Bluffs combined; more than Cincinnati, more than Louisville, and much more than Columbus, Ohio." By 1890, its population topped fifty thousand, making it more than 50 percent bigger than Dubuque, Iowa's second-largest city. Of course, like many other cities across the country, Des Moines's surging growth and rapid expansion changed the urban landscape: larger brick and stone buildings rose, replacing wooden structures, and as streetcars became more prevalent, the city began to spread out. But as elsewhere, growth caused problems for the city's infrastructure, and as municipal officials dealt with such issues as expanding sewer systems, paving streets, or providing water at a reasonable cost, there were murmurs of corruption.[21]

Shortly after the decade opened, the *Iowa State Register* proclaimed that 1881 was the "greatest epoch experienced in the city's building history." Actually, the phrase was apt for the decade as the boom extended over the entire period. And Charles was involved. Whether it was in construction, investing in local institutions, or serving as an alderman, he played a prominent role in the city's transformation of the 1880s. Curiously, he was not part of the new state capitol project, the most significant and expensive structure erected during the period. Begun in 1871, the $2.8 million edifice rose under the watchful eye of general contractor Robert Finkbine, but early problems with the foundation combined with funding it on a "pay-as-you-go" basis meant that it was not completed until 1886.[22]

Meanwhile, as the statehouse was rising, it became clear that Des Moines had outgrown its city hall, and bids were solicited for a new municipal building in the spring of 1882. Charles was one of five to bid the job, but the $25,000 contract went to competitor James Garrety, who completed the new facility that December. It was not a total loss for Charles, however. Almost immediately after the structure was finished, the new city jail, located inside the municipal building, became overcrowded, and several years later, in 1886, Charles was hired to expand it.[23]

Although he did not get the city hall job, the 1880s proved very good for him. Much of his work was done along what had often been referred to as "Rat Row" or "Rum Row," a rundown stretch of several blocks along Walnut Street where, the *Iowa State Register* reported, "rat and worm-infested shanties remain." However, the paper noted, "The Des Moines boom is too much for Rat Row, and it is going, going, going!"[24]

In 1882, Charles built the fine, $12,000 Goldman & Hyman Block at Fourth and Walnut Streets and the $14,500 Des Moines National Bank two blocks away at Sixth and Walnut. Afterward he bought several properties and lots along Walnut, leased the buildings, and over time refurbished them. On the vacant lots, Charles and a Mrs. Mattes announced their intentions to erect new office buildings, a plan the *Register* applauded, calling the idea "splendid." Charles erected both buildings in 1883 and 1884, the Mattes Block at Walnut and First Streets and the Weitz Block, an office building and warehouse, on Fourth Street between Walnut Street and Court Avenue. He did most of the work on this latter building, but contracted out some jobs, with Conrad Youngerman doing the brick and stone work. Later in 1884, Youngerman constructed a similar building at Locust and Fifth Streets. Not surprisingly, it was known as the Youngerman Block, and Charles did the carpentry work for his old friend.[25]

Charles had not intended his work on Walnut Street as an urban renewal project, but that was essentially what resulted. The new buildings he erected, the properties he bought and renovated, and his own business block went a long way to transforming the once decrepit "Rat Row" into the major business thoroughfare in the city. It was soon followed by Locust Street, after a new Savery Hotel on Locust and Fourth Streets—the original on Walnut and Fourth had closed in 1878—opened amid much excitement in 1888.[26]

Actually, other jobs kept Charles focused on Des Moines's new, thriving commercial street as well. His lodge connections probably got him some remodeling work at the Knights of Phythias Hall at Walnut and Sixth Streets, but his biggest contract came from the Masons, a fraternal group to which he did not belong. They hired Charles to erect a building a block west of Pythias Hall. Hailed as "new and magnificent" by the *Iowa State Register*, the $30,000 Masonic Temple opened in June 1884. The structure was damaged by fire in 1886, and Charles returned to do extensive repairs to the grand hall.[27]

Charles's work involved him in other areas of the city as well. For instance, in 1887, he made extensive repairs to the Des Moines Saddlery Company on Court Avenue, now the home of the Court Avenue Brewing Company. He also remained active in the residential housing market, and because of the expanding economy, he was hired to build a number of large, upscale homes. These included new residences for George Hippee, Conrad Youngerman, livestock dealer Ben F. Elbert, and Manassah Sheuerman of Capital City Woolen Mills. Unfortunately, Sheuerman was unhappy when his home was finished and disputed the $12,000 bill because he claimed the wrong flooring was laid and the cistern was installed with mortar instead of cement. It is unclear how this issue was resolved, although Charles does not mention placing a lien on the property, and it must have been eventually settled amicably.[28]

Amid these projects, Charles needed more space, and instead of expanding his shop at 119 Third Street, he opted to move to a larger facility. He kept the property on Third Street; part of the shop was already leased and he would continue to rent it, but in March 1886, he relocated in a two-story building he bought several blocks west at 713 Mulberry Street. He announced the move with a notice that proclaimed, "I desire to inform my old as well as my new friends and patrons alike, that in the future, as in the past, I shall feel pleased to see them on business at the above named place and I guarantee prompt attention to any and all orders left with me and full satisfaction in Material and Worksmanship employed." Although Charles could not have known it, the company would remain at this location for nearly sixty years.[29]

But Charles did know that the Des Moines transportation sector was growing, and he was successful in getting jobs with both railroad companies and the city's streetcar firms. In August 1884, Charles did some work for the Wabash, St. Louis & Pacific Railroad (the Wabash), which had reached the capital city two years earlier. The following year, he won a bigger job with Fred Hubbell and Jefferson Polk's St. Louis, Des Moines & Northern Railway—a narrow-gauge line that carried mostly freight between Des Moines and Boone, a town forty miles to the north—and had an agreement with the Wabash. Charles was hired to add four car stalls to its roundhouse.[30]

Meanwhile, new facilities were required for the city's expanding streetcar systems. Several companies were operating at the time, and although Charles did not specify which firm hired him, he put up a streetcar barn in 1886 and did miscellaneous work for the Des Moines Broad Gauge Street Railway and the Sevastopol (a Des Moines suburb immediately south of downtown) Street Railway. Two years later a change in technology led to more work. Up to that time, streetcars in Des Moines were pulled by horses, but in December 1888, the Broad Gauge Street Railway Company became the first in the city to electrify a line. Shortly after that, Polk consolidated the city's various streetcar companies into the Des Moines City Railway, and in 1890, Charles was hired to erect a powerhouse for the new operation.[31]

As the 1880s progressed, Charles continued overseeing his flourishing construction business, but two other endeavors took up an increasing amount of his time. First was banking. Sometime in the late 1870s or early 1880s, maybe as he became a shareholder in the syrup business, he began buying bank stock, initially in Valley Bank. Charles had also done significant work on its building, located at Court Avenue and Fourth Street, and when the banking concern was reorganized as Valley National Bank in 1883, he accepted an invitation to join its board of directors. He also began investing in other area financial institutions including Des Moines Savings Bank. Charles became even more involved in the industry with the creation of the German Savings Bank in the 1890s.[32]

Charles's personality seemed perfectly suited for his work with local banks. He was regarded as a serious, solid citizen and an upstanding, conservative businessman. Friends, however, sometimes saw a more lighthearted figure who enjoyed a friendly wager every once in a while. In 1884, for example, betting commenced on election outcomes. That October, Ed Edinburn bet E. L. Smith that Democratic nominee Grover Cleveland would carry the state of New York in that year's presidential election. Charles was charged with holding the money. Cleveland carried the state, won the election, and Edinburn pocketed $10. In a separate wager, Charles bet Robert Fullerton of the Chicago Lumber Company a silk hat that Ohio would go Democratic in the same presidential election. It did not, and Charles bought his friend the fashionable accessory.[33]

Then in a more important move that seemed out of character, Charles threw his own hat into the ring for a seat on the city council. Up to that point, he had focused almost exclusively on his business, and except for a brief stint on the city's library association board in the early 1870s and again in the 1880s, he had not taken up public service. Nor had he ever sought leadership roles in the organizations he joined. In this case, it seems most likely that friends or associates pressed him to seek the office, and interestingly, although he was a Democrat, Charles ran for alderman at large in March 1886 on the "Citizens' ticket." Des Moines was, as the *Iowa State Register* explained, a Republican city, and this may have encouraged Charles and several other Democrats to run under that banner as opposed to their own party. Such reform-oriented third parties, in fact, were increasingly popular across the country as a growing number of people saw excesses and corruption in their local governments and found the entrenched parties unresponsive. Whatever his or his backers' reasoning for aligning with the Citizens' Party, the strategy worked. Charles defeated Republican businessman W. T. Heywood and began his position in May. He would go on to serve two terms, from 1886 to 1890, and like many other city councils at the time, Charles and his fellow aldermen took up the pressing issue of expanding public services. In particular, key topics they addressed included street paving, acquisition of the waterworks, and growing Des Moines through annexation.[34]

Des Moines's poor roads had long caused problems. By the 1870s, "many thousands of dollars had been expended in cutting and filling, grading them up or down as the surface of the ground required....But no attempt had yet been made at paving, and at times in certain seasons of the year, some of the principal streets of the city were almost impassable." In 1878, the city council took action and invited a highly regarded Chicago engineer to recommend a comprehensive plan for sewers and street paving. The city adopted the proposals and began laying sewer lines; street paving commenced in 1882 using cedar block.[35]

Paving had become an even bigger issue by the time Charles took office. The cedar block did not hold up as expected. Although they initially provided a smooth surface, the wooden pavers soon became rough and uneven, and they were easily broken by spikes used to secure the expanding street railway tracks. Worse still, all cedar blocks were susceptible to water, and after being in the ground for a while, accumulated moisture caused them to rot from the bottom up. As they decomposed, the cedar blocks gave off the pungent, unpleasant odor of rotten eggs. Charles knew and understood the characteristics of building materials, and he apparently suggested the city consider switching to a hardened brick paver, recently developed by the local brick industry. The city council created and sent a paving committee, made up of Charles and fellow aldermen Michael Drady and Frank Morris, to see how brick paving was holding up in several cities to the east.[36]

The group went on the fact finding mission in June 1888. After visiting Wheeling, West Virginia; Columbus and Cincinnati, Ohio; Galesburg and Bloomington, Illinois; and Pittsburgh, Pennsylvania, the committee drafted a report explaining that the brick-paved streets they examined were performing well and should "no longer be seen as an experiment." Some sections of brick pavement they examined were six years old, and although they were "under constant travel with heavy transfer wagons and tremendous loads," the roads were in remarkably good shape. The report concluded with a recommendation to switch to brick on Des Moines's roads because it "stands up to heavy wear and tear," would not rot or emit any stench, and would be a boon for the local brick industry. The council as a whole agreed, and the first brick pavers were put down in Des Moines later that year. Brick was certainly more durable than the cedar pavers, and as expected, its use on roads led to an expansion of Des Moines's brick manufacturing business. However, by the mid-1890s, the advantages of asphalt were being discussed, and it would soon become the paving material of choice.[37]

By the time brick pavers were being laid, Charles was involved in another big issue confronting the city: the waterworks. The city and the private Des Moines Water Works had had a contentious relationship since the company's founding in 1871. Like many other late-nineteenth-century municipal governments, Des Moines officials had battled the waterworks over rates and struggled with the issues of regulation, buying the utility, or building one of their own. At one point in 1876, the city considered leasing the waterworks, but the idea never gained traction, and the struggles continued.[38]

By 1888, the waterworks was reorganized with stockholder Fred Hubbell becoming the majority owner. In the midst of this restructuring, the city appointed three aldermen, Charles, George Sheldon, and Michael King, to investigate its ongoing problems with the waterworks. Deciding that buying the works was in order, they approached Hubbell in February 1889. Although he had tried to sell it a year earlier, he told them he was no longer interested in disposing of the property. The city council dropped the matter, but it was far from over. Amazingly, the two sides remained at odds and continued squabbling for thirty years. Finally an agreement was reached in 1919, and the city bought the waterworks for $3.45 million.[39]

The last major item on the council's agenda was the issue of expanding Des Moines through annexation. As the city had grown, a number of small, independent communities developed around it, including Sevastopol, North Des Moines, Greenwood Park, Gilbert, University Place, Capital Park, Grant Park, and Easton Park. Beginning in the late 1880s, a greater Des Moines movement emerged, calling for municipal expansion by combining the central city of Des Moines with its suburbs through annexation. The merger was pushed by the city council, the Commercial Exchange—a business organization founded in 1888 that would become the city's chamber of commerce—and key community figures like businessmen Jefferson Scott Polk and Conrad Youngerman. The merger, it was hoped, would even out property taxes, which were lower in the suburbs because they did not provide services, such as police or fire protection, as Des Moines did. At the same time, the larger tax base would bring down taxes in Des Moines by spreading the burden among more people, and it would encourage the spread of municipal services to the suburbs. By February 1890, North Des Moines became the last suburb to vote in favor of merging, and in the following month, the Iowa General Assembly recognized the annexation. Des Moines grew by forty-six square miles to encompass an area of fifty-six square miles. These new city boundaries would remain unchanged for the next seventy years.[40]

By almost any measure, Charles's years on the city council were productive and successful, and after four years of service, he decided to step down and did not seek reelection in 1890. Soon, however, his work and that of his colleagues was clouded by charges of misconduct for appropriating extra pay. This was not the first time the council had come under suspicion. In 1884, two years before Charles joined the council, the *New York Times* raised the specter of corruption: "The Des Moines city government for many years has been wasteful, but not until last night has Tweedism [a reference to the infamous political boss William Marcy Tweed, who ran Tammany Hall, a Democratic political machine and was convicted of stealing millions from New York city taxpayers] been formally charged upon the city officers." Allegations, which included accepting illegal pay, abating their own property taxes, and allowing "gambling and prostitution to increase without effort to check them," were leveled against three aldermen and the mayor, but apparently nothing ever came of them.[41]

Then six years later, in the spring of 1890, a grand jury issued indictments against eleven city officials and ex-officials for willful misconduct in office. In what was soon referred to as the "Des Moines Boodle Cases," Charles and fellow former aldermen Drady, King, Morris, John Macy, Mark Egan, and Alvin Hammer, and current aldermen Sheldon, J. P. Smith, and H. R. Reynolds, as well as Adam Baker, clerk of the board of public works, were charged with taking $7,200 of city money beyond their salary. Two other indictments were filed against Drady, one for malfeasance and one for obtaining money under false pretenses. Interestingly, Drady had also been one of the accused councilmen in 1884.[42]

In November, Alderman Drady was acquitted of the two additional charges; then the larger case went to trial. Earlier that fall, attorneys for the defendants—by then down to eight; Reynolds and Smith were under indictment in another case and charges against Hammer had been dropped—submitted a demurrer to dismiss the case on the grounds that no crime had been committed. They contended that 1888 law under which city officials were charged did not provide any penalty for taking excess pay nor even define such an act as a crime. Judge Marcus Kavanagh, however, was not convinced. He rejected the demurrer, and the case moved forward. Once the trial began, attorneys for the aldermen continued with the same defense; they did not deny that the clients took the money but claimed that the 1888 statue in question did not identify their clients' action as illegal and was, at best, drafted in "vague and uncertain" language.[43]

Closing arguments for the ten-day trial ended on Thursday evening, December 4, with Judge Charles Bishop promising a decision the next day. As the crowded courtroom awaited the judge's opinion, the *Iowa State Register*, which was already convinced that the men should be found guilty, described some of the defendants: Sheldon sat with his "brow furrowed looking troubled," Drady's "keen little face was anxiously drawn and his sharp eyes blinked nervously," and King, "the brains of the council of 1888," sat "self-collected and imperturbable." When it got to Charles, the Republican paper could not resist the irony that this man of upstanding reputation was charged with misconduct; it sarcastically referred to him as "'honest' Charles Weitz."[44]

In contrast to Judge Kavanagh, Bishop found in favor of the aldermen, agreeing with their attorneys that the taking of extra salary had not violated any Iowa statue, and hence the councilmen had not committed any crime. He therefore instructed the jury to return a verdict of not guilty. The *Register* called the acquittal a "grievous disappointment to the citizens and taxpayers of Des Moines," but the issue soon dropped out of the headlines, and it was reported that most of the aldermen "refunded to the city certain amounts of money," although the specifics of who returned how much is not clear.[45]

The case is not mentioned in any of Charles's remaining business records, but he must have been mortified by the charges and trial. He would have been happy with the acquittal and that the case was behind him but likely remained disturbed that his character had been sullied. He had worked long and hard to build a solid reputation, and this had clearly played a role in his successful rise. Fortunately, if the number of jobs that came into the firm was any indication, the incident did not affect Charles's business or his standing as a builder. Several large contracts, in fact, were on the horizon, and success would continue for the sixty-four-year-old, now one of a handful of leading contractors in Des Moines. But Charles was beginning to think about slowing down, especially as his two eldest sons and eventually his youngest learned the various aspects of the business and were making their way up the ranks of the company.

Chapter Four

TRANSITIONS

Ever since Charles arrived in Des Moines, his personal story had been intimately intertwined with the company. But by the 1890s, Charles was in his midsixties, and as he became more engaged in banking, he started pulling back from work. Maybe the spate of court cases starting in the late 1880s had worn him down or maybe it was the natural aging process, but whatever the reason, Charles's priorities changed over the course of the decade. Like many other prosperous business figures of the period, he gradually began disengaging from the firm and started enjoying some of the fruits of his labor.

This meant that although Charles remained in charge, he was preparing the groundwork to turn the company over to the next generation. The process began in mid-decade and picked up steam, especially as Charles became frailer after the turn of the century. By 1903, the change in ownership was complete, and his three sons, Charles, Frederick, and Edward, took over the company reins. Led by Fred, the brothers built on their father's successes and expanded the firm's work in larger commercial and office buildings, but most important was a new emphasis on government contracts. The seamless transition must have buoyed the elder Weitz before he passed away in 1906.

The Weitz succession took place during a twenty-year period of change in Des Moines. The rapid growth of the 1870s and 1880s had slowed. Instead of doubling every ten years, the city's population over the next two decades rose from 50,100 in 1890 to 86,400 in 1910. The economy slowed as well, rocked by a depression in the mid-1890s. Commercial activity picked up at the end of the decade and was followed by some minor dips, until a deep decline was set off by the Panic of 1907. This slower growth actually allowed urban services and amenities to catch up, and as the city matured, some of the ugly, rough edges of uncontrolled expansion were softened.

The city's first parks, such as Greenwood, Waveland, Union, and Grandview, were laid out in the mid-1890s; new city, county, and state government facilities were opened; modern hospitals rose—Mercy in 1893 and Iowa Methodist in 1901—the five-story Younkers department store replaced its much smaller retail establishment; and the downtown became more visually appealing when the tangle of overhead electric wires were put underground. Soon thereafter, Des Moines's landscape was influenced by Chicago's 1893 Columbian Exposition as municipal leaders took design cues and architectural styles from this world's fair and employed them in what was in essence an urban renewal project. The result was part of the City Beautiful Movement, eventually leading to seven Beaux-Arts public buildings along downtown Des Moines's riverfront. Other important projects changing the face of the city included the ornate Polk County Courthouse, completed in 1906, and the third Fort Des Moines, a new cavalry post, initially dedicated in 1903.[1]

Against this backdrop of activity, first Charles and then his sons went after and won a number of these larger, more important jobs, but the 1890s opened with Charles losing out on a couple of significant bids. The first must have been particularly difficult. By the last few decades of the nineteenth century, institutions designed to care for the poor and those with physical and mental disabilities began going up across the country. Such a facility for the blind was being discussed at the Iowa statehouse in the late 1880s, and soon the legislature approved the building of a state-owned Industrial Home for the Blind. Here, the visually impaired could learn a trade, and the goods they produced were sold to defray the cost of the institution. The small town of Knoxville, roughly forty miles southeast of Des Moines, was selected as the site.[2]

Seven contractors bid the job, including Charles and his nemesis, F. S. Whiting, the contractor he had challenged in court because of the lost high school contract. Charles not only failed to win the job, he lost it to Whiting, who was paid over $29,000 for the work. This must have been particularly disturbing, but if there was a silver lining, it was that Whiting and his wife were also hired to serve as the first "superintendent and matron" of the Industrial Home for the Blind when it was completed in 1892. Charles was probably upset by the appointment as well, but at least it took Whiting out of Des Moines activity for a while.[3]

As he was preparing his bid for the Industrial Home for the Blind, Charles also sought what he called the "Children's Home" contract. This was the Des Moines Home for Friendless Children, the city's first orphanage, which eventually evolved into today's Orchard Place. The organization was planning a new facility on High Street in 1890 and solicited bids. But the process dragged into the following February, when the organization called for changes in the building's design and contractors had to revise their estimates. Unfortunately for Charles, his $8,800 proposal was on the high end, and Des Moines builder Storm T. Roberts won the job with a bid of $7,835.[4]

63

These loses notwithstanding, Charles and his company kept busy with what they had been doing for years—remodels and renovations, some commercial buildings, and private homes. Weitz crews, for instance, were renovating the Younker Brothers Dry Goods warehouse and had a variety of small jobs at Valley National Bank and Cottage Hospital on Fourth Street, reputed to be the city's first hospital. The Weitz firm had done some of the original carpentry work on the Cottage Hospital medical building two decades earlier, and when it later went out of business because it could no longer compete with new Mercy Hospital, Charles was again hired to work on the building; this time to convert it into row houses. Other projects in 1892–93 included construction of private residences, such as a $3,300 home for merchant William Jaquith, a smaller $1,300 cottage for Simon Casady, and the original Homestead Building on Locust Street—today this building houses Splash Seafood Bar and Grill and includes an addition that was constructed in 1905 by the Weitz company.[5]

More important than any of these individual jobs, however, was the gradual managerial transition taking place at the company. Charles's two eldest sons, Karl Heinrich, known as Charlie, and Frederick—Fred or Fritz to family members—had been working their way up through the ranks of their father's construction operation. After attending local schools, Charlie began working for the firm in 1876, learning various aspects of the operation and making $1 per day. He loved working with his hands and became a skilled carpenter who had an interest in architecture as well, and in the late 1870s, he also worked as a draughtsman for Des Moines architect William Foster. Fred, who was eight years younger than his brother, also studied architecture at a local firm and joined the family business sometime in the mid-1880s. By 1894, Charlie had become the company foreman and was paid $10 a day, while Fred was working as a carpenter earning $5 per day. By that time, sixteen-year-old Edward, the Weitzes' youngest child, had finished school and joined the firm as well.[6]

Meanwhile, in 1888, Charlie had married Lena Vote, originally from Fairfield, a small town 110 miles southeast of Des Moines, and the couple took up residence on Fourth Street. Although he was not the eldest, he was the first of the Weitz children to wed. The rest still resided at Charles and Helena's home at Eighth and Pleasant Streets. In addition to Fred, there were Lizzie and Rosa, who never married; Lizzie was a milliner at Riegelman & Co. and Rosa was a clerk at the Merchants Retail Association. Their sister Emilie "Amelia" remained at home until she wed John McPherrin in 1897; Emma, who taught at Julia Ward Howe School, also lived at home before marrying George Mahnke late the next year. Finally, Edward, who had just started working for the company, was still at home as well.[7]

By that time, many of the city's elites had joined their wealthy peers across the country in building grand homes, which were generally clustered in upscale neighborhoods. Terrace Hill (then owned by F. M. Hubbell) and Herndon Hall, Jefferson Scott Polk's English manor-styled home, established the area along Grand Avenue west of downtown as the city's most fashionable. Over the next couple of decades, the posh residential area spread south of Grand Avenue and just north and west into the Waterbury neighborhood. Although Charles did not follow others to the western edge of town, he did decide on a bigger house. Part of his thinking must have been practical; he and Helena had six adult children living at home, and their current house probably seemed increasingly small. At the same time, he was probably affected by the culture, which suggested that those of the upper classes maintain large residences. Still, his conservative nature would not allow him to erect a showy palace. Instead, he built a comfortable, substantial home befitting his success as well as his understated personality. And for whatever reason, Charles chose not to move west to the Grand Avenue area, as all of his sons eventually did, but instead built a new home on his current land on Eighth and Pleasant Streets.[8]

Before he could build, Charles sold his frame house to insurance agent John J. Ryman in July 1894, and then hired Joseph Blakeslee to move the structure to Ryman's lot two blocks to the west at Tenth and Pleasant Streets. A final part of the agreement gave Charles and his family the right to live in the house "without charge" from August 1894 until September 1895 and then pay Ryman rent if the Weitzes' new home was not yet completed. The classical-styled, three-story brick home "with distinctive arched windows and large front porch" took eighteen months to complete, and the family moved into their new residence in December 1895. Maybe its most memorable aspect was in the formal dining room, which granddaughter Greta Weitz Brown remembered as "the heart of the home." Here stood a floor-to-ceiling china cabinet with beautiful leaded glass doors. According to Brown, when Charles could not find the glass he desired for the cabinet in Des Moines, he purchased crystal wine glasses in Columbus, Ohio, broke off their stems, and "cut the bases to be set in lead" for the cabinet doors.[9]

As the house was being built, Charles renamed the company "Charles Weitz & Sons" to reflect the growing role Charlie, Fred, and now Edward were starting to have in the business. And probably because he felt increasingly comfortable ceding additional company responsibilities to his eldest sons, he became more involved in banking. Already an active board member of Valley National Bank, Charles invested in the new German Savings Bank and became a director in 1894. Capitalized at $50,000 (this was relatively small; Des Moines National Bank was six times larger and Citizen National Bank four times its size), it had been established two years earlier and opened an office on Fifth Street. The bank struggled through the difficult economy and was forced to shut down temporarily in 1897. When it reopened later that year, Charles became the vice president, a position he held for five years, before being named president in 1902.[10]

Meanwhile, now operating under its new moniker, the construction firm began getting bigger contracts. Company records are relatively scant here, and it is difficult to say whether these larger jobs reflected a rebounding economy, more aggressive bidding, or both. But there was a subtle shift, and it began with a couple of institutional projects.

The first was not a large job, but it was a state contract and may have represented Charles's sons' introduction to dealing with a government agency. It consisted of building a chapel for the Girls' Department of the Iowa Industrial School in 1896. The reform school was located in Mitchellville, a town eighteen miles northeast of Des Moines, and housed troubled girls, largely between thirteen and fifteen years of age. Maybe the most interesting element of the job, however, was that Fred evidently served as the on-site manager and signed all the checks for his father from an account established at Citizens Bank in Mitchellville. He had initially been listed as an "architectural foreman" for the company in the previous year's city directory, and this was likely his first substantial management experience. The following year, Fred and his brother were tied up on a larger project closer to home, when the company won the contract for the new Polk County Insane Asylum, located on the grounds of the Polk County Poor Farm, northeast of downtown Des Moines on what became Northeast Fourteenth Street.[11]

In addition, Weitz & Sons remained in the residential market, erecting a number of large, upscale houses just west of downtown Des Moines. Two notable homes built in the first decade of the twentieth century sit south of Grand Avenue on Thirty-Seventh Street: a brick mansion for Gardner Cowles, then publisher of the *Des Moines Register and Tribune*, and another for Clyde Herring, an automobile dealer who later served as the state's governor and then a United States senator.[12]

Several years earlier, in 1897, Weitz & Sons built one of their first homes in the south of the Grand Avenue area, when they erected a new house for Fred. Situated several blocks west of where the Cowles and Herring homes would be located, the structure was originally named "The Dormers," clearly a reference to its four large dormer windows and situated south of Grand Avenue on what was then Park Lane but is now Forty-Second Street. With his background in architecture, Fred probably designed the home himself, and according to Ann Weitz, his great-granddaughter, the style was likely inspired by German farmhouses, although he must have taken his cues from photographs or drawings because he had never been to Germany. Family lore also holds that he actually built the spacious two-story brick home as a wedding gift for his bride, Alice C. Wilson, whom he married in Des Moines in the summer of 1898.[13]

The next year, the economy began to pick up, and many companies started considering expansion. That May, Weitz & Sons began excavation for an addition to the Des Moines Saddlery Building on Court Avenue, but much more important was a contract the firm had just landed with Younker Brothers, a dry goods retailer. The company's origins went back to 1856, when three Younker brothers established a general store in Keokuk, a Mississippi River town in southeastern Iowa. Eighteen years later, they sent a half brother to open a branch store in Des Moines. Their operation in the capital city did well, but business in the original store declined, and in 1879, the brothers closed their Keokuk store and consolidated their business in Des Moines.[14]

Despite stiff competition, which by the 1890s included retailers Harris-Emery Dry Goods, Simon Clothing, Mandelbaum Dry Goods, and Utica Clothiers, Younkers had already moved into larger quarters twice since arriving in the city. In 1899, Younker Brothers had secured an eighth of the block on the northwest corner of Seventh and Walnut in preparation for another move; this time the brothers would build their own five-story department store. The Des Moines architectural firm of Liebbe, Nourse & Rasmussen was selected to design the building, and Weitz & Sons beat out thirteen other general contractors for the work. The job was estimated to be $85,000, the company's largest to date.[15]

Demolition of the old buildings on the corner began that April, and initially the project moved along quickly. The Weitzes employed three shifts of men working around the clock, and the new structure reached five stories in July. But then progress slowed. In August, a storm flooded the construction site, and then in October, a nearby fire melted the building's cornice and broke many of its recently installed plate glass windows. These setbacks delayed the store's completion by a month, but in November, Younker Brothers proudly announced the opening of its "great store." "SIX IMMENSE FLOORS [this included the basement]," the *Des Moines Leader* ad explained, "brilliantly lighted, comfortably heated, and thoroughly ventilated—Its comforts and conveniences of the highest type—its hundreds of aisles, its electric elevators, its spacious balcony—Its numerous departments—together with many other bright and exceptional features" made this new store the "Ideal Shopping Place."[16]

Clearly a triumph for Weitz & Sons, the downtown Younkers building would be expanded over the years and become a Des Moines landmark, only to be devastated by fire in 2014. Shortly after this job, Charles opened a companion business, starting the Century Lumber Company in January 1901. Century had office space in the Weitz Building on Mulberry Street, and its lumberyard was set up a couple blocks to the southeast at Sixth and Market Streets. Charles served as operations president; he hired nonfamily members James Watt, who by that time was also the cashier of the German Savings Bank, as vice president and William Wood as secretary.[17]

Century Lumber was likely part of the transition process as Charles prepared to hand over the construction business to the second generation. Sons Charlie and Fred were now both working as foremen at Weitz & Sons, and Charles must have realized that only one of them could run the business. Fred was evidently the heir apparent of the construction company, and the founding of Century Lumber headed off potential problems between the two eldest sons. It provided a leadership opportunity for Charlie, opened up more possibilities for youngest son Edward, and created a business that the family understood because it was closely tied to the building trade.

As if indicative of his faith in his sons' ability to run the businesses, but also motivated by his declining health—Charles had suffered from a "nervous condition" in 1901—and to escape cold weather, he and Helena took what appears to have been their first major vacation when they went to Saint Petersburg, Florida, in 1902 into 1903. There are no other specific references to his illness, and unfortunately the phrase covered a variety of maladies. Whether called a nervous condition, neurasthenia, a term that had been in vogue in the nineteenth century, or nervous breakdown, which was coined in 1901, the ailments categorized as such were frequently associated with overwork and the pressure and stress of modern life. Symptoms included anxiety, fatigue, and memory loss. Sometimes physical or mental collapse occurred as well. So although the exact nature of Charles's illness is not known, it was serious enough to have led to his first extended vacation, and before leaving town, he transferred ownership of his companies over to his sons.[18]

Each received one-third of the construction business as well as Charles's shares in Century Lumber Company. Several months later in 1903, the brothers signed a partnership agreement and renamed Weitz & Sons to reflect their ownership; henceforth it was Charles Weitz' Sons. Fred became the managing partner, although he very likely had been running the firm for a while, and Charlie became the president of Century Lumber.[19]

Of the two eldest sons, Fred had the most dominant personality, and it was probably no surprise that he ended up heading the construction operation. Like his father, he was strong and determined but "reticent and undemonstrative." He preferred working behind the scenes and "rarely became publicly identified with civic programs or movements." Outside of work, his passions were architecture and design, and his "fervor was in talking and dreaming of achieving in Des Moines a city of architectural perfection." Fred was clearly an ardent civic booster, but he was also a pragmatic businessman, and as Des Moines moved toward this better, well-planned future, he and Charles Weitz' Sons would be there to do the building.[20]

Even before the transition to the second generation was complete, it was clear that government contracts were a growing priority for the company. The increased emphasis in this direction was probably Fred's doing and initially involved his interest in urban renewal and city planning. In the late 1880s, the city's newly formed Commercial Exchange began pushing for cleaning up the Des Moines riverfront, which had become an unsightly dumping ground, lined with derelict buildings and ugly billboards. Other groups, including the Des Moines Women's Club and the Des Moines Park Commission, soon joined the effort. Meanwhile, new thinking about urban structures came out of the 1893 Columbian Exposition in Chicago. The world's fair had featured the so-called White City, a stunning array of chalk-white buildings erected in the Beaux-Arts neoclassical style set amid landscaped grounds, fountains, and a lake, emphasizing balance, beauty, and order. Such architecture and design grew out of an increasing belief that graceful public grounds and structures could create civic spirit and social harmony. These ideas blossomed into the City Beautiful Movement and bore fruit in Des Moines as the riverfront reclamation was getting underway.[21]

Eventually the project would include the elegant seven-building civic center district—the Des Moines Public Library (now the World Food Prize headquarters), the post office (now a county building), the coliseum, an arena that burned down in 1949, city hall, and the municipal courts building (now the police station). Later, the US Courthouse and the armory (now a city hall annex) were added—as well as new bridges, landscaping, fountains, and a river walk. The district began piecemeal in 1899, with initial plans calling for only the three-story neoclassical public library building. This would be the first new structure to grace the Des Moines riverfront. Fred was enthusiastic and would remain so through the planning and erection of the other buildings along the waterfront.[22]

The Weitzes bid on the library job, but the work went to Capital City Brick and Pipe, another Des Moines contractor. Construction began immediately. Unfortunately, it dragged on for years, because, according to Des Moines historian John Zeller, "The city kept running out of money. When the building finally opened [in 1903], it was only partially lit, partially occupied, and, as late as 1904, there were few books." Lack of funds remained an issue, and it was not until 1907 that the Weitz brothers were hired to finish the building's interior. That same year, Charles Weitz' Sons was the only local contractor to bid on Des Moines's new post office, the second neoclassical building set along the Des Moines riverfront. Again, the job went to someone else, but by that time, the Weitzes had already landed several valuable state and federal contracts across the city.[23]

In 1902, the Weitz firm was back working on the Iowa State Fairgrounds, where years earlier, Charles had erected a hall for the McCormick Harvesting Company. Many of the fair's original frame buildings were now in need of repair or replacement, and fortunately the Iowa state legislature began appropriating funds for the construction of permanent buildings. Plans for the new Livestock Pavilion were announced in 1902, and Charles Weitz' Sons won the contract. It was the fairgrounds' first masonry structure, topped with its signature three-tiered roof. The pavilion opened that summer. Two years later, Charles Weitz' Sons built the Agriculture Building, well known today for its butter cow exhibit. Not surprisingly, some of its key design features, such as its two domed entryways, were inspired by the Columbian Exposition's neoclassical architecture. The building's dark red brick façade and stone trim were similar to the recently erected Livestock Pavilion. In 1907, Charles Weitz' Sons also built the horse barn and a powerhouse on the grounds. The company would build additional facilities at the fairgrounds in the years ahead, but in the midst of these first projects, the three sons took a moment to observe their aging parents' fiftieth wedding anniversary.[24]

On July 4, 1904, Charles and Helena celebrated their golden anniversary. The couple had invited the entire family to their home for dinner, but the children and grandchildren surprised their parents with a visit at 8:00 a.m. that morning. Later after dinner, the children and grandchildren again surprised Charles and Helena with a program paying homage to their parents. Fred hosted the evening, and many family members offered the couple toasts and tributes, which were, interestingly enough, given in German.[25]

If this party was a highlight for the family patriarch, so too was seeing the firm continue under his sons. When Charles passed the company on to them in 1902, he poignantly noted doing so "for and on account of love and affection, and other good and valuable consideration, to me in hand paid, by Charles H. Weitz, Frederick W. Weitz, and Edward Weitz." And for several years he had the pleasure of watching his sons grow and expand the business, taking on bigger private and public projects. But his health continued to decline until his condition became serious in the summer of 1906. Charles lingered until November 8, when the eighty-year-old slipped into a coma, and with his family gathered around him, he died at home two days later.[26]

The *Register* eulogized the loss of the "prominent businessman" and "pioneer builder," writing, "Charles Weitz, Sr. built better than he knew. Upon the business streets of Des Moines are hundreds of buildings which have been constructed by him. The big office buildings, department stores and even some of the important public buildings stand substantial and well made, fitting monuments to the memory of the man who laid them stone by stone and brick upon brick." Then the paper, which had taken a jab at the builder's upstanding reputation when he was among the city councilmen charged with misconduct in the 1880s, praised Charles as "thrifty, sturdy in character, and honest in purpose, who came to Des Moines in an early day and with business sagacity and the strict application of the golden rule in all his affairs both public and private lived to a ripe old age, beloved by his family, respected by his fellow citizens and liked by everybody."[27]

Indeed, Charles had played a significant role in building Des Moines, and because he knew the market and made the necessary adjustments over the years, his company prospered along with it. Maybe more important, however, he had laid the foundation for the firm to continue and even thrive once he was gone. This was no easy task; less than 30 percent of family businesses were successfully passed on to the second generation, and the Weitz firm was among those Des Moines companies that made the transition. Others that went through the process at roughly the same time included Hubbell Realty, Gilcrest Lumber (now Gilcrest-Jewett), Kurtz Hardware, Amend Packing Company, and Joseph's Jewelers.[28]

Once they had put their father to rest, the Weitz sons forged ahead in the construction business, remaining on the path that managing partner Fred had already laid out—an emphasis on government work. One project, set in motion four years earlier, was a huge undertaking on the south side of Des Moines. Actually, its origins dated back to 1888, when bringing an army post to the city was among the primary objectives of the Commercial Exchange. Winning the installation, however, was a long and arduous process. Iowa congressman John A. T. Hull began lobbying for such a fort in the early 1890s, and after several failed efforts, he finally succeeded in pushing through a cavalry post bill in 1900, but it was subject to Des Moines donating the requisite land for the facility. With funds raised by the Commercial Exchange, the city purchased four hundred acres for the post, which at the time was south of the city limits, and turned it over to the federal government. The first phase of Fort Des Moines's construction eventually began in the spring of 1902, and although Charles Weitz' Sons must have bid on these jobs, the initial work went to three other firms—Atchison Brothers, Hamilton and Hamilton, and S. A. Robertson. The following year, builders C. E. Atkinson and his brother Guy Atkinson won contracts for additional barracks and stables, and Fort Des Moines was dedicated that November. It would later serve as the first training camp for African American officers during World War I and, during World War II, as the first training center for the Women's Army Auxiliary Corps (WAACs), which later became the Women's Army Corps (WACs). [29]

In 1905, however, Charles Weitz' Sons won its first contract at the fort, building "two double stable guard houses" and a "double set of civilian employee's quarters" at the post. Two years later, it was awarded a $70,000 job, and more followed. In 1917, the firm began expanding and remodeling the base hospital and converting the fort's gymnasium/exchange into a medical facility. Although this work was significant, more important were the connections Fred and company managers made with government officials and the experience they garnered working with the military. These contacts and the knowledge gained would prove valuable when the

Weitzes went after another massive military contract calling for the expansion of Camp Dodge, ten miles northwest of Des Moines, in 1917.[30]

But that was down the road. Shortly after obtaining the 1907 work, Fred and Charlie, along with sisters Rose and Lizzie, who together served as trustees of their father's estate, decided to invest some of the monies from the estate in an apartment complex. All would have been aware of their father's success in buying and renting property, but it was probably Fred as the de facto leader of the family who oversaw the project from inception to completion. In January 1908, the trustees bought an old brick residence in the Sherman Hill neighborhood on the northeast corner of Eighteenth and Pleasant Streets. Charles Weitz' Sons tore down the home and erected what was considered the first high-rise apartment building west of the Mississippi River. The luxury six-story structure was completed in March 1909 and featured "every modern convenience known to contractors." Named the Lexington, the apartment's most notable amenity was its "automatic boyless elevator," which passengers could operate without the need of an attendant. It was the only apartment building in Iowa with such an elevator.[31]

The Lexington kindled Fred's interest in real estate, "a weakness" he believed he had inherited from his father, and he began constructing and managing other apartments in the Sherman Hill area. In 1910, he put up the Emerson next door to the Lexington on Eighteenth Street. Then, after World War I, he built two more buildings on Eighteenth Street: the five-story Concord Apartments in 1919 and the Lowell Apartments in 1920. He later erected the Poncele Apartments at Twentieth-Eighth and Ingersoll Streets. And although he would later admit having "a weakness for owning and speculating in real estate," Fred kept Weitz' Sons focused on government contracts. As the Lexington was being completed, city officials began discussing construction of another Beaux-Arts-inspired public building.[32]

The implementation of the Des Moines Plan—a commission system of city government—in 1908 led to growing concerns about the inadequacy of the current city hall. Plans for a new municipal building soon jelled, and a consortium of four Des Moines architectural firms—Liebbe, Nourse & Rasmussen; Hallett and Rawson; Wetherell and Gage; and Bird and Proudfoot—working together under the name Associated Architects, drafted plans for a new facility. It was to be located along the Des Moines River with the other public facilities in what was soon called the civic center district. The striking neoclassical building was intended to reflect the reformers' ideals of the commission form of government; particularly its interior, which boasted "large and open" spaces "where city business could be conducted on an open business-like basis."[33]

Fourteen contractors bid on the job, but Charles Weitz' Sons' proposal of $301,960 came in the lowest, and the firm won the work. It soon became complicated, however. Each company submitted two bids, one for using the less-expensive Tennessee marble and one using Kasota marble. Charles Weitz' Sons was the lowest bidder using the former material, while Benson & Marxer was the lowest using the latter. Fortunately for Fred and his brothers, when the city council gave the contract to Charles Weitz' Sons, it also passed a resolution giving the architects the right to choose which marble would be used. The architects chose the Kasota stone, Benson & Marxer protested, but the contract stayed with Charles Weitz' Sons.[34]

Construction went forward, but was slowed initially by a dispute between councilmen over who had the right to supervise the project. It was settled when John MacVicar, as the superintendent of streets and public improvements, received the job. The project then picked up steam, and the building's cornerstone was laid in June 1910. Late that year, however, the city council tried asserting its authority and asked for bids on the building's hardware, after Charles Weitz' Sons already had a contract with Garver Hardware for this material. Weitz and Garver cried foul, the city solicitor Robert Brennan agreed with them, and in February 1911, the city council finally backed down and rejected all hardware bids it had requested. That was the last major glitch, and the municipal building was completed that December. Called the "crown jewel of the Civic Center" by Des Moines historian John Zeller, the new city hall opened with a dedication ceremony and parade on January 2, 1912.[35]

Large Des Moines jobs such as this one, the Iowa State Fair facilities, and the Younkers Building put the firm in the public eye and suggested how far Charles Weitz' Sons had come since being established fifty-five years earlier. These bigger jobs, and the company's increasing volume of work, also meant that the firm had outgrown its two-story building that dated back to the 1880s. Therefore, even as they were erecting city hall, the Weitz brothers decided to replace their current shop at 713 Mulberry Street with a larger and more distinguished edifice.

When the five-story terra-cotta and brick-faced structure was completed in July 1910, a local newspaper called it "one of the handsomest buildings erected in the downtown district… this season." And as Fred and his brothers certainly intended, the building exuded a solid and dignified air, one of a company with a strong record in the past and a commitment to the future.[36]

Taken together, these projects closed a long and successful transition period for the Weitz company. It had begun in the 1890s with founder Charles taking a variety of jobs but then starting to pursue larger contracts, all the while building on the firm's reputation for quality work. At the same time, he brought his sons into the business, and when Charles retired and transferred the enterprise to them, it did not miss a beat. Under Fred's direction, the company grew, securing bigger jobs and increasingly working on government facilities. It would continue to do so in the years ahead.

Charles Weitz, ca. 1870s.
Courtesy of Fred Weitz.

Helena Weitz, ca. 1870s.
Courtesy of Fred Weitz.

Charles Weitz, ca. 1904. Courtesy of the Weitz Company.

Frederick, Edward, and Charlie Weitz, ca. 1904. Courtesy of the Weitz Company.

Weitz office building at 713 Mulberry Street, Des Moines, ca. 1890s. Courtesy of the Weitz Company.

The downtown Des Moines Younkers Building, ca. 1905. It was built by Charles Weitz' Sons in 1899. Younkers expanded the structure with additions in 1909 and one in 1924 that linked it to the adjacent Wilkins Building, vastly increasing the store's size. A 2014 fire destroyed the original structure built by Weitz. Courtesy of the State Historical Society of Iowa, Des Moines.

Livestock Pavilion under construction on the Iowa State Fairgrounds, Des Moines, 1902. Courtesy of the State Historical Society of Iowa, Des Moines.

Livestock Pavilion, Iowa State Fairgrounds, Des Moines. Courtesy of the Iowa State Fair Blue Ribbon Foundation.

Agriculture Building, Iowa State Fairgrounds, Des Moines, erected 1904. Courtesy of the Iowa State Fair Blue Ribbon Foundation.

Des Moines City Hall, completed 1911. Courtesy of the Weitz Company.

The second Weitz office building on Mulberry Street, Des Moines, erected in 1910 at the same location as the company's earlier building there. Courtesy of EMC Insurance Companies.

Hubbell Building (now the Hubbell Tower Apartments), Des Moines, erected 1913. Courtesy of the Hubbell Realty Company.

Weitz jobsite, picturing company's early use of a steam shovel, ca. 1915. Courtesy of the Weitz Company.

Century Lumber Company advertisement, 1916. Courtesy of Polk City Directories.

Panoramic view of Camp Dodge, showing construction material unloaded at rail yard. Des Moines, Iowa. 22 August 1917. Photographer: Bandholtz Photo Co., Woodward, Iowa [No. 50 in series]. Courtesy of the State Historical Society of Iowa, Des Moines.

Hotel Fort Des Moines, erected 1918. Courtesy of the Weitz Company.

Frederick Weitz, ca. 1920.
Courtesy of Fred Weitz.

Drake University Stadium and Field House, Des Moines, completed 1925–26.
Courtesy of the Weitz Company.

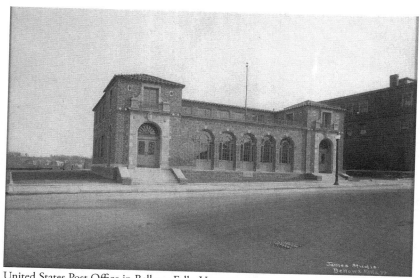

United States Post Office in Bellows Falls, Vermont, 1931. This was one of dozens of post offices the Weitz Company built around the country from 1915 to 1940. Courtesy of the Weitz Company.

United States Appraisers Stores Building, Houston, Texas, completed 1940. Courtesy of the Weitz Company.

Des Moines Ordnance Plant under construction, 1942. Courtesy of the Weitz Company.

Des Moines Register and Tribune Building addition, Des Moines, 1949. Courtesy of the Weitz Company.

Heinrich Weitz, 1956. Courtesy of Robert Weitz.

Rudy Weitz, ca. 1960s. Courtesy of the Weitz Company.

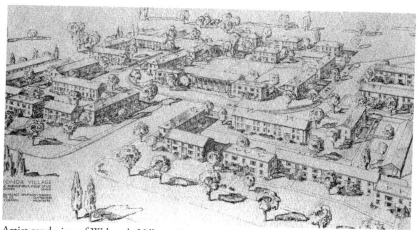

Artist rendering of Wakonda Village, Des Moines. Courtesy of the Weitz Company.

Part of Drake University dormitories and dining hall complex, designed by architect Eero Saarinen and erected in the 1950s, Des Moines. Courtesy of the Weitz Company.

Iowa Electric Light and Power's Marshalltown power plant under construction, 1954. Courtesy of the Weitz Company.

Chapter Five

FROM BOOM TO BUST

Construction of buildings like city hall suggested that Charles Weitz' Sons was in capable hands and its future looked bright. Fred's strategy of seeking larger jobs and contracts from local, state, and federal governmental agencies was paying off. As the company won sizable Des Moines projects, such as the Hubbell Building or another Homestead publishing facility, it also looked outside the city for work. The move was prompted by a developing relationship with the United States Treasury Department, and the firm began building post offices first in Iowa and the Midwest and eventually across the country. These jobs expanded the company's increasingly impressive resume and led to solid recommendations, including one in 1917, which referred to the contractor as "the largest, best equipped, and most reliable in the state." Such positive words and the firm's substantial catalog of fine buildings helped Fred obtain an important World War I contract—the major expansion of an army camp located just outside Des Moines.[1]

The job led Charles Weitz' Sons into the paving business, and soon thereafter the company expanded into other related businesses as well. At the same time, city growth and the boom of the 1920s propelled the urban economy forward and brought the firm significant work, including the construction of the Hotel Fort Des Moines, several large churches, and significant additions at Drake

University. It was amid these jobs that the third generation of Weitz family members joined the company. But even as Charles Weitz' Sons continued winning federal contracts, the onset of the Great Depression revealed financial cracks in the company's otherwise shiny veneer. The company had become overextended and was forced to go through a lengthy and difficult reorganization.

Since roughly the turn of the century, Fred Weitz had successfully guided the company, but keeping it on track had not been easy. It had required long hours, and he worked incessantly. Early on, his daily routine included a full day at the office, followed by dinner at home with the family. Then it was up to his study, where he worked late into the night, poring over records, reviewing the company books, and examining building plans. Son Heinrich once recalled that he saw very little of his father.[2]

Fred's overzealous work ethic was matched by his wife, Alice. She had been one of the city's first female journalists, writing for the *Des Moines Capital* and the *Des Moines Daily News*, and although she no longer worked full-time by the time the children were born—Rudolph "Rudy" in 1901, Greta, 1903, Heinrich, 1905, and Elsa Rose in 1914—she remained as busy as her husband. While she still contributed articles to city newspapers, most of her time was devoted to club work. She played prominent roles in the Des Moines Women's Club, the local YWCA, the Iowa Press and Author Club, and the Iowa Federation of Women's Clubs, including serving as editor of *Iowa Club Woman*, the federation's magazine. Alice also helped establish the Little Theater in 1919, now the Des Moines Community Playhouse, and served on the Des Moines Public Library Board of Trustees for more than twenty years.[3]

Fred's focus on business and Alice's devotion to club work meant that they had a somewhat distant relationship with their children. This was accentuated by an air of formality, which Fred and Alice shared, and was epitomized by the family's annual Christmas party. Beginning in 1907, Fred and Alice held a formal dinner party at their elegantly decorated home on Christmas Eve. Forty or more family members attended the extravagant event; the men in tuxedoes, the women in evening gowns and furs. The black-tie gathering was a family tradition for nearly fifty years.[4]

But the strain of putting in long hours at the company was catching up with Fred. According to Heinrich, his father felt he needed to work harder than his rivals because he lacked a college degree, which a growing number of his competitors possessed. Although clearly intelligent, Fred was largely self-educated. Years of experience taught him all facets of the contracting business, but his lack of formal education evidently gnawed at him. His wife, Alice, had gone to college, and a number of second-generation business leaders in Des Moines—F. M. Hubbell's son F. C. or Phineas Casady's son Simon, for example—had at least some college experience. Whatever his motivation, overwork apparently wore him down, and by 1911, even as the municipal building was going up, Fred realized he needed a break and took his family on an extended vacation to get out of the Iowa cold and recuperate.[5]

His poor health had precipitated the trip, but the destination certainly grew out of a desire to connect himself and his children with their heritage. Charles and Helena had steeped Fred and his siblings in the culture and traditions of their homeland even though neither ever returned to Europe. Fred had continued the practice of emphasizing German customs at home but went one step further than his parents by planning a family trip to Germany. In February 1911, Fred, Alice, and their children, Rudy, Greta, and Heinrich, took a train to New York, where they boarded a ship and sailed to Bremen. Heinrich later recalled that he and his siblings especially relished the time the trip afforded them with their father, a major exception to the formality and distance that usually existed between the children and their parents.[6]

From Bremen, the family toured through Germany until arriving in Munich, where they planned to remain a few months before returning to Iowa. While he was gone, Fred's brothers oversaw the company and its building projects. Fred returned to Des Moines early that summer, but plans changed for his wife and children, who remained in Germany through the summer of the following year. The children enrolled in school and, much to Fred's delight, learned the language and absorbed German culture.[7]

Meanwhile, Fred returned refreshed and oversaw the completion of the municipal building. He also had become an outspoken advocate of the German social insurance system, which had impressed him during his visit. The compulsory program provided workers an old age pension, medical care, and accident insurance, with the premiums being shared by both employers and employees. The system provided basic protections for workers and helped ensure a reliable workforce for employers, and Fred believed that "Americans must sooner or later follow the lead of the Germans." Ironically, the United States would not take serious steps in this direction until the Social Security Act became law in 1935, the same year Fred passed away.[8]

But that unexpected event was well in the future. Shortly after his return to Des Moines, Fred bid on a large office building for F. C. and Grover Hubbell. The brothers planned a ten-story $300,000 structure at Ninth and Walnut Streets and went to great lengths to hire local companies for the job. Charles Weitz' Sons was named the building's general contractor, while Des Moines

Clay Manufacturing supplied the brick, Des Moines Bridge & Iron Works provided the structural steel, Iowa Portland Cement the cement, and L. H. Kurtz the hardware, while the Des Moines branch office of the Crane Company furnished the plumbing fixtures. When the project was completed in the spring of 1913, the contracting firm proudly advertised, "The Hubbell Building was erected by Charles Weitz' Sons, Specialists in High Grade Building Construction." It then suggested, "Let us build a Hubbell building for you."[9]

Yet a recession ran through the rest of 1913 and 1914, and there was not much work for the firm. While the Hubbell Building added to the company's reputation, Charles Weitz' Sons also benefited from Fred's adeptness at making connections and getting contracts. One such job that helped carry it through the slow economy was the new Crane Company building. The Chicago-based plumbing and fixture firm had come to town by acquiring a Des Moines enterprise in 1908. It was initially located at Second Street and Court Avenue. While the Hubbell Building was under construction, the Crane Company, which had furnished the facility's plumbing needs, considered building its own Des Moines structure. It was probably here that Fred built a relationship with local Crane officials, although he certainly would have known the manufacturer and used its products in previous construction.[10]

When Crane unveiled plans for a five-story office, showroom, and warehouse at Fifteenth and Walnut Streets, it looked to Weitz to erect the building. Construction began on July 4, 1914, and the project was immediately noteworthy because it marked the first time a steam shovel was used for a building excavation in Des Moines. Charles Weitz' Sons' other important job during the recession involved retailer S. S. Kresge. The Detroit-based chain of five-and-dime stores had been interested in the Des Moines market since 1910, when it bought land for a building several blocks east of the Crane structure on the northeast corner of Seventh and Walnut Streets. After a few delays, Kresge hired Charles Weitz' Sons to put up a four-story building with its discount store on the first floor and three floors of office space above.[11]

Fortunately the economy began picking up the next year, as Des Moines's population surpassed one hundred thousand for the first time in 1915. The *Register and Leader* noted these positive signs and that spring reported a "much better construction season" for the city. There was renewed interest in commercial construction downtown, and transportation within the city was being improved. Access to the business district, for example, was enhanced with the building of the Seventh Street Viaduct—a bridge over busy rail yards, which provided an arterial entry to downtown from the southern part of the city—and the planning of a new Grand Avenue bridge. Together, these opened a brighter period for Charles Weitz' Sons. Besides finishing projects from the previous year, the firm won a $200,000 renovation and addition for the Harris-Emery Department Store, just across Walnut Street from the Kresge Building, and erected a new facility for Globe Machinery & Supply Company on Court Avenue.[12]

Fred also obtained a remodeling job for the city's post office. The work itself, which included installing larger windows in the building's granite-walled basement, was not nearly as significant as the Harris-Emery remodeling contract, but it connected Fred with a federal supervisor, who was so impressed with the company's work, he told him there was more such work available. He suggested Charles Weitz' Sons subscribe to the *U.S. Government Advertiser*, a weekly publication that listed federal building projects to be let. Fred did so and almost immediately began bidding to construct post offices in Iowa and adjacent states.[13]

In November 1915, the company landed its first contract through the federal publication, winning a bid for remodeling the post office in Kirksville, Missouri. Others soon followed; in 1916, Charles Weitz' Sons began building post offices in Falls City, Nebraska; Grinnell, Iowa; Redfield, South Dakota; and Dickinson, North Dakota. The next year, it started erecting post offices in Chariton, Cedar Falls, and Glenwood, Iowa; Bonne Terre and Butler, Missouri; and Cherryvale, Kansas. Of course, the firm did not get every post office contract it sought. It failed, for instance, in obtaining such work in Aurora, Nebraska, and Washington, Iowa. Still, Charles Weitz' Sons won many more of these jobs than it lost, and this proved only the beginning. The company would erect many more in the 1920s and in the lean 1930s.[14]

Even though Fred must have been excited about the potential for this type of work, and while he occasionally took other jobs outside Des Moines—in 1917, for example, the company built the State Savings Bank in Lamoni, a small town eighty miles to the south—his focus remained on Iowa's capital city. Over the next few years, Charles Weitz' Sons took on a number of local projects. Several years earlier, in 1911, Valley Investment Company acquired additional land for a new Valley National Bank Building on the northwest corner of Fourth and Walnut Streets. Plans to tear down the existing structure and replace it with a new, larger one were announced but did not go forward until 1916, when Charles Weitz' Sons was hired to put up the $600,000 ten-story building. The company's experience on large commercial facilities clearly gave it an edge in getting the contract, but the firm's connection to the bank and its management—founder Charles was a longtime board member of Valley National—certainly helped as well.[15]

Other work keeping Charles Weitz' Sons busy comprised the building of a warehouse for Carpenter Paper Company on Southwest Seventh Street, a new interurban freight depot for the Des Moines City Railway at Second Street and Grand Avenue, a three-story nurses' home at the Iowa Methodist Hospital complex on Pleasant Street, and a two-story factory for Mark's Hats on Third Street. Larger projects included a distribution center for Standard Oil south of Walnut Street near the railroad tracks and a second facility for Homestead publishing on Grand Avenue (now Central Academy of the Des Moines Community School District). Besides these 1916 commercial jobs, the company also erected a gracious home for Edward Weitz west of downtown in the Waterbury neighborhood. Actually, it was the second home the firm built for a family member in the area. Three years earlier, in 1913, it constructed a house for Charles Weitz a block east of where Edward's residence would be located.[16]

While these projects were underway, Fred was selected chairman of the group of twenty-five contractors of the Des Moines Master Builders Association. The group was under the umbrella of the city's chamber of commerce, of which the Weitz firm was a charter member, when it was founded as the Commercial Exchange in 1888. Shortly after Fred's appointment, the United States declared war on Germany in April 1917, and the following month, the US Army announced plans for developing sixteen regional training camps to prepare recruits for battle. As the search for the sites began, the Des Moines Chamber of Commerce saw an opportunity for Camp Dodge, an Iowa National Guard post just north of the city, which they believed a perfect facility to expand into one of the new army cantonments. It lobbied aggressively for the site, while thirteen contractors of the Des Moines Master Builders Association, including Charles Weitz' Sons, proposed submitting a bid for developing the camp together as a consortium.[17]

It soon became clear, however, that the federal government would only consider bids from individual contractors, and on June 15, Iowa congressman C. C. Dowell met with Des Moines builders and urged them to pick one contractor to submit the bid. They did so, and asked Fred to go to Washington, DC, to see if there was any way around the government's unwillingness to take a bid from the association, and if unsuccessful, he should submit a bid for the camp expansion from Charles Weitz' Sons. All at the meeting supported the idea, believing that the job would be so huge they would all participate, and although Fred had not volunteered, he accepted the group's invitation.[18]

That evening, Fred, businessman Clyde Herring; Ralph Bolton, secretary of the Greater Des Moines Committee, an advisory group within the chamber of commerce whose members were all past presidents of the chamber; and several others traveled to Washington to lobby for locating the cantonment at Camp Dodge and for the Des Moines consortium or Charles Weitz' Sons to develop it. When the Des Moines delegation arrived, members were told that the army selection board was leaning toward Fort Snelling in Minnesota for the regional cantonment and giving the construction contract to a Saint Paul firm, but Secretary of War Newton Baker had not yet signed the deal. Given this glimmer of hope, the Des Moines delegation went from office to office with well-prepared presentations selling the merits of Camp Dodge and a local contractor. And because the federal government remained adamant that it would not deal with a consortium, Fred bid the job on behalf of Charles Weitz' Sons. Remarkably, the group's persistence and that of Congressman Dowell, who had been laboring for weeks to bring the facility to Iowa, paid off. The selection board and Baker picked Camp Dodge over the Minnesota option, and on June 21, the contract was let to the Weitz firm. Bolton explained the Des Moines group's success as "good merchandising."[19]

Part of the delegation's sales pitch likely involved Prohibition. Besides emphasizing the advantages of the Camp Dodge location and the experience of the Weitz firm, representatives surely raised the point that the state had passed a strict Prohibition law the previous year, and construction workers in Iowa would not face the temptations of alcohol as they would elsewhere. This proved significant, and according to historian Fred Emory Haynes, "Undoubtedly, the fact that Camp Dodge was located near a saloonless city and at the center of a prohibition State influenced the decision of Secretary Baker."[20]

Fred Weitz believed this was critical as well, and after construction was winding down, he candidly explained to the *Des Moines Tribune*: "Had we saloons in Des Moines the past three months, Camp Dodge cantonment would have never been completed [in the time required], ready to receive the various allotments of men as directed by Secretary of War Baker."[21]

Beyond supporting Prohibition, Fred's comments also alluded to the required rapidity of construction. Plans called for erecting a massive facility to house and train thousands of army recruits from Iowa, Minnesota, Nebraska, and North and South Dakota as quickly as possible. As expected from the outset, Charles Weitz' Sons hired subcontractors from the Des Moines Master Builders Association, and together the builders oversaw an army of workers who began construction at Camp Dodge in July. Standardized plans were provided by the army, and over the next four months, thirty barracks rose, each designed to accommodate 150 soldiers, as well as two headquarters buildings. Crews also constructed a 3,000-seat auditorium, fire stations, a hospital, libraries, post offices, a railroad depot, eight YMCA halls, a YWCA Hostess House, where soldiers could meet visitors, as well as centers for other organizations such as the Knights of Columbus, the Lutheran Brotherhood, and the Jewish Welfare Service.[22]

Even as this work was completed, plans were being made for another expansion of the camp in early 1918, and Weitz and the other contractors continued enlarging the training venue. The camp would in essence become a "self-sufficient community of approximately 40,000" in 1918, housing the Eighty-Eighth Infantry Division and later the Nineteenth Infantry Division. To keep the frantic pace of construction moving forward and motivate the more than five thousand workers on the job, Charles Weitz' Sons posted a patriotic sign at the building site entitled, "Time is Precious." It reminded the workforce of the war and the need to complete the camp quickly so American soldiers would receive adequate training before going off to fight. "One day's delay may cause precious lives to be lost; one week's delay might lose the war," it warned. Then, in a nod to the increasing anti-German sentiment stirred up by the federal government that cast all Germans as enemies and placed a cloud of suspicion over German Americans, the placard explained, "We have the most generous employer the world has ever known—the Government of the United States. So let us prove to our employer that there are no slackers or friends of the Kaiser among us, and that we, together with Major Butler's [the army's construction quartermaster assigned to Camp Dodge] assistance, will complete this cantonment on time."[23]

Besides providing encouragement to the workers, the placard also suggested Fred Weitz's interest in publicly professing his and his company's loyalty. Given the family's German background and the increasingly hostile environment to those of such heritage, it is not at all surprising. By this time, a number of school boards across the nation had banned teaching of the German language, German books were burned, German music ceased to be played, many German-language newspapers were closed down, and German foods were renamed; sauerkraut, for example, became liberty cabbage and hamburgers, liberty steaks. In addition, "'100% American' campaigns enlisted ordinary people to sniff out disloyalty." As citizens began eying each other's behavior for signs of treason, the hysteria reached new heights when Iowa governor William Harding issued his Babel Proclamation in May 1918, prohibiting the use of any foreign language in public.[24]

Sometime after the decree had been issued, a maid at Fred Weitz's house became concerned when she overheard the family speaking German at dinner. Even though the conversation took place in the privacy of the home, the maid contacted police, who followed up by visiting with Fred and Alice and asking a few questions. That ended the incident, which was considered merely a misunderstanding by officials, but it did suggest the difficult environment German Americans faced during the war. Maybe most interesting, though, was the irony of the episode, given that Charles Weitz' Sons was building one of the nation's sixteen cantonments for the US Army. Others who lived near the Weitzes would have thought the suspicion incongruous as well considering Fred had been hosting a large annual Fourth of July picnic and fireworks for the neighborhood since 1909, while in 1917, Alice, as president of the Iowa Press and Authors Club, had established *Prairie Gold*, an anthology highlighting Iowa authors and artists, which would be produced at the club's expense and sold to benefit the American Red Cross.[25]

At about the same time, Fred and Charles Weitz' Sons were receiving praise for their work at Camp Dodge. Six weeks into the process in August 1917, *American Contractor* magazine noted that the construction was proceeding with "wonderful speed and efficiency." By 1918, Colonel Peter Junkersfeld of the Quartermaster Corps, which oversaw the construction division of the US Army, believed the firm's "final showing was as good as any of the other camp constructors." Indeed it was; Charles Weitz' Sons met every War Department deadline and finished the project under budget. Major I. P. Shelby of the Quartermaster Corps was impressed and wrote the Des Moines company, thanking the Weitz brothers for their "consistent courtesy and fair dealing." He was familiar with five other contractors on cantonment projects, but the Weitzes, he explained, expended "more effort to get efficiency out of the labor and equipment and to keep the cost of construction down…than any of the others."[26]

But then two lawsuits cracked the shiny veneer of the Camp Dodge experience. First was a dispute with several members of the Des Moines Master Builders Association who believed Charles Weitz' Sons had breached a joint venture agreement it had made with them on June 15, 1917, to build the camp. When Fred received the camp contract six days later, he appointed an advisory committee, which included three contractors from the group, John Benson, J. E. Lovejoy, and John Mardis, and work began. The other contractors of the Master Builders Association were hired to do a variety of work at the camp and were compensated accordingly, but they thought that because of the agreement, they were entitled to share in the profits equally with Weitz and those on the advisory committee. Fred did not believe any such contract existed, and when he refused to alter the way the revenue had been divided in early 1918, the contractors who felt wronged—John Tusant & Sons, James Maine & Sons, Segner Anderson, Arthur Neumann & Co., W. F. Kucharo Company, A. Sugarman, N. D. Garner, and Edward Baty and William Brereton—sued Charles Weitz' Sons, individuals Fred and Charlie Weitz, and the companies represented on the advisory committee—Benson & Marxer, J. E. Lovejoy, and the John C. Mardis firm.[27]

Des Moines District Court Judge Joseph Meyer ruled in Charles Weitz' Sons' favor, but the case was appealed to the Iowa Supreme Court, which in February 1923 finally settled the issue by affirming the lower court's decision. It argued that although there was clearly an understanding that if Weitz secured the Camp Dodge job, all contractors at the June 15 Master Builders Association meeting would participate in the work and benefit from it, there was no evidence of a contract between Charles Weitz' Sons and members of the builders group. Thus Fred's original plan for divvying up the fee for building the camp—$250,000, less $75,000 in overhead expenses, which went to Charles Weitz' Sons—remained in place and was divided into seven equal portions, with Fred Weitz receiving one share, Edward Weitz, one share, Charles Weitz, one share, Benson & Marxer, one share, Lovejoy, one share, and Mardis, one share. A last share was divided among the rest of the contractors who participated in the construction.[28]

Before the Master Builders Association case was settled, the situation grew worse when Charles Weitz' Sons was hit with another lawsuit. The action stemmed from an eighteen-month federal probe into concerns of excessive charges during the building of all sixteen cantonments. Initially, after Fred heard reports of the planned investigation, he welcomed the query. There would not be any problems with Camp Dodge work, he reasoned, because it had been cheaper to build than all but one of the camps, and the company had received a commendation from Colonel Millard Butler of the Quartermaster Corps stressing "the economical and efficient manner in which this work had been handled."[29]

Nonetheless, in the late fall of 1922, Charles Weitz' Sons was among the ten cantonment contractors the Department of Justice sued to recover up to $50 million that the federal government claimed it was fraudulently overcharged for the camps. In the Weitz case, the government was amazingly suing for $4.5 million, or two-thirds the total cost of the $6.8 million to erect Camp Dodge. Fred vehemently denied any wrongdoing, explaining, "We built Camp Dodge like we would build a plant for any private citizen. We watched the expenses and kept it as low as possible." He added that every government directive on the building of Camp Dodge had been followed "to the smallest detail," and all of the work had been overseen and endorsed by War Department representatives.[30]

The day after the lawsuit against Charles Weitz' Sons was filed, the *Des Moines Tribune* wrote a sympathetic editorial. The paper suggested that the allegations against cantonment builders were brought by Attorney General Harry Daugherty amid demands for "his impeachment because he would not prosecute the real war profiteers." It called for dropping of the "sensational" suit against Weitz, finding the demand for a $4.5 million refund "theatrical." Then it reminded readers, "the well and cheaply built" Camp Dodge was less expensive than "any but one of the camps, and that was in the south, where heating was not installed." Finally, the paper opined, "If Camp Dodge wasted any $4 million, the other camps must have been most colossal steals."[31]

In fact, Daugherty, a member of President Warren G. Harding's infamous Ohio Gang, had been facing charges of wrongdoing for some time. Besides being criticized for not scrutinizing possible fraud during the war, Daugherty faced a House Judiciary Committee inquiry in 1922 for using an injunction against striking railroad workers to keep the trains running. The investigation led to impeachment proceedings against him, but they failed that December, and in January 1923, he was exonerated by the entire House. Charges of misconduct continued to dog Daugherty, however, until fallout from the notorious Teapot Dome Scandal finally led Calvin Coolidge, who as vice president had succeeded Harding in office when the president died unexpectedly in August 1923, to demand his resignation at the end of March 1924.[32]

Unfortunately for Charles Weitz' Sons, the lawsuit continued past Daugherty's downfall and would drag out until 1927, when Attorney General John Sargent finally dropped the case when it was found that government officials had approved all the Camp Dodge charges at issue. The *Des Moines Tribune-Capital* remained convinced that the allegations were trumped up anyway, as the *Tribune* had hinted five years earlier. At Charles Weitz' Sons' exoneration, it wrote, "There was never any reason to believe that the suit was brought for any other reason than to divert attention from Attorney General Daugherty's other troubles over war profiteering."[33]

Although Fred and Charles Weitz' Sons were ultimately vindicated, the litigation had been costly in terms of time, money, and aggravation. But as the suits ground on, the company had found success with local projects, starting in 1918. While it was still doing work at Camp Dodge, the firm won the $1.2 million contract to build the Hotel Fort Des Moines, an elegant new ten-story hostelry at Tenth and Walnut Streets. Designed by Proudfoot, Bird, and Rawson, the U-shaped hotel would boast four hundred guestrooms, increasing the city's hotel room capacity, the *Tribune* bragged, by more than 10 percent. Construction began in March and was expected to take fifteen months to complete.[34]

One of the workers on the job was Heinrich Weitz, Fred's thirteen-year-old son, who served as a water boy, providing cold water to the construction crew that summer. The previous summer, he had been a mail clerk, shuttling mail twice a day to the company's Camp Dodge office via trolley car. Like his father, Fred was clearly grooming his sons to work at the business. Several years earlier, he first introduced his older son Rudy to construction, also by having him help as a water boy for the Crane Building job. After these experiences, both boys continued working for the firm during their summer vacations, learning other aspects of the business, including carpentry and the brick masonry trade. But unlike his father, Fred thought higher education important and sent both his sons to Grinnell College. Rudy graduated in 1921, Heinrich in 1927, but then their interests took them in different directions. Rudy's focus on management landed him at Harvard Business School, and Heinrich's penchant for engineering led him to graduate work at Massachusetts Institute of Technology. As expected, both returned to join the company. Rudy worked his way up on the administrative side, while Heinrich began in a more hands-on capacity, first as a bricklayer, then as a masonry foreman.[35]

Rudy and Heinrich were the only members of the family's third generation who would work full-time at Charles Weitz' Sons. While Fred and his two brothers had remained equal partners in both the business and their Century Lumber Company, from the outset they had divided the duties between the two. Fred was the managing partner of the construction business, while Charlie and later Edward oversaw the lumber operation, which appeared to be doing fairly well. In 1913, Century bought Peoples Lumber Company, giving it a branch lumberyard, located north of downtown in the Highland Park area. The following year more expansion occurred, and the company apparently built a new facility, advertising it as the "the Largest Fireproof Lumber Warehouse in the United States," which was "60 feet wide, 505 feet long, and Three Stories High."[36]

With both Charles Weitz' Sons and Century Lumber showing signs of success, there may have been a tacit agreement that the same arrangement between the three Weitz brothers would carry over to the next generation; thus Fred's family would remain involved in the construction business, and Charlie's and Edward's families would work at Century. Charlie's sons, Carl and Harold, were eight and five years older than Rudy, and although they may have done some summer work for Weitz, it is more likely they did so for Century, where they began their careers in 1915 and 1921 respectively. The division was simpler because Edward Weitz had no children, although his father-in-law, Orlando M. Brockett, an attorney and partner in the Des Moines law firm of Brockett, Strauss and Shaw, did the legal work for Charles Weitz' Sons and was especially busy from 1918 to 1927 fighting the firm's two Camp Dodge lawsuits.[37]

While Fred's sons were learning the family business, construction on the Hotel Fort Des Moines moved ahead even as the Camp Dodge job and the war itself were winding down. Heinrich, in fact, was in the unfinished hotel building on November 11, 1918, when the announcement came of World War I's end. He saw the spontaneous mass celebration as thousands of people jammed Walnut and Locust

Streets, the main thoroughfares of the business district, rejoicing in the news. The "carnival spirit" ensued for hours, but the ending of the war also led to growing social tensions, especially between labor and management. Organized labor had backed the war effort, and because of its cooperation and its stand against strikes, it had won high wartime wages, reduced workdays, and, in a number of cases, union recognition. But inflation resulted in rapid increases in the cost of living—food prices doubled and clothing costs tripled from 1915 to 1920—and after the war, many employers tried to roll back concessions workers had won during the conflict. These issues led to a wave of labor unrest in 1919, when nearly 3,600 strikes took place across the nation. Over four million workers, or roughly 20 percent of the country's workforce, participated in these stoppages. Among the most well-known of these were a general strike in Seattle in February, the Boston police strike in September, and the steel strike, which started in the fall and went down in defeat in January 1920.[38]

Similar labor strife erupted in Des Moines in the spring of 1919. When the city's Master Builders Association did not meet the wage demands for area bricklayers, painters, hoisting engineers, and electricians, the four groups went on strike April 1. Carpenters joined the work stoppage the following day and pledged to remain so until their wage concerns were addressed. Within a week, workers from the rest of the building trades walked off the job in sympathy for their fellow laborers. Approximately five thousand workers stayed home, and ongoing construction projects, including the Hotel Fort Des Moines, a new Hotel Savery at Fourth and Locust Streets, and the Des Moines Municipal Court and Public Safety Building, came to a standstill.[39]

The costly strike lasted nearly eight weeks, finally coming to an end in late May after a group of businessmen who owned unfinished buildings that had been under construction when the strike began pushed contractors and labor back to the bargaining table. Committees representing the builders, workers, and building owners were formed (Fred headed the contractors' committee), and the three hashed out a two-year labor agreement. Full terms were not disclosed, but all appeared satisfied with the compromises—unions were recognized, wage increases provided, and there was an agreement that no strikes would take place before arbitration efforts were exhausted—and all were happy that construction resumed.[40]

Charles Weitz' Sons went back to work, finishing the hotel in July and beginning a number of other projects, including a factory for Blackhawk Tire Manufacturing Company and an addition to the Des Moines Hosiery Mill, both located east of the capitol. But the big contract came that December with a $500,000 job to build the Wilson Rubber Company factory just west of Sixty-Third Street and River to River Road (now Ashworth) in what is today West Des Moines.[41]

This work, coupled with the city's growing population—which had risen to over 126,000 by 1920—and area business expansion, boded well for the company as it entered the new decade. Unfortunately, not everything proceeded as planned. Work at the Wilson Rubber facility commenced with Charles Weitz' Sons preparing the ground, pouring a concrete slab, and beginning on the building. The first floor was nearly completed when the rubber company went bankrupt. Charles Weitz' Sons was not compensated for its work, and the unsightly, weed-filled lot and unfinished building stood as a reminder of the failed project for nearly twenty years until Tom Archer bought it in 1939 and opened the ValAir Ballroom.[42]

Bad luck with the Wilson Rubber job notwithstanding, Fred remained optimistic about the company's future and moved into a couple of sideline ventures he hoped would prove successful. One was the concrete paving business, prompted by the Camp Dodge job, which had required building a road within the facility and then paving Merle Hay Road, the north–south route into the camp from Des Moines. As an automobile enthusiast, Fred was well aware of the need for better roads and certainly of the Good Roads Movement, which had been lobbying to lift Iowa out of the mud and on permanent roads for year-round use. Initially Fred's company received some paving work, including other Iowa jobs in Ames and West Burlington, but competition was stiff and not many additional contracts followed.[43]

Although paving was not the moneymaker he had hoped, Fred continued trying new things. During the construction of Hotel Fort Des Moines, he worked with Weller Manufacturing to develop a more efficient on-site concrete mixing operation, which was used successfully for the first time at the hotel. Sand, gravel, and stone were delivered to the site and placed in an elevator, which distributed the three different materials into individual storage bins. Spigots underneath the bins allowed operators to discharge the proper amount of each material into a mixture, which then moved down a conveyor belt where cement was added before the aggregate ended up in the mixer. Touted by a trade publication, the plant was said to cut labor costs by doing "away with wheelbarrows and shoveling."[44] Clearly a success, this innovation must have helped Fred hold down costs on future jobs.

Another worthwhile move was the addition of an electrical shop. Established in 1918, the subsidiary quickly proved its worth by often attracting work when the general construction side of the business did not. Then there was Fred's interest in concrete bricks. Shortly after the Hotel Fort Des Moines was completed, he became intrigued by the possibility of producing them, which he surmised the company could manufacture, use in its own jobs, and also sell to other contractors. Hence, in the early 1920s, Charles Weitz' Sons designed its own factory based on the Hamilton Concrete Machinery Factory in Cleveland. The facility was built on Sixth Street, just up the road from Century Lumber's large yard. Unfortunately, Fred had misjudged the market. A lot of people were already in the industry, and profits were slim. However, one of the company's few deals with these concrete bricks was noteworthy.[45]

In 1923, Fred signed a contract to use some of his manufactured bricks in erecting reinforced concrete storage bins for Pyramid Portland Cement Company in what is today West Des Moines. According to the deal, Charles Weitz' Sons was to build the facility for its costs plus 10 percent (total costs were estimated at $60,000) to be paid in cement when the contractor needed it. After a short time, Century Lumber signed a deal with Pyramid as well, allowing it to purchase cement at a below-market rate.[46]

Charles Weitz' Sons built the facility in 1923, which ultimately cost nearly $90,000 to construct, and then began ordering cement in payment. Century Lumber also placed cement orders, which were credited to the Charles Weitz' Sons account and deducted from the amount Pyramid owed the contracting firm. But in 1924 and 1925, the cement company told Weitz and then Century Lumber that it could no longer fulfill the cement orders. As a result, Weitz looked to the United States Fidelity & Guaranty Company, a surety firm that had guaranteed the contract, for payment. When the insurer balked, arguing that the original contract had been altered twice—once when the construction costs exceeded the estimate by nearly 50 percent and once when Century Lumber became involved—Charles Weitz' Sons sued the United States Fidelity & Guaranty

Company and Pyramid for what it was owed on the contract. The contractor won in district court, but the case was appealed and finally settled in 1928, when the Iowa Supreme Court affirmed the lower court's decision and ordered the surety firm to pay Charles Weitz' Sons the outstanding amount it was due.[47]

Despite Charles Weitz' Sons missteps in paving and concrete bricks, the 1920s seemed otherwise bright for the company, which kept busy with both local and out of state construction. Fred's connections continued to help him land these jobs. Relationships made during his Camp Dodge work, for example, must have helped him get a 1921 job building a four-story shop facility for recuperators—mechanical parts using springs or pneumatic power to return a gun or artillery piece to the firing position after recoil—at the Rock Island Arsenal in Illinois, while his experience with the Treasury Department led to more post office work. Over the decade, the company built thirty-five post offices in twenty-three different states.[48]

Then there was a job for the Des Moines Women's Club. Fred's wife, Alice, was serving in her second term as president (1921–22), when the organization decided to add a large auditorium to Hoyt Sherman Place, the mansion of deceased Des Moines businessman Hoyt Sherman, where the club had met since 1907. It probably came as no surprise when Charles Weitz' Sons was awarded the $100,000 contract and completed the ornate 1,200-seat theater in 1923.[49]

Meanwhile, there had been another setback. In March 1922, a fire broke out on the third floor of the Weitz Building on Mulberry Street. Although the front half, where the offices of Charles Weitz' Sons and Century Lumber were located, was fireproof and largely undamaged, the rear of the structure was completed gutted by flames. The fire was attributed to faulty wiring and the loss estimated at $60,000 (the machinery and products destroyed were valued at $35,000, while building damage was $25,000). Insurance covered 60 percent of the loss, and Charles Weitz' Sons rebuilt the structure immediately. The day after the fire, Century Lumber ran an ad in the *Des Moines Capital* assuring customers that it was open for business despite the "big fire," which "only temporarily inconvenienced us." But rebuilding proved more than an inconvenience for Charles Weitz' Sons' finances, which were stretched thin at the time. This was suggested in the negotiations when Fred and Pyramid were hammering out a contract in early 1923, when Fred told his counterparts at the cement company that Charles Weitz' Sons did not have "the available funds to carry out the work" and did not want to borrow from its bank because it would need "a large amount of credit when road work begins." Instead, Fred proposed that Pyramid ask its bank to extend credit to Charles Weitz' Sons for doing the job.[50]

But financial trouble was not imminent because Fred was good at getting jobs and able to keep the company's cash flow positive through most of the 1920s. Significant projects included a three-story $100,000 warehouse at Third Street and Court Avenue for commission merchant operation Todd & Kraft Company and the $150,000 Saint Gabriel's Monastery at Merle Hay Road and Douglas Avenue, which was torn down for the Merle Hay Mall in the late 1950s. City growth also meant that more schools were needed, and by mid-decade, Charles Weitz' Sons had built Amos Hiatt Junior High School and Woodrow Wilson Junior High, both located east of the capitol. These were followed by other large undertakings, including Drake University's stadium and field house in 1925 and 1926 as well as the Basilica of Saint

John on University Avenue and the Grace Methodist Episcopal Church (now Grace United Methodist Church) on Cottage Grove Avenue, all northwest of downtown.[51]

But as the economy slowed late in the decade, construction jobs dried up, and Des Moines contractors struggled. Some, like William Knudson & Son, Lovejoy Construction, Garmer & Stiles, and the A. H. Neumann Company, tightened their belts, survived through the ensuing depression, and remained important contractors in the area. Others were not as fortunate, as several prominent builders that had worked with Charles Weitz' Sons on the Camp Dodge facility closed their doors. These included John Mardis, who had gone out of business earlier in 1924, as well as James Maine & Son in 1927, Ed Marxer—once in business with John Benson; the partnership had split up in 1920—in 1928, and Edward Baty in 1929.[52]

The Charles Weitz' Sons contracting firm survived the late 1920s but went through an arduous reorganization process. Problems first became clear in the middle of the decade, when Fred won a number of large contracts but material and labor costs were rising rapidly, making it difficult to develop accurate estimates. As a result, the company lost large sums of money on several big jobs, particularly Saint Gabriel's Monastery and Drake Stadium; Charles Weitz' Sons was now in desperate need of working capital. Fred's eldest son, Rudy, who had been working full-time at the company since 1922 after a year at Harvard Business School, suggested that his father take out second mortgages on some of his apartment buildings to fund the company. Fred did so, and another firm called Weitz Realty was created to hold and manage the properties.[53]

Fred would have been the sole owner of Weitz Realty, but because he had borrowed money from his two brothers to build several apartment buildings years earlier, the amount he still owed them was deducted from his shares of the new company and distributed to Charlie and Edward, thus making it a partnership. Meanwhile, Century Lumber was evidently experiencing difficulties as well, and although its situation was not as dire as Charles Weitz' Sons, the brothers also provided it with additional capital via the real estate company. But the money sent to the construction company was not enough for it to survive. In an effort to generate additional income, Charles Weitz' Sons established another subsidiary in 1929. Called the Weitz Company Inc., the firm was headed by Rudy and intended to sell and install Oil-O-Matic oil burning furnaces. And although the reason is unclear, it set up two offices, one in Des Moines and another in Saint Louis, Missouri.[54]

In the midst of these challenges, Fred and his brothers dealt with their mother's death. The ninety-five-year-old widow had been in a wheelchair for several years but was in otherwise good health before she fell ill for a few days and passed away in May 1929. Because of her advanced age, her death was certainly not a complete surprise. Still, burying his mother must have been especially poignant for Fred as he struggled to keep the company founded by his father alive.[55]

But indebtedness for Charles Weitz' Sons remained a problem, and the new furnace subsidiary did not make as much money as had been hoped. By this point, the Depression had set in, and the construction industry, which had been down since the late 1920s, continued suffering. Nonetheless, the firm still found work. From 1929 through 1931, Charles Weitz' Sons built post offices in Conway Arkansas; Boise, Idaho; Decatur and Metropolis, Illinois; Anderson, Indiana; Elizabeth, New Jersey; Salem, Oregon; Corinth, Mississippi; Mitchell, South Dakota; Wenatchee, Washington;

Fitchburg and Pittsfield, Massachusetts; and Washington, Pennsylvania. In Tulsa, Oklahoma, it landed a $700,000 contract to renovate and expand the federal building, and in Des Moines, the company erected the Temple B'nai Jeshurun at Fifty-First Street and Grand Avenue.[56]

Unfortunately, these jobs did not solve company problems, and by 1931, the consulting accountants recommended that "radical measures" be taken. With few options open, Charles Weitz' Sons went into receivership, and Rudy, who had just been appointed company treasurer, was named the receiver. Working with creditors that included Weitz Realty, another family firm called Weitz Investment Company, Valley National Bank, shareholders (Fred and his two brothers), and suppliers to pay off accounts equitably, Rudy laid the groundwork to launch a reorganized firm. Meanwhile, he refocused the company on its core business, shedding the paving subsidiary, the concrete brick venture, and the recently established furnace enterprise. The electrical division, however, had proven successful and remained part of the company.[57]

As the reorganization moved forward, there were other hiccups. First was the company's proposal for erecting a post office in Pampa, Texas, a small town in the middle of the state's panhandle. When the bids were initially opened, Charles Weitz' Sons appeared to have won the job, but when late proposals were reviewed the following day, the Des Moines firm was no longer the lowest bidder and did not get this much-needed work. More bad news followed from Helena, Montana, where the firm was erecting a federal building. The structure was supposed to be completed in January 1933, but was delayed three months because the firm could not get the sandstone required. Then in March, construction was suspended because the firm's payroll funds were "tied up in a closed Iowa bank." Both issues were finally rectified, and by June, Heinrich Weitz, who was supervising the job, reported that the building was "nearly complete" and ready for federal inspection, but the delay must have been costly.[58]

The planned restructuring had gone forward, and the leaner contracting firm was launched in February 1933 under the Weitz Company Inc. name, which had been used by its now defunct furnace enterprise. Fred was elected chairman, Rudy, president, P.S.M. (Munk) Pedersen—the company's chief engineer—vice president, and Andrew Johnson, vice president for the electrical division. In addition, the Weitzes also reconsidered the ownership issue. Up to this point, the three Weitz brothers shared ownership of both the Weitz contracting firm and Century Lumber Company, although Fred had run the former, while Charlie and Edward had operated the latter. However, after Charles Weitz' Sons was liquidated and reorganized as the Weitz Company, Charlie and Edward pulled out completely, leaving the construction operation solely owned by Rudy and Fred (Heinrich would soon buy shares as well), with Pedersen and Johnson holding minority positions. But Fred continued holding his shares of Century Lumber and remained a vice president.[59]

Fred and his sons were hopeful the streamlined contracting firm could survive the continuing difficult times, but its first few months did not look promising, as the company lost three post office jobs in Iowa and Missouri to lower bidders. The stress wore on Fred. He had devoted his life to the company and was clearly upset by its problems, so much so that he apparently was unable to discuss them with his wife. Instead, he wrote her a detailed, four-page, single-spaced typed letter in 1932, explaining the firm's inauspicious circumstances and his culpability. Following the reorganization, Fred redoubled his efforts to make it a success, but the strain proved too much, and he suffered a stroke while in his office in February 1935. He was taken to Iowa Methodist Hospital, where he remained in a coma until he died five days later on February 17.[60]

The restructuring of the firm and then Fred's unexpected death signaled the closing of an era for the company. For the past twenty years, he had directed Charles Weitz' Sons as it became an increasingly prominent player in Des Moines's commercial construction. At the same time, the firm effectively moved into federal contract work, building a number of post offices around the country as well as the World War I cantonment at Camp Dodge. But growth did not necessarily translate into success, and even as Rudy and Heinrich began moving up the company hierarchy, financial trouble was brewing. A series of lawsuits, although they were all won, drained the company of cash. Several subsidiary businesses proved unprofitable, and substantial losses on several big jobs threw the company into a tailspin. Reorganization seemed the only answer. When Fred died, the future of the Weitz Company fell to Rudy and Heinrich. Time would tell if the family's third generation could right the ship and navigate the troubled times.

Chapter Six

FROM BUST TO BOOM

The Depression years were bleak. Businesses failed, workers lost their jobs, and many wondered if good times would ever return. But for all the fear and uncertainty, there were success stories. Major national companies such as Fisher-Price, Rubbermaid, Tyson Foods, and GEICO had their beginnings in the Great Depression, and there were similar triumphs in Iowa as well.

Partners Charles Hyde and David Vredenburg opened a general store in Beaconfield, a small town sixty miles south of Des Moines, in 1930, but closed this operation three years later. The men had opened several other stores, and by 1938, they were operating fifteen in Iowa and Missouri. This was the beginning of Hy-Vee, now a West Des Moines-based supermarket chain with 235 stores. In Des Moines, meanwhile, tough times and the death of his father had forced eighteen-year-old John Ruan to drop out of college in 1932 and find work. He bought a used truck and began hauling gravel for a road builder in southeast Iowa. Ruan soon switched to carrying coal, bought more trucks, and eventually got into petroleum hauling. This became the basis for a Des Moines-based business empire that today embraces trucking, banking, and real estate.[1]

Unlike these Depression-era start-ups, Charles Weitz' Sons' past gave it an advantage over new businesses. Despite its restructuring, the firm had years of expertise in the field, longstanding relation-ships with suppliers, a reputation for quality work, and a solid customer base. Fred and then Rudy planned to build on this with a straightforward, simple strategy of focusing on the core construc-tion business while using the electrical division to attract any jobs possible. Ultimately they hoped to hang on until the economy turned around.

With a skeleton staff, the company struggled forward. As Rudy recalled years later, "Work was a little quiet, but we were never entirely without work." Indeed, Charles Weitz' Sons stayed afloat with small jobs until the mid-1930s, when business finally started recovering. And by the latter half of the decade, as historian Joseph Wall explained, the Depression "was no longer the all-absorbing topic of conversation." It looked as if, he noted, "the seven years of famine" were over. No one, however, could have anticipated "the feast" that was to come. World War II pumped billions of dol-lars into the economy, pulling the Weitz Company and countless others out of the doldrums.[2]

That proved only the beginning of a great turnaround. Although many feared a return to depression, an unprecedented boom followed the war. Fueled by government spending, pent up demand, wartime savings, and the baby boom, which pushed the nation's population from 141 million in 1946 to 160 million in 1955, a new prosperity spread across the country. Productivity rose, incomes surged, unemployment remained low, and consumer spending reached new heights. Output of goods and services nearly doubled over the period, and for most Americans, in the words of historian John Diggins, it was a time of "unbounded possibility." Together, the economic expansion and the baby boom reconfig-ured the nation's cities with countless suburbs developing on their fringes. And all the while, new homes and schools, churches and shopping centers, as well as office buildings and factories sprouted across the country. The construction of this abundant postwar world created great opportunities for contractors, and the Weitz Company was well-positioned to take advantage of them.[3]

Years earlier, however, the future had not appeared so bright. Fred and Rudy had worked closely together on the company's drastic reorganization. While Rudy remained an officer of the firm, first as president but soon as treasurer, and was active at board meetings, when the business was reincorporated as the Weitz Company in 1933, he no longer worked full-time. He and his father must have discussed the need to pare down, and as a result, the thirty-two-year-old left the family firm and began work as a vice president at Valley Bank and Trust Company. Here he helped oversee the reorganization of the firm's banking operations. Its Valley National Bank was in trouble. Ultimately it was consolidated with the holding company's stronger Valley Savings Bank during the national bank holiday in March 1933, but weeding out bad debt and ensuring that the institution had the required assets to meet new state banking restrictions was a long and complicated process.[4]

Meanwhile, by 1934, Fred was running the Weitz Company with a full-time staff of four and then three—Munk Pedersen was vice president and chief engineer, but he resigned that July and was not replaced. Heinrich was the construction superintendent; Andrew Johnson headed the electrical division; and Cleo Davis ran the office, though her named changed to Anderson after she married in 1936. The dwindling staff was now situated in only a portion of the third floor of the Weitz Building, where in the 1920s it had occupied the entire second and third floors. And for a while, because it was so expensive to heat their space, Fred and his team cut costs by turning the furnace off and wearing heavy clothing and boots in the office during the winter months. The situation was indeed grim, and that February the board noted that "there does not seem to be much prospect of making a go of it." But the company limped along and recorded a net profit of $509 in 1934, up from $235 the year before.[5]

Even though Rudy was working at Valley Bank and Trust, there was no question that he was the Weitz Company's heir apparent and would head the company when the time came. He had clearly been groomed for the position; raised around the firm, Rudy had been involved in various aspects of the construction business since he was young. He had also taken graduate courses at Harvard Business School and then, under his father's tutelage, gained years of experience in management at the firm. Thus, when Fred died suddenly after suffering a stroke in 1935, Rudy left the bank and took the reins of the Weitz Company. Smart and self-assured, Rudy did not suffer fools easily and could be domineering, but he proved an effective, natural-born leader both inside and outside the company. From his father, he had inherited his love of the contracting business and his proclivity for experimenting with new building techniques and ideas, while from his mother he had picked up an artistic bent and a penchant for civic organizations. These latter interests had led Rudy to serve as editor of the Grinnell College newspaper and, years later, take up photography. They also meant that, unlike his father, who focused almost exclusively on the firm, Rudy became active in the community, first in the 1920s as a board member and then president of the Des Moines Community Drama Association. This group operated the Little Theater (now the Des Moines Community Playhouse), which his mother had helped found. He was also a member of organizations like the Des Moines

Chamber of Commerce (now the Greater Des Moines Partnership) and the Community Chest (now United Way), and served on the boards of various companies and nonprofits.[6]

Nine years before taking over leadership of the Weitz Company, Rudy had married Sarah "Sally" Stevenson in September 1926. Born in 1902, she was the daughter of Des Moines attorney Jesse F. Stevenson and Lora Ankeney. Sally was very bright, and after attending Des Moines public schools, she attended Grinnell College for two years. There she roomed with Greta Weitz, Rudy's sister, but although she knew Rudy, who was a Grinnell senior at the time, the two did not date while at college. After her sophomore year, Sally moved back to Des Moines and worked for a year as a copywriter at Harris-Emery Department Store. It was here in Des Moines that she and Rudy began seeing each other when he returned from Harvard.[7]

After working for a year at Harris-Emery, Sally went back to college that fall of 1923, but transferred to the University of Wisconsin, possibly following in the footsteps of her sister Helen. There she graduated Phi Beta Kappa in 1925 and went into advertising work for the Standard Corporation in Chicago. She kept in close touch with Rudy, however, and a year later the two were married in a "simple" ceremony at Sally's parents' Pleasant Street home in Des Moines. The newlyweds spent the night at the Hotel Fort Des Moines and then enjoyed a "northern motor trip" to Mason City, Minneapolis, and on to Lake Superior.[8]

Once back in Des Moines, the two settled into the Lowell Apartments, then owned by Rudy's father, Fred, on Eighteenth Street. Three years later, the couple needed more space. In April 1929, Frederick William, their first child, was born, and that fall they moved into a two-story home—also owned by the Weitz family—next door at 726 Eighteenth Street.[9]

But the young family was not there very long. In 1930, Rudy and Sally bought sixteen wooded acres south of Grand Avenue on Fifty-Sixth Street. There they planned to build their "dream house" and initially erected a picnic cabin on the property. But hard economic times changed their plans. Instead they gradually added onto the cabin before moving into the expanded structure in the spring of 1932. Three years later, a second son, Stevenson "Steve," rounded out the family.[10]

In an unusual twist, Fred and Steve were raised to refer to their parents by their first names, Rudy and Sally, as opposed to mother and father or mom and dad. The origin of this peculiarity is unclear, although it may have stemmed from Rudy's reaction against the formality of his family. Regardless, Fred and Steve were both close to their cultured and doting mother and had admiration for their hardworking and intellectual father.[11]

While Rudy and his father, Fred, had been managing the company in the late 1920s, his younger brother, Heinrich, had been largely out of state, overseeing post office construction after doing some graduate work at the Massachusetts Institute of Technology. Warm, genial, and more affable than Rudy, Heinrich was an engineer who had deferred to his older brother's domineering personality for years. The pattern continued, and he naturally settled into a secondary role at the company. After completing a post office in Greensburg, a suburb of Pittsburgh, Pennsylvania, Heinrich returned to Des Moines briefly in 1930, when he married Elizabeth "Betty" Carter, the daughter of insurance agent Edwin E. Carter and Theo Ethel Lierle. Like Sally, Betty attended college, graduating from the University of Iowa. The newlyweds were not in Des Moines long, however. Shortly after the July wedding, the couple headed out to Bellows Falls, Vermont, followed by Helena,

Montana, where Heinrich continued supervising the firm's post office work. The couple's older son, Edwin, was born in Montana in 1932, before the growing family returned to Des Moines the following year.[12]

Here they briefly took up residence at the Concord Apartments at 732 Eighteenth Street—another one of Fred Weitz's apartment buildings, located next door to the house where Rudy and Sally had lived—before moving to 6003 Waterbury Circle, which had been Betty's parents' home and was around the corner from both uncles Charles and Edward. In 1936, Heinrich and Betty's second son, Robert "Bob," was born.[13]

Now under Rudy's leadership, the Weitz Company stuck with its long, successful strategy of seeking federal contracts. The efforts paid off in 1936 and 1937, when the company's experience helped land five more post office contracts; three in Iowa and two in neighboring Illinois. These jobs signaled the company's recovery, and from that point on it was back on track. Two additional federal jobs were in the offing. In 1938, the firm secured a Public Works Administration (PWA) contract. The PWA was a New Deal program that built large-scale public projects and provided employment working through private contractors. The Weitz Company's PWA job was to build a new elementary school in West Des Moines on the former Lincoln School site at Locust and Seventh Streets. The Weitz Company tore down the old school and erected the new structure, called West Des Moines Elementary, which opened in the fall of 1939. It was renamed Phenix Elementary School in 1955 and remained in use until budget cuts led to its closing in 2014. Current plans call for converting the building into apartments.[14]

The firm won a second significant federal job in 1939, when it was awarded the contract for a US Appraisers Stores building to be erected in Houston, Texas. Completed in 1940, the three-story art deco structure sat on the Houston shipping channel and was operated by customs officials who inspected imports and assessed duties and taxes.[15]

In the midst of this federal work, construction in Des Moines started picking up as well. Building permits issued in the city nearly doubled from 1934 to 1938. Although the company was no longer seriously involved in building homes, it took on some residential construction jobs in 1935 and 1936, erecting several houses for well-to-do families in Des Moines. One in particular stood out. Des Moines physician Helen Johnston, convinced of the advantages offered by an "all-electric" home, decided to build one in 1936 in the "south of Grand" Avenue neighborhood west of downtown. By the 1930s, General Electric and other utilities companies began publicizing the advantages of such homes as a way to generate sales. These structures were generally modern in style with bold shapes and flat roofs. Inside, efficiency was emphasized, and, of course, the homes featured all the latest electrical innovations and devices including indirect lighting, the newest kitchen appliances, such as automatic dishwashers, ranges, refrigerators, and garbage disposals, as well as clocks, radios, and hall chimes. The Weitz Company constructed the unique home, probably because Rudy, like his father, was drawn to design and new ideas.[16]

Commercial jobs followed. These included a renovation at the Meredith Publishing offices at Seventeenth and Locust Streets, an addition to the Des Moines Power Plant at First and Center Streets, the Hills Department Store Building along the 300 block of Walnut Street, and a telephone exchange building in Marshalltown, fifty miles northeast of Des Moines. But the biggest local job of the period and maybe the best signal of the recovery in downtown

Des Moines was Bankers Life's move to a new home office. The company had been in the Liberty Building since 1924, when it signed a fifteen-year lease. After initially considering the erection of a new building west of downtown on Grand Avenue, the company eventually decided to stay in the city's business core. Early in the Depression, Bankers Life had acquired some properties between Seventh and Eighth Streets along High Street, just north of Grand Avenue. In 1937, it bought several other buildings along the block, including the old Weitz home, which had been empty since Helena died in 1929.[17]

The Weitz Company bid the $1.5 million project, but in this case, rival Des Moines builder A. H. Neumann Company was named the general contractor. Fortunately the firm did not walk away completely empty-handed; it submitted and won a separate bid to do the electrical work. The building was begun in the summer of 1938 and dedicated in the spring of 1940. Despite getting only the electrical contract, the Weitz Company's fortunes were clearly looking up. In 1939, it posted a net profit of $5,445, up more than ten times from 1934.[18]

Like the Weitz Company, many Iowans were enjoying economic recovery by the end of the decade, but nationally, unemployment was still high, remaining over 14 percent as late as 1940. Ultimately it was World War II and conversion of the economy to a wartime footing that pulled the country out of the depression. In 1940, for instance, the total federal budget was just shy of $10 billion, but that rose as President Franklin Roosevelt prepared for war and soared following the attack on Pearl Harbor, when the United States entered the global conflict in December 1941. New facilities were built to produce weapons, and countless existing factories converted to war production. And there were jobs. Seven million American civilians moved into the workforce, while over fifteen million served in the US military. By the time the war ended in 1945, the annual federal budget edged up over $100 billion, ten times what it had been five years earlier, and unemployment had fallen to just 2 percent.[19]

As the war transformed the nation, so too did it alter the Iowa landscape. When fighting began in Europe, demand for foodstuffs jumped, and farmers prospered as they mechanized, setting production records throughout the conflict. Change was also evident in Iowa cities. New plants or additions to existing ones rose to meet the wartime need for weapons, munitions, and other goods required for the military effort. In Waterloo, for example, 115 miles northeast of Des Moines, seventeen factories dedicated to war production employed over seventeen thousand workers. Another twelve thousand workers assembled artillery shells and aerial bombs at the Iowa Ordnance Plant in the southeastern Iowa city of Burlington. Smaller towns like Newton, forty miles east of Des Moines, were also affected, with the Maytag Company switching from producing washing machines to aircraft parts. All told, this war activity had a huge impact on Iowa's industrial capacity, and the state saw the number of these enterprises rise from 2,540 employing nearly 65,000 workers in 1939 to 2,970 facilities with 112,500 employees in 1947.[20]

Demand for wartime plants and additions created real opportunities for the Weitz Company. Shortly after the federal government chose Burlington for the ordnance facility in 1940, state officials, including Iowa's US senator Clyde Herring and Governor George Wilson, began lobbying hard for a second defense facility in Iowa, while Des Moines mayor Mark Conkling and local business organizations such as the chamber of commerce and the Greater

Des Moines Committee had been working specifically to locate an armament plant in their city. Rudy was active in these booster groups, and although there is no record of it, he was most likely involved in these state and municipal efforts. Besides the potential benefits for the city and state, Rudy knew that if they landed a big military contract, the Weitz Company would likely participate in the work. He also knew that the company was probably not large enough to handle the work itself, so he began piecing together a consortium of Iowa contracting firms in case the opportunity presented itself. By March 1941, the military was considering twelve Midwestern locations for additional munitions plants. Three months later, news of three small arms plants were announced: one for Des Moines, with identical complexes to be built in Saint Paul, Minnesota, and Salt Lake City, Utah. The project required a large piece of land, and over the next couple of weeks, military officials reviewed several Des Moines metro area sites before settling on 2,445 acres just south of Ankeny, a small town of 780, ten miles north of the capital city's downtown.[21]

As the site selection process went forward, Rudy formed a joint venture with three other firms: J. S. McLaughlin & Sons of Des Moines as well as Central Engineering and Priester Construction, both based in the eastern Iowa city of Davenport. Together the four companies submitted a $32 million proposal for the Des Moines Ordnance Plant job. The group won the cost-plus deal and signed the contract on July 14. Weitz, McLaughlin & Sons, and Central Engineering would divide the profits equally, each receiving 30 percent, while Priester, whose involvement in the project was significantly less, was allotted 10 percent. Like the Iowa Ordnance Plant in Burlington, the Des Moines facility was built and owned by the Defense Plant Corporation—a federal agency created within the Reconstruction Finance Corporation (RFC) in 1940—to expand the nation's war production capability, but each plant was managed by a private contractor. United States Rubber Company, which became Uniroyal and was later purchased by Michelin, ran the Des Moines facility.[22]

Much of the job was curiously reminiscent of the Weitz Company's Camp Dodge experience twenty years earlier. As with the World War I contract, it was the Weitz Company, in this case Rudy, who took the lead, put the deal together, and worked the federal bureaucracy to win the contract. The Weitz firm then acted as managing partner and oversaw the massive project, which because of the urgency of war was erected with amazing rapidity. Construction of the Des Moines complex began in late July, with site preparation that included mowing down any corn remaining in the fields—for which the government paid the former landowners—grading the soil, and building a fourteen-mile chain-link fence encompassing the entire facility. The site was guarded around the clock, and security passes were required for entry.[23]

After remodeling the old Fitch barn—the F. W. Fitch Company's 750-acre dairy farm was the largest single piece of land acquired for the plant—as an on-site office for Weitz Company and the rest of the contractors, a permanent administration building and warehouses went up. By September, over 3,500 workers were busy at the site, and Rudy said the plant would be completed in January. But problems slowed progress. A fire burned down an on-site warehouse, and unusually wet weather impeded construction. In October, floodlights allowed for two, ten-hour shifts, and even though the project was half completed by the end of November, it remained behind schedule.[24]

The work pace picked up after the Pearl Harbor attack in December, and in March 1942, a little more than seven months after construction began, the enormous, 219-building Des Moines Ordnance Plant began producing both .30- and .50-caliber machine gun cartridges. As with its work at Camp Dodge, the Weitz Company's efforts were praised, but unlike the earlier experience, which was tarnished by two lengthy and costly lawsuits, the accolades reverberated widely. Although the company had begun recovering when Rudy landed this work, the contract singlehandedly transformed the firm. The immense size and scope of the job was like nothing it had done before, forever changing the still struggling operation into a large and profitable business. And almost immediately, more lucrative defense work resulted. Shortly after the Des Moines facility opened, the Weitz Company was given a contract for building another munitions plant in Eau Claire, Wisconsin, "on a fixed-fee basis without competition." The only stipulation was that Rudy "take charge and direct the operations."[25]

Because the Eau Claire job entailed remodeling and expanding an existing facility, it was not nearly as large a project as Des Moines, and it also involved U. S. Rubber, whose ties to the Eau Claire factory went deeper than its connections to the central Iowa plant. By the time the United States entered World War II, Japan had consolidated its hold on much of the world's raw rubber resources, and when the federal government restricted the sale of rubber goods for civilian purposes, tire production at the Gillette Tire Company's Eau Claire plant fell off sharply. The U. S. Rubber Company had purchased a large share of Gillette in 1931 and acquired a controlling interest in 1940. With orders diminishing, U. S. Rubber sold the Gillette complex to the government in early

1942. This facility became the basis for the Eau Claire Ordnance Plant, which, like Des Moines, would produce small arms ammunition and would be managed by U. S. Rubber.[26]

Rudy and the Weitz Company directed the project, partnering with a local contractor, Fox Valley Construction, out of Appleton, Wisconsin. The $10 million revamping and expansion of the Eau Claire complex went forward rapidly, and it began producing munitions that August 1942. Six months later, the Weitz Company started the first of three additional war projects, each involving the commodity of rubber. Lack of raw rubber pushed the federal government to establish a synthetic rubber program, for which industrial alcohol was needed. In February 1943, the Defense Plant Corporation went ahead with plans to build a grain alcohol works in Muscatine, an Iowa city on the Mississippi River, 150 miles east of Des Moines. Local businessmen G. A. Kent and S. G. Stein formed Grain Processing Corporation to manage the facility, and the $3 million construction contract was let to the Weitz Company. The plant was up and running by December. Weitz also erected a smaller industrial alcohol facility in Clinton in 1943. The following year, the contractor was hired by the Defense Plant Corporation to install machinery for the production of military tire casings and tubes in Des Moines's new Firestone Tire and Rubber factory that opened north of downtown on Northwest Second Avenue in 1945.[27]

The company's last defense contract during the war was its expansion of the Cornhusker Ordnance Plant in Grand Island, Nebraska, which loaded and assembled high-explosive artillery shells as well as fragmentation bombs and larger, general demolition bombs. The $2.6 million job included adding a fourth munitions loading line, enlarging two existing loading lines, expanding existing buildings, and erecting two new warehouses. The project was completed in 1945.[28]

Besides defense contracts, the Weitz Company was kept busy with other war-related work. Grinnell College modified its curriculum because of the conflict, and in cooperation with the federal government, it began offering a number of military education programs, including Officer Candidate School, the US Navy's Flight Preparatory School, and specialized training for the army. Such undertakings required new facilities. Since Rudy, Heinrich, their sister Greta, and Sally had all gone to Grinnell, the family had close ties to the college, and when the institution decided new buildings were in order, it looked to the Weitz Company to erect them. Thus the firm constructed Cowles Hall, a new men's dormitory, in 1941 and the Darby Gymnasium and Field House the following year.[29]

Meanwhile, at Iowa State College (renamed Iowa State University in 1959) in Ames, thirty-five miles north of Des Moines, a secret research and development project required a new building. In 1941, chemistry professor Frank Spedding was recruited by the War Department to develop a process that could produce pure uranium metal. The Ames group worked in conjunction with the Manhattan Project—the code name for the program that developed the first atomic bombs—and operated out of the former women's gymnasium, which was renamed the Physical Chemistry Annex. Once the scientists worked out the details and began significant production of uranium in 1943, they began looking for ways to recover uranium from scrap metal. This process required another structure, and Weitz won the contract for the Physical Chemistry Annex Two, which was completed in 1944.[30]

In the midst of all this activity, Rudy moved the company offices, which had been located in the Weitz Building at Seventh and Mulberry Streets since the family constructed it in 1910. Actually, the firm had been in an older building at that location going back to the 1880s. But the poor economy of the mid-1930s made the weight of the building's mortgage payments too much to bear, and in 1934, Rudy and his uncle Edward cut a deal with Bankers Life, the note holder, transferring the building to the insurance company in exchange for being released from the mortgage. Yet the Weitz office, as well as that of Century Lumber, remained in the building as they continued leasing space there for eight more years. That changed in May 1942, when Rudy relocated the firm to the fourth floor of the Fleming Building at Sixth Avenue and Walnut Street. Century Lumber, which was still held by members of the Weitz family but was completely separate from the construction company, also moved, setting up office at its lumberyard, just south of downtown at Southwest Sixth and Murphy Streets.[31]

The move may have been prompted by the expiration of the lease, Bankers Life's interest in disposing of the building—which it did the following year, selling the structure to L. M. Bolton and H. M. Hay—or maybe a desire of Rudy's to be closer to the heart of downtown. This last possibility seems likely. Rudy was a networker and a joiner. His company reaped the benefits of relationships he built with various organizations, and Rudy liked nothing better than serving on boards and associations, often moving up to positions of leadership. He was active, for instance, in the Master Builders Association of Des Moines and was its president in 1945, and also served as a director of the Association of General Contractors of America and a director of the local Community Chest (now United Way). He was also actively involved in the Greater Des Moines Chamber of Commerce, serving on a special postwar committee to address potential problems in the conversion to a peacetime economy. A decade later, in 1956, Rudy became president of the chamber. Connections and his growing prominence in the business community also led to a number of board appointments, including positions with Solar Aircraft, Delavan Manufacturing Company, Bankers Trust, and Employers Mutual Casualty Company (now EMC Insurance Companies).[32]

Another change had taken place as well. When the Weitz Company relocated, the electrical division was no longer a part of it. The previous year, Rudy and Andy Johnson, head of the electrical division, had evidently negotiated a deal, with Johnson buying the subsidiary and renaming it Johnson Electric. By that time, the company was coming out of the doldrums of the Depression, and Rudy must have figured it best to focus on the company's core business.[33]

Actually, the company's turnaround was palpable for Rudy and his family. While the Weitzes were among the city's well-to-do, the Depression had hit the construction industry hard, and as Sally Weitz recalled, although they certainly did not suffer, they were more careful with money and "cut down on spending." The family did not, for example, do much traveling over the course of the 1930s, but when the Weitzes did, they resorted to modest automobile trips as opposed to the luxurious first-class rail travel. Two vacations stood out in eldest son Fred Weitz's mind. First was the trip he took with his mother and aunt to visit their good friends the Delavans, who had a summer cottage on Cayuga Lake, one of the Finger Lakes in upstate New York. Later in the decade, as the company's fortunes were improving, Fred's mother and father took him on another car trip, driving to Texas to visit friends and check the firm's progress on the US Appraisers Stores Building in Houston. Now with more disposable income, Rudy and Sally had more to spend, and in 1939, they remodeled their home, adding a dining room and a "fine kitchen," expanding their guest room, and converting the lower level into an "English basement" for their sons with two bedrooms, a bath, and a playroom.[34]

But it was the Des Moines Ordnance Plant contract in 1941, Fred remembered, that really changed the family's lifestyle. "Dad drove a Ford [regarded as an entry-level automobile] but once we got the ordnance job, he got a Buick." More dramatic for twelve-year-old Fred, however, was a change that took place that summer. The previous few years, he had gone to the local YMCA camp in Boone, northwest of Des Moines, for a week or two each summer, but after the Weitz Company landed the huge defense contract, the youngster went to Camp Minocqua in northern Wisconsin. Here he enjoyed eight-week stints over the next five summers, the last two serving as an assistant counselor and then a counselor, respectively. Another important change involved education. Up to this time, Fred had gone to Des Moines public schools–first to Hanawalt Elementary, then Callanan Junior High, and finally Roosevelt High School. But as Fred was finishing his sophomore year, Rudy grew dissatisfied with his son's education. With greater discretionary income, he sent Fred to the Cranbrook School, an exclusive preparatory boarding school in Bloomfield Hills, Michigan. Younger son Steve would follow in his brother's footsteps both at Camp Minocqua and later at the Cranbrook School.[35]

While World War II defense work proved a godsend and guaranteed the Weitz Company's comeback, the vast economic expansion that followed created an ideal environment for the firm's continued success. "Economic growth," wrote historian James Patterson, "was indeed the most decisive force in shaping of attitudes and expectations of the postwar era. The prosperity of the period broadened gradually in the late 1940s, accelerated in the 1950s, and soared to unimaginable heights in the 1960s." Such growth was influenced by several factors, with the pump being primed by federal government spending. Although it had dipped below wartime levels, this spending remained well above outlays in the prewar years and then rose with the Korean War and the growing Cold War. State and local government spending rose as well, doubling between 1945 and 1948, largely to erect schools and build roads. And private investment climbed commensurately as the baby boom and a new acquisitiveness made possible by wartime savings and rising wages opened a new era of mass consumption and affluence.[36]

As the postwar period began, policymakers and private citizens alike had questions regarding the reconversion from a wartime economy to a peacetime one. Concerns ranged from the closing of defense plants and people being thrown out of work to the millions of soldiers facing demobilization. Many wondered if there would be jobs, housing, or educational opportunities for the returning GIs. As with the rest of the nation, these issues and the prosperity that followed were evident in central Iowa, and the Weitz Company found itself right in the middle of the transition.

Shortly after the war ended, the Des Moines Ordnance Plant was shuttered, and a number of other factories that had converted to manufacturing military goods were anxious to return to their production of consumer goods. With the Weitz Company's experience in building defense facilities and installing the required machinery, it was only natural that the firm received contracts to "remove, preserve, and pack for storage" millions of dollars' worth of machines and tools used to build munitions, aircraft parts, and other war-related products. In 1945 and 1946, the Weitz Company kept crews busy doing such "plant clearance" work for a number of clients, including Bendix Aviation, Packard Motor Company, Maytag Company, and Deere & Company. Then in a bigger job that received more attention, Weitz was hired by the RFC, which had taken over the Des Moines Ordnance Plant after the war, to serve as the facility's custodian. This $1 million contract entailed clearing out machinery, salvaging and rebuilding equipment, maintaining the site, and readying it for sale to a private entity.[37]

Unfortunately, the job got off to bumpy start, as labor unrest swept the nation. Workers and unions had done well during the war and had largely eschewed strikes. But the year immediately following the conflict was different. Faced with postwar inflation and determined to protect their wartime advances, unions across the country became strident, calling strikes with much greater frequency. In all, five million workers in most major industries walked off their jobs in 1946. The Weitz Company experienced some of this militancy during its custodianship of the Des Moines Ordnance Plant. Problems began in January 1946 with a dispute between Local 235 of the United Rubber Workers—part of the CIO—which had acted as the bargaining agent for the plant when U.S. Rubber operated it during the war, and the Weitz Company, which replaced some of these employees with AFL workers because it had a contract with construction workers tied to that union. Local 235 responded by calling a strike and set up picket lines outside the plant. Maybe the most memorable part of the standoff took place when, according to the *Des Moines Register*, Weitz Company officials used airplanes "to bring food over the picket line to employees remaining on the grounds." The seventeen-day strike ended in early February when the Weitz Company and union officials agreed that the CIO union could bargain for maintenance workers at the plant (about 75 percent of the workers on site) but not for the construction workers or those dismantling equipment or buildings.[38]

Weitz Company workers spent nearly a year preparing the complex for sale, and at the end of 1946, Deere & Company purchased a large part of the former ordnance plant—the buildings and over five hundred acres—from the RFC for $415 million. The Weitz Company's work at the site continued when the farm machinery manufacturer hired it to remodel the facility over the next few years. And although many were concerned about the loss of thousands of defense jobs when the ordnance plant closed, they cheered Deere & Company's arrival, which employed over 1,400 people during its first full year of operation. The Deere facility produced cultivators and corn pickers.[39]

Given the large number of veterans who had returned home after the war, job creation was only one of the pressing issues. Housing was another, and just like cities throughout the country, Des Moines faced a serious shortage. Few homes had been built during the Great Depression and World War II, and demobilized soldiers and sailors struggled to find places to live. The problem was compounded by city growth, which saw Des Moines's population rise from 160,000 in 1940 to 209,000 in 1960. As an emergency stopgap measure, city leaders opened the decommissioned Fort Des Moines as temporary housing for nine hundred veterans and their families. Fortunately, help was already in the works. A year before the war ended, the federal government enacted the GI Bill, which would provide veterans $20 billion of benefits over the next decade, including long-term, low-interest mortgages. The program set off a boom in home building. In Des Moines, for example, housing starts surged from only fifteen in 1944 to 1,842 by 1950. Because the Weitz Company had moved away from residential construction, it did not initially participate in this thriving market. That changed in 1950, when Rudy took a page from his father's playbook and entered the apartment business.[40]

Demand for housing remained high, and the federal government—in particular the Federal Housing Administration (FHA)—tried to lure builders to erect midpriced apartments by revamping a portion of the National Housing Act. Section 608 of the law, originally drafted in 1941 to assist private contractors in building housing for defense workers, was altered after the war and encouraged the construction of multifamily dwellings. Developers agreed to building standards set by the government and were offered guaranteed loans up to 90 percent of the project's value.[41]

At the same time, architects, planners, and developers were becoming interested in garden apartment complexes, which at a minimum were made up of several two- or three-story apartment buildings with central entrances set amid landscaped courtyards and green spaces. The concept had originated in both England and Germany in the early twentieth century and became increasingly popular in the United States in the 1930s and 1940s. Rudy may very well have encountered and been inspired by Colonial Village, a large garden apartment complex in Arlington, Virginia, and the first FHA-backed apartment project, during one of his wartime trips to Washington, DC. Because he was also well connected in Washington and plugged into the industry through the Master Builders Association of Iowa and the Associated General Contractors of America, he would have been well aware of the increasing popularity of garden apartments and the FHA programs. Thus, with Des Moines housing still in short supply in 1950, Rudy took the company into the apartment business, deciding to build and then manage two FHA-insured apartment projects.[42]

Wakonda Village went up first. With 224 apartments, it consisted of thirty-three, two-story brick buildings arranged throughout sixteen rolling, landscaped acres and included playgrounds, a tennis court, fire pits, and parking. The complex was situated in the southwestern part of Des Moines along Watrous Avenue, just south of the Wakonda Club. This was followed by the University Terrace Apartments, located on a few blocks west of Drake University on Thirty-Sixth Street between Forest and University Avenues. Roughly half the size of Wakonda Village, it had 120 apartments in twenty buildings spread over six-and-a half acres of lushly planted grounds.[43]

The decision proved a good one; Rudy had used low-interest federal money to build the complexes, which were immediately popular. University Terrace, in fact, was completely occupied by the time it was finished, and the apartments provided a steady source of income. Subsidiaries were created to oversee the two complexes, and Rudy hired his brother-in-law Charles Godfrey (his sister Elsa Rose's husband) to manage them. But it was another federal program that had a greater impact on the company's bottom line.[44]

Besides offering low-cost loans, the GI Bill also provided full tuition and a subsistence stipend to former soldiers and sailors to further their education. This pushed open the doors of colleges and universities as never before. Enrollments shot up as 2.2 million veterans took advantage of the program and attended college or graduate school. At Iowa State College, for instance, the number of students tripled from 1945 to 1948, while at the University of Minnesota, World War II veterans made up more than half of its thirty thousand students in 1947. Such rapid growth overwhelmed colleges and universities, and as Iowa institutions looked to expand their facilities, a number turned to the Weitz Company.[45]

First was Grinnell College, where the firm had erected a couple of buildings early in the war. By now, however, Rudy's relationship to the college had grown closer. In 1944, the alumnus was named to the school's board of trustees, and this connection certainly helped the company win several significant contracts, including Loose Hall, a women's dormitory, in 1947, Younker Hall, a men's dormitory, in 1950, and a new science building two years later. Because he and his brother Heinrich both had a fondness for the institution, they took a special interest in the construction, often driving to their alma mater to check on its progress.[46]

Rudy served as president of the college's board from 1952 to 1954, and several years later, the Weitz Company built a new library for the institution. As it turned out, though, this did not add to the firm's earnings. Chicago architects Skidmore, Owings & Merrill designed a striking and functional contemporary building with soaring ceilings and glass walls, but it was clear the structure would exceed the $1.2 million the college allocated for the project. Although the plans were redesigned to cut costs, it was only because Rudy decided to build the library on a "nonprofit basis" that the project stayed within the budget. Burling Library opened in the fall of 1959.[47]

In the midst of its work at Grinnell, the Weitz Company also erected an electrical engineering building at Iowa State College in 1949, and two years later it completed a $1.6 million main library at State University of Iowa (now the University of Iowa) in Iowa City, 115 miles east of the capital. Meanwhile, Drake University in Des Moines was also struggling to keep up with rising enrollments and hired the firm for what became its largest higher education job of the period. Here in the mid-1950s, the Weitz Company completed a complex of three dormitories—Carpenter,

Crawford, and Stalnaker Halls (a fourth, Herriott Hall, was added in 1957)—and Hubbell Dining Hall, designed by nationally regarded architect Eero Saarinen, whose notable architect father, Eliel Saarinen, was locally known for his work on the original Des Moines Art Center building.[48]

Other institutional work went the Weitz way as well. Communities that had put off constructing schools during the Depression and World War II now went forward with new buildings. In Des Moines, the company erected Park Avenue Elementary School and Benjamin Franklin Junior High; in Chariton, fifty-five miles south of Des Moines, it built a high school, and in Eldora, seventy-five miles northeast of Des Moines, an elementary school. It also completed a major addition to the high school in Washington, a county seat town 115 miles southeast of Des Moines, and put up two elementary schools in Iowa City. Hospitals also went up in the postwar years, and the Weitz Company constructed one in Muscatine County on the Mississippi River and another in Boone County, fifty miles north of Des Moines.[49]

Overseeing all these jobs required a growing office staff, which had shrunk to just three when the firm hit its nadir in the depths of the Depression. Now that the economy was flourishing, the company rapidly expanded its personnel, but not only in size. Similar to many other firms, the Weitz Company moved toward hiring professional managers, who coordinated and supervised increasingly complicated operations. Company officials now had college educations, while duties became more specialized and lines of authority more distinct. By the early 1950s, the company boasted more than fifty full-time employees. Besides Rudy and Heinrich, key managers included Harold Carlson, vice president and chief engineer, who had been with the firm since 1936; Henry Howell, secretary of the company and a cost control engineer; Buell Rocky, chief office engineer; M. A. "Jim" Tanner, purchasing engineer; William Metzger, general superintendent; Norman Hall, engineer and estimator; and James Sillers, the comptroller.[50]

While these managers were certainly kept busy with construction prompted by the GI Bill, it was private sector work that now dominated company time. Complex wartime defense projects had served as a training ground for the firm, and when the conflict ended, it was ready and able to tackle large-scale commercial and industrial jobs as businesses scrambled to keep up with growing demand. For the Weitz Company, one such huge construction job began in 1946 on the Cherry-Burrell plant. One of the largest manufacturers of stainless steel dairy processing equipment at the time, Cherry-Burrell wanted a new, efficient facility in Cedar Rapids. Weitz won the $3 million contract for the 400,000-square-foot plant, which took over two years to build. As this structure was going up, the company landed a number of other commercial jobs, but a shortage of bricklayers slowed construction and led Rudy and his engineers to consider alternative building methods employing greater use of concrete.[51]

They initially experimented with tilt-up construction. Using this technique, workers poured concrete into horizontal forms to make wall slabs on the ground at the jobsite. When the concrete slabs had cured, they were tilted up into position around a concrete floor, which had already been poured. Although this system was first used in the early twentieth century, it did not become economically feasible until World War II, when mobile cranes were developed that could lift the wall components into a vertical position, where they were braced until secured to other structural elements.[52]

With this method now available, Weitz Company engineers redesigned construction plans to use tilt-up concrete walls instead of masonry ones for the Luthe Hardware Company's distribution center, built in 1947 on Aurora Avenue in northeastern Des Moines. The following year, the firm used the same technique to erect the Merchant Transfer and Storage Company's warehouse on Ninth Street, just south of downtown.[53]

Then, in an effort to increase efficiency and speed up the process of finishing concrete, the firm's engineers began using a technique for vacuum drying concrete, employing vacuums to remove excess water from the concrete mix. First developed in the 1930s, the method was adopted across the construction industry in the 1940s and 1950s. Essentially, the process strengthened finished concrete more rapidly without losing the flexibility necessary for placement. Using vacuum drying, the Weitz Company shortened the construction time needed for the Cherry-Burrell plant, Luthe Hardware's facility, Merchant Transfer's building, and the large Armstrong Furnace complex—a subsidiary of Lennox—it completed northeast of downtown on East Euclid Avenue in 1949.[54]

Many more industrial and commercial jobs followed. One of the most notable was the Register and Tribune building's $3 million addition. The Weitz Company was hired in 1947 to build a new annex to replace the old one on the northeast corner of Eighth and Locust Streets. Original plans had called for a seven-story structure to replace the old one, but it was pared down to four stories that housed the newsroom, editorial departments, and the presses in the basement levels. The challenge was to erect the new building "around and over" the existing building so as not to interrupt production and printing of the newspaper. The construction thus took place from the top down, encasing the original structure, and when it was completed, the old building was removed.[55]

Other significant contracts in Des Moines included a plant for Iowa Pipe and Tile Company, located where the Greater Des Moines Botanical Garden now sits, an addition to Wood Brothers implement manufacturing facility just north of downtown, and a new office building for Iowa Power and Light Company (now MidAmerican Energy), at Ninth and Walnut Streets. Next were two jobs for another utility, Iowa Electric Light and Power Company (now Alliant Energy), constructing a major addition to its power station in Boone and building a large steam turbine electric generating plant in Marshalltown, fifty miles northeast of the capital city.[56]

Just as the thriving postwar consumer society created a number of opportunities for the Weitz Company, so too did the Cold War, which emerged from mounting tensions between the United States and the Soviet Union in the late 1940s. American anxiety grew as the Iron Curtain descended over Europe, the Soviets tested their own atomic bomb, and China "fell to communism." In response, the US peacetime military budget soared, rising even more rapidly when the Korean War broke out in June 1950. The Cold War and the conflict in Asia led to a big demand for weapons and was a boon for defense contractors. Two such contractors in Des Moines saw business jump and soon required larger facilities. The Weitz Company got the contracts.

By 1951, the Solar Aircraft operation in Des Moines needed more space. The San Diego-based firm had been lured to the city in 1942 by the Des Moines Chamber of Commerce, which convinced Solar it could use the old Ford auto plant at 1800 Grand Avenue (now Des Moines's Central Academy) to build aircraft parts. Although military orders dipped after the war, they picked up late in the decade with the expanded use of jet aircraft, and by 1951, Solar was the largest manufacturer of jet aircraft engine components in the country. That year the firm decided to more than double its capacity by building a new plant three miles southeast of Fleur Drive on Bell Avenue. The Weitz Company won the $1.7 million job.[57]

Because it was a defense contract, building the 290,000-square-foot complex as rapidly as possible was important. Weitz engineers, working with architect Brooks-Borg, chose to use precast concrete panels for the structure. Several years earlier, the company had successfully sped up the construction process on a couple of jobs by using tilt-up concrete wall slabs—poured outdoors on site—but the possibility of freezing temperatures, which slowed the curing process and made it much more expensive, meant that the Weitz Company and other contractors in northern-tier states were forced to look for other, more reliable means of using concrete for construction year-round. Precast concrete panels were the solution. These were produced indoors, thus avoiding any weather-related problems, transported to the jobsite, and then tilted up into position.[58]

The precast concrete panels on Solar's new facility worked well, and Rudy would become so enamored with the technique that he would take the company into the precast concrete business several years down the road. Meanwhile, Solar's new Wakonda Works Plant opened in October 1951, although it continued using its Grand Avenue plant as well. In 1952, Des Moines Community Schools bought the building but agreed to lease it to the aircraft parts manufacturer for another four years. At that point, plans to remodel the building as Des Moines Technical High School went forward, and the Weitz Company won the remodeling contract in 1956.[59]

Rudy certainly understood the significance of defense jobs like the Solar plant, and he maintained close relations with the military. These connections, for example, played a role in Rudy being among fourteen prominent Iowans invited by the navy to participate in the shake-down cruise of the recommissioned USS *Iowa*. The group, which included Fred Maytag, president of Newton appliance maker Maytag; F. W. Hubbell, president of Equitable Life Insurance Company; E. T. Meredith Jr. of Meredith Publishing Company; Craig Sheaffer, president of the Fort Madison Sheaffer Pen Company; and University of Iowa president Virgil Hancher, flew from Des Moines to Long Beach, California, where they boarded the battleship and sailed to Pearl Harbor. During the two-week trip in the fall of 1951, the Iowa leaders toured their state's namesake from stem to stern and were updated on the navy's capabilities and most pressing needs.[60]

Shortly after returning from the cruise, Rudy obtained another defense-related contract; this one was with Des Moines-based Delavan Manufacturing Company, the brainchild of Nelson Delavan, a close friend of Rudy's. The Cornell University graduate had worked for an electric switch company and established his own firm to represent manufacturers, but in 1942 he had founded Delavan Manufacturing Company, which began producing aircraft parts as a military subcontractor. In the postwar years, Delavan specialized in precision nozzles for furnaces, agricultural implements, and jet aircraft. The high-tolerance parts for such planes led to lucrative defense contracts, and in 1952, the company hired Weitz to erect a 27,000-square-foot plant at Fourth Street and Grand Avenue in West Des Moines.[61]

This was immediately followed with another defense job three hundred miles to the west, when in 1953 the firm began adding warehouses and utility lines at the Naval Ammunition Depot in Hastings, Nebraska. As Weitz Company crews were finishing the job, Rudy himself became news. He was named deputy assistant secretary of defense in December 1953, and he and his wife, Sally, moved to Washington, DC, the following month. A Republican, Rudy was pleased Dwight Eisenhower was in the White House and also must have been happy to be serving under Secretary of Defense Charlie Wilson, a businessman and engineer who had previously headed General Motors.[62]

Once ensconced at the Pentagon, Rudy's immediate boss was the assistant secretary of defense for properties and installations Franklin Floete, a friend and retired Des Moines businessman who had secured Rudy's appointment. During his fifteen months in Washington, Rudy acted as the maintenance director or, as the *Des Moines Tribune* put it, "the chief caretaker for thousands of army, navy, and air force buildings and depots."[63]

His sabbatical in the nation's capital was significant and closed out a period that had opened twenty years earlier when Rudy had also left the company. Then the situation was dire, and because it was unclear if the firm could sustain all the family members involved, Rudy had taken another job. By the mid-1950s, however, the situation was completely different. The firm was prospering, it was enjoying a healthy balance of private sector and government work, and a solid management team was in place. With the operation in good hands, Rudy felt comfortable stepping aside for a while. And because he liked running things, the job at the Pentagon gave him the opportunity to manage on a much greater scale. Finally, the timing of the hiatus seemed right, as it appeared the family's fourth generation was about ready to take up the mantle at the company.

Initially Rudy might have thought all four Weitzes—his two sons, Fred and Steve, and Heinrich's sons, Ed and Bob—would move into the firm. Each had worked on company jobsites during their high school or college summers, but Rudy's sons seemed much more interested in joining the firm and were clearly being prepared to do so.[64]

Fred began with the company as a timekeeper/clerk on the Luthe Hardware warehouse site in the summer of 1947, and over the next couple of summers, he worked at the Benjamin Franklin Junior High and Iowa Pipe and Tile construction projects. After finishing at the Cranbrook School in 1947, Fred was off to the Massachusetts Institute of Technology, where Rudy had strongly encouraged him to go. He majored in business/engineering administration, but when the Korean War began in 1950, he altered his path by joining the Air Force ROTC program. The following spring, Fred graduated from MIT as a second lieutenant, but his military service was deferred because he followed in his father's footsteps and went to the Harvard Business School. After completing his MBA in 1953, Fred began his two-year stint in the service at Wright-Patterson Air Force Base in Dayton, Ohio, as a contracting officer. That same year, his younger brother Steve graduated from Cranbrook. He had spent his past few summers at the company as well, first as a water boy at the Wakonda Village and Solar Aircraft jobs and then as a carpenter's apprentice on the Drake dormitories. In the fall of 1953, he went to Yale, planning on majoring in civil engineering or architecture and then joining the company.[65]

Thus it was a satisfied Rudy Weitz who that winter headed off to Washington. He had overseen an incredible rebound, reorganizing the company and returning to run it after his father passed away. Rudy had nudged it from the brink of collapse in the mid-1930s and positioned it to take advantage of huge defense spending during World War II. Winning large military contracts ensured the firm's future, provided it with the experience of carrying out huge, complex projects, and padded its commercial/industrial construction resume. These factors, combined with Rudy's connections and interest in innovation, gave the Weitz Company an edge, and it rode the wave of postwar prosperity, becoming one of the leading contractors in the state. With plenty of work coming across the transom, Rudy surely felt good about the present, and with son Fred soon ready to come on board and Steve in the wings, the future of the family firm appeared bright as well.

Harold Carlson, Weitz Company vice president and general manager, 1940s until 1956, when he left the firm to go into business for himself. Courtesy of the Weitz Company.

Leonard Howell became the first non-Weitz family president of the company in 1957. Courtesy of the Weitz Company.

Construction at Grand Forks Air Force Base, Grand Forks, North Dakota, 1958. Courtesy of the Weitz Company.

Burling Library at Grinnell College, Grinnell, Iowa, completed 1959. A Grinnell alumnus, Rudy Weitz agreed to build the structure at cost for his alma mater so the project could stay within the college's budget. Courtesy of the Weitz Company.

Dr. Kenneth Berg, ca. 1963. Courtesy of the Berg family.

Calvin Manor, Des Moines, completed 1964. Courtesy of the Weitz Company.

Export grain elevator under construction at Ama, Louisiana, ca.1968. Courtesy of the Weitz Company.

Grain elevator under construction in Ashuganj City, East Pakistan (now Bangladesh), 1969. Courtesy of the Weitz Company.

United States Post Office, Des Moines, under construction, 1969. The Weitz Company constructed the building using architectural precast concrete panels provided by its subsidiary, Midwest Concrete. Courtesy of the Weitz Company.

Concrete core of Colorado
State Bank Building under
construction, Denver,
Colorado, 1969. Courtesy of
the Weitz Company.

Skyline Manor, Omaha, Nebraska, completed in 1969. Courtesy of the
Weitz Company.

Friendship Village Dayton, Dayton, Ohio, 1974. Courtesy of the Weitz Company

Fred Weitz, ca. 1975. Courtesy of the Weitz Company.

Fred Weitz and Richard "Dick" Oggero at Des Moines jobsite, 1975. Courtesy of the Weitz Company.

Weitz Building 800 Second Avenue, Des Moines. Courtesy of the Weitz Company.

The Weitz Company's construction group management committee, 1979. From left to right are Jack Hall, executive vice president; Fred Weitz, president; Jerry Gosselink, vice president–construction; Roscoe Paulson, treasurer; Bill Bontrager, vice president–estimating; Dick Oggero, vice president–marketing and real estate development; Mike Carlstrom, vice president–construction; and Glenn DeStigter, vice president–Vulcan. Courtesy of the Weitz Company.

Des Moines Civic Center and Nollen Plaza, 1979. Courtesy of the Greater Des Moines Partnership.

Capital Square, Des Moines, completed in 1983. Courtesy of the *Business Record*.

Larry Laird of Life Care Services, 1986. Courtesy of Life Care Services.

Fox Plaza, Los Angeles, California. Completed in 1987, the building was featured as the fictional Nakatomi Plaza in the original *Die Hard* movie. Courtesy of the Weitz Company.

Prairie Meadows, Des Moines. The Weitz Company built the horse track and grandstand, completing it in 1989. Courtesy of the *Business Record*.

Glenn DeStigter joined the Weitz Company in 1968 and succeeded Fred Weitz as the company's president and CEO. Courtesy of the Weitz Company.

Sandhill Cove, Palm City, Florida, 1993. Courtesy of Life Care Services.

Stan Thurston, chairman, president and CEO of Life Care Services, 1995 – 2006; Fred Weitz; and Ed Kenny, current chairman and CEO of Life Care Services, 2011. Courtesy of Life Care Services.

Current Weitz Building, Des Moines. Courtesy of the *Business Record*.

Leonard "Len" Martling, Weitz Company president and CEO, 2010 to the present. Courtesy of the Weitz Company.

Iowa Fertilizer Company plant under construction, Wever, Iowa. Courtesy of the Weitz Company.

Cowles Commons, Des Moines. Courtesy of Des Moines Performing Arts.

Chapter Seven

THIRD TO FOURTH GENERATION

The year 1955 was noteworthy for the Weitz Company as it reached its one hundredth anniversary, a feat few businesses attained. According to the *Des Moines Register*, it was now the oldest construction firm in the state. Given the Weitz family's formal and understated nature, it was not surprising that the company's celebration consisted of a quiet, unassuming party at the Wakonda Club, the city's south side country club bastion of old-money conservatism.[1]

Throughout the year, the firm ran a number of advertisements across a variety of publications using the milestone as an inducement to win work. The general template opened with the header "The Weitz Guide To Modern Industry..." followed by a photograph and a paragraph or two about a particular past project—Cherry-Burrell, Solar Aircraft, Maytag, Delavan, Iowa Pipe and Tile, for example—and the phrase "How to cut costs THE MODERN WAY." The ads concluded with the Weitz Company name (the "W" was draped with a one-hundredth anniversary banner) and the simple words "Over 100 years of service in the construction industry."[2]

The ad campaign captured the way the Weitzes and top managers felt about the centennial. It merited acknowledgment and some self-satisfaction, but present and upcoming jobs were obviously the focus. In August 1955, the *Weitz Surveyor*, the firm's in-house magazine, emphasized the pragmatic, unsentimental view: "Company officers, while expressing obvious pride in the company record, have stated that they are much more interested in the future than the past." This forward-looking mentality was embedded in the company culture. In 1980, for instance, the 125th anniversary of the company, Fred Weitz, Rudy's eldest son and then company president and CEO, said of the firm's long history: "It's fun and it's interesting to talk about. In a sense, I suppose I have a degree of pride that we have that kind of record, but...you can't sell that. Nobody's going to buy it. They're only going to buy the last five years. That's what's important, what you've been doing."[3]

If the anniversary aspect of 1955 was downplayed, Rudy's return to the company and Fred's beginning at the firm were surely noticed, for their presence ensured certainty and managerial continuity. Rudy kept the organization moving down the same successful path. The Weitz Company would stay focused on its home market of Des Moines, where it had been building and rebuilding the city since 1855. This remained a lucrative market, and as *Mid-West Contractor* put it, the firm "prefer[red] to work close to home," while Rudy stressed that "we have no ideas about being a national construction company." However, he kept his eyes open for opportunities beyond the city and remained interested in new technologies; after acquiring a design and engineering firm, for instance, he took the Weitz Company overseas in the grain elevator business.[4]

Meanwhile, he and son Fred—representing the family's fourth generation to join the Weitz Company—went through a lengthy process of learning to work together. After several years of struggling, they eventually found an effective division of labor. Rudy concentrated on the international component of the business while Fred developed and managed the domestic side. And develop he did; it was Fred who saw potential in the retirement home business, and in the early 1960s, he involved the company in the industry. The firm's activity in this sector grew, and the following decade, even as the Weitz Company was shedding other once promising subsidiaries, it became increasingly reliant on the building and then management of retirement communities. This would be the beginning of a reconfigured Weitz operation, which Fred would lead from the mid-1970s.

Although Rudy had kept in close touch with Weitz officials while serving as maintenance director at the Department of Defense, and although the company had done well during his tenure in Washington, DC, his authoritarian streak made it difficult for him to be away from the family business so long. After his planned one-year term dragged on a few more months, he had, according to his wife, Sally, "felt the need to get back to the Weitz Company," and even though his boss, Assistant Secretary of Defense Frank Floete, urged him to stay longer, Rudy resigned in April 1955 and returned to his desk in Des Moines.[5]

During his absence, though, the firm had not missed a beat. Relationships Rudy had cultivated over the years and the company's continued strong reputation, coupled with a robust local economy, had all but ensured constant work for the firm. While his younger brother and partner Heinrich had remained in Des Moines, management of the operation during Rudy's absence fell largely to company veteran and vice president Harold Carlson and secretary and estimator Henry Howell. Heinrich was consulted on major company decisions, but he stayed in the background, generally overseeing smaller projects and finishing up the "odds and ends jobs."[6]

Despite the recessions of 1953 and 1957–1958, the decade was another one of expansion for Des Moines. Over the period, the city grew by 17 percent, reaching its apex of 209,000 by 1960. The downtown remained vibrant while the city's suburbs grew even more rapidly. Ankeny and West Des Moines, for example, more than doubled in size, while Urbandale and Windsor Heights more than tripled. Such an environment was good for the Weitz Company, and when Rudy returned in 1955, the firm was in the midst of several projects. Prior to his Pentagon position, Rudy usually took the lead in securing contracts for the firm and continued to do so once he returned. Interestingly, however, it was Rudy who had obtained one of the bigger jobs the Weitz Company began that spring, and he did so while still in Washington.[7]

A few years earlier, in 1952, Employers Mutual Casualty Company (EMC) began developing plans for a new home office building. The insurer wanted to replace its current headquarters in the Brinsmaid Building on Seventh Street, just north of Mulberry Street in downtown Des Moines. The Weitz Company, in fact, had remodeled this building for EMC in 1938. Once Chicago architects Childs & Smith were hired to design the $1.25 million structure, the firm looked to board member Rudy Weitz's company to erect the three-story building in March 1955. Rudy's ties to this firm remained important, and fourteen years later, it again looked to the Weitz Company to build its ten-story new home office, immediately to the west of its existing facility. Interestingly, one of the properties EMC acquired along Mulberry Street was the old Weitz Building (called the Bolton & Hay Building when the insurer bought it in 1957). It was torn down in 1969 to make way for EMC's new office.[8]

Later in 1955, Rudy's connections also helped land other jobs. These included additions for the Wallace-Homestead publishing facility (formerly known as Homestead) on Grand Avenue in Des Moines and new buildings for Maytag, the appliance maker based in Newton, a small town forty miles to the east. Emblematic of his interest in networking and engaging with others in the business community, Rudy was elected president of the Des Moines Chamber of Commerce (its name had been changed to the Greater Des Moines Chamber of Commerce in 1955) for 1956. Rudy would continue working with the chamber as well as the Greater Des Moines Committee, an elite business promotional group, where he would serve as president a decade later. This adeptness at networking bore fruit again and again. Later in the 1950s, Rudy's connections led to contracts for additions at Solar Aircraft and Delavan Manufacturing, as well as the LOOK Building—headquarters for the Cowles-owned biweekly magazine, which emphasized photojournalism—at Tenth and Mulberry Streets. Two other projects were the fine arts building at Grinnell College and an addition to the Bankers Trust building at Sixth and Locust Streets, where Rudy was a member of the bank's board.[9]

The company secured other important jobs across the state. In a joint venture with contractor J. D. Armstrong of Ames, the Weitz Company won the contract for the third phase of construction of the Coralville Dam and Spillway in the fall of 1955. Situated several miles north of Iowa City and begun six years earlier, the US Army Corps of Engineers project was designed to regulate runoff from the Iowa River and was part of a larger flood control program for the Mississippi River. Work was completed in 1958. Meanwhile, the firm also erected two buildings for the Rolscreen Company, a manufacturer of windows (renamed the Pella Corporation in 1992) in Pella, a small town forty-five miles southeast of Des Moines; won the downtown Des Moines riverfront YMCA

job, beating out rivals Arthur H. Neumann & Brothers and Rin-
gland-Johnson for the honor; and constructed a new post office/
federal building in Burlington, Iowa.[10]

Meanwhile, the ongoing Cold War also created opportunities for the Weitz Company. Concerned that a mounting defense
budget would be a drag on the economy, President Dwight Eisenhower called for a reformulation of America's national security
policy, eventually dubbed "the New Look." Instead of maintaining
a huge and expensive army to prevent Soviet aggression, the Eisenhower administration chose the more cost-effective strategy of rely-
ing on the country's superior nuclear capability in tandem with the
doctrine of "massive retaliation," which threatened the immediate
use of these weapons in response to Soviet or Soviet-backed prov-
ocation. This shift required beefing up certain bases and facilities
connected to atomic weaponry. Rudy had been at the Pentagon
when the new strategy was rolled out, and his connections within
the current defense establishment as well as his intimate knowledge
of the military bureaucracy and its process for letting work certainly gave the company an edge when it came to bidding for some
of these contracts.[11]

Beginning in 1956, the firm won the first of three contracts
at the Strategic Air Command (SAC)'s Ellsworth Air Force Base
in Rapid City, South Dakota. There it enlarged hangars for the
B-52 aircraft—long-range bombers designed to carry atomic
bombs to their targets—erected a Nike missile air defense launch
site designed to protect the facility, and put in a "ready aircraft
shelter" for fighter aircraft also based at Ellsworth. That same year,
it was the low bidder on a job for the Atomic Energy Commission
in Burlington, where the AEC had taken over the former Iowa
Ordnance Plant for the production and final assembly of atomic

weapons. Two more AEC contracts were awarded for additional work at the Burlington plant in 1957 and 1958, and over the next few years the company constructed buildings at the SAC's Grand Forks Air Force Base in North Dakota and Offutt Air Force Base near Omaha, Nebraska.[12]

By the end of the decade, these defense contracts, combined with various commercial and industrial jobs, put the Weitz Company's annual construction volume between $8 and $10 million while usually working on twelve to fifteen projects at a time. But Rudy was an activist by nature and not content merely overseeing the status quo. Instead, he aggressively sought out other money-making opportunities, and over the last half of the 1950s, he took the firm down three new paths.[13]

These moves began in 1955, while the firm was building a new apartment complex for developer Arthur Sanford & Company west of downtown Des Moines at 3660 Grand Avenue. The elegant ten-story luxury building was faced with glass and dark green exposed aggregate panels. These decorative panels were relatively new to the industry and had been produced by Midwest Concrete Industries, a Des Moines firm owned by Perry Wells. Rudy was so taken with the panels and what he saw as their potential for the business that he contacted Wells and began negotiating to purchase the operation. At the same time, the Weitz CEO saw another business prospect: the postwar population boom had pushed communities to expand and upgrade their infrastructure, which included the widening and building of new roads. In response, Rudy moved the firm back into the paving business after a twenty-year absence, although this time it was asphalt instead of concrete.[14]

As these two options were being investigated, Fred Weitz joined the company following the completion of his two years of active military service at Wright-Patterson Air Force Base outside Dayton, Ohio. There on a blind date, he had met Emily Booton in May 1954. She was a mechanical engineer who had graduated from Virginia Polytechnic Institute and State University and was working at General Motors' Delco plant in Dayton. The two soon became a couple, and when Fred's air force service was over, they married in April 1955, in a small service in Emily's hometown of Chester, Virginia. After a honeymoon in Myrtle Beach, South Carolina, the newlyweds headed to Des Moines, where they took up residence in a Weitz-owned Wakonda Village apartment.[15]

Although Rudy and his eldest son never actually discussed the matter, it was clearly understood that after completing his education, Fred would return to the firm, which, if all went well, he would eventually take over. However, when Fred came on board in the spring of 1955, Rudy was just fifty-four years old, and leading the company, not succession, was uppermost in his mind. He clearly had not given much forethought to his son's duties or job description, and the issue was initially solved by happenstance. Rudy's interest in new lines of business now occupied Fred's time. He was given the rather nebulous title of assistant secretary and assigned to the financial side of the operation where he did some forecasting and cost accounting, but most of his attention went to supervising the company's growing subsidiary operations.

At the outset, this only entailed overseeing the firm's apartment complexes—Wakonda Village and University Terrace—which were managed by his uncle, Charles Godfrey. Almost immediately an issue arose, when Godfrey told Fred in June 1956 that an African American couple had inquired about the availability of an apartment in Wakonda Village, which only had white residents. Godfrey assumed he should respond that the complex was full, but Fred said no and thought they should lease to the couple. He talked over the matter with his father, who agreed, even though Rudy figured the move would cost them some white tenants.[16]

The Weitzes opened the doors to the couple and did not lose any tenants. The following spring, another African American couple moved into Wakonda Village without incident. Thus, in their quiet and nonchalant manner, Fred and Rudy made the complex one of the first integrated apartments in Des Moines.[17]

Another subsidiary soon fell to Fred as well, when he and Henry Howell were put in charge of Century Construction, the company's new asphalt paving concern. In 1957, the Weitz Company bought Stade Construction, another paving enterprise, out of Fairmount, Minnesota. This operation was rechristened Carson Construction Company—named after Carson, a small Iowa town 115 miles southwest of Des Moines where the subsidiary did its first work after the Weitz Company bought it—and soon absorbed the previously created Century firm. In fact, it was here at Carson that Heinrich's oldest son, Edwin "Ed," became the second member of the Weitzes' fourth generation to join the family firm, starting work for the paving company in 1957. Ultimately he decided the business was not for him and left the firm even as Rudy was reconsidering the paving business. Although the asphalt enterprise pulled in a small profit, Rudy recognized it was a distraction, and in 1962, he pulled the plug on the business, noting that it was "no longer proper to risk our capital in this highly competitive undertaking" and fearing that it might "dilute our management strength" from more important operations.[18]

Ed Weitz's brother Robert, Heinrich's youngest son, meanwhile, understood that he wanted no part of the construction business after working on jobsites during high school summer vacations. Shortly after graduating from Grinnell College, Bob moved to New York in 1960. This left only one other fourth-generation family member, Steve Weitz, Rudy's younger son. Like Fred, he had also been groomed for the company—sent to the elite Cranbrook School and then Yale. Summers he spent at Weitz construction sites, and like his brother, he expected to join the Weitz Company.[19]

But he did not. At Yale, Steve decided on a career in architecture, which was certainly compatible with working at the family business. It was a six-year program when combined with an undergraduate degree, which he was awarded in 1957. Before completing the last two years, however, Steve took a year off and returned to Des Moines, where he served in the US Army Reserve and worked at Brooks-Borg (now Brooks Borg Skiles), an architectural and engineering firm.[20]

He returned to Yale the following fall, but after a few weeks, he was "overwhelmed" by the demanding coursework and decided architecture was not for him. Steve dropped out and came back to Des Moines, but instead of joining the Weitz Company, he pursued a growing interest in urban planning and began working for the city planning office.[21]

Neither Rudy nor Fred discouraged Steve's move away from the business. Maybe Rudy decided having only one son at the firm was best, eliminating any potential conflict between the siblings. Fred certainly understood it in those terms. He did not think his uncle Heinrich "had a very good situation at the company" because Rudy was so domineering, and because Fred, a leader by nature, wanted to run the business someday, he worried that if Steve joined the operation, he might treat his younger brother as Rudy had Heinrich. Steve had a similar perception of the work relationship between his father and uncle and did not want to see this dynamic repeated in his generation. Consequently, as his brother Fred was becoming established at the company, Steve followed his developing interest in urban planning. After graduate work at the University of Washington, Steve worked at Wilbur Smith & Associates (now part of CDM Smith), a traffic engineering firm in Columbia, South Carolina. In 1967, he took a job with the US Department of Housing and Urban Development (HUD) in Washington, DC, where he remained until retiring in 2000.[22]

Although Fred did not know it at the time, he would be the sole family member of his generation to remain at the Weitz Company. Here he oversaw the paving division and was actively engaged with Midwest Concrete Industries (MCI), the precast concrete firm Rudy had become aware of during the 3660 Grand apartment job. Fred had been involved with MCI from the very beginning, as Rudy had him evaluate the business and go over its books prior to making an offer. Despite Fred thinking it did not "look particularly attractive," Rudy saw great potential and went ahead with the purchase in March 1956. He then assigned his son to MCI, telling him to make "development of this outfit his principal interest."[23]

Overall, though, Fred was frustrated and felt he "was really being wasted." And while Rudy undoubtedly wanted Fred in the company and expected him to run it one day, the authoritarian father had great difficulty seeing his son as a business colleague or putting him on the leadership path. Likewise, there were no open management slots for Fred at the firm, and Rudy made no effort to create one.[24]

In fact, in 1956, he created a business manager position, to be filled by an outsider, which would have crowded the company hierarchy even more. However, the new job never really materialized but became a replacement for vice president and general manager Harold Carlson, who would leave and go into business for himself the following year. That December, Rudy hired Des Moines city manager Leonard Howell, who had been popular with civic groups but had been fired by the city council over an apparent dispute over lines of authority in a controversial 3-2 vote. Howell replaced Carlson, and in early 1957, Jim Tanner was also promoted to a vice presidency. In July, Rudy moved over to chairman and focused on expansion, new work, and general policy, while Leonard Howell assumed the presidency, becoming the first non-Weitz family member to act as "operating head" of the company. The board was expanded from merely Rudy and Heinrich to include Howell and Joe Brody, an attorney from the Brody, Roberts firm (now Davis Brown) who did most of the Weitz Company's legal work.[25]

Left out of this reorganization, Fred remained the liaison between the Weitz Company and its growing subsidiaries, giving special attention to Midwest Concrete. His first major decision came in 1956, when he recommended Greg Gentleman as manager for the business. Rudy agreed, and Gentleman joined the firm that spring. A mechanical engineer who had been a fraternity brother of Fred's at MIT, Gentleman had worked in product development for Sears, Roebuck in Chicago before coming to Des Moines that spring.

Unfortunately, Midwest Concrete fell short of expectations. It was in a highly competitive industry, and local contractors were averse to purchasing products from the company because it was owned by Weitz, a rival contractor. Business was sluggish, and MCI had lost money ever since the Weitz Company bought it. Gentleman soon argued that the current facility on the east side of Des Moines was too small; more space was needed to fabricate larger precast panels as well as possibly manufacturing prestressed concrete beams, thus increasing the company's product line. Fred and Rudy agreed, and a new $150,000 plant was built in West Des Moines south of Railroad Avenue on Fuller Road in 1958, with MCI's operations consolidated there the following year.[26]

But mediocre performance continued, and Rudy kept tinkering with Fred's role at MCI, giving him additional duties at the Weitz Company and then rescinding them and restoring his son's focus to Midwest Concrete. At the same time, Rudy was always looking over Fred's shoulder, monitoring the operation and second-guessing his son. This lack of clarity and constant shifting of Fred's responsibilities led to growing disagreements and arguments between Rudy and his son. Fred's frustration mounted, and matters grew worse. After Rudy considered but then dropped the idea of selling MCI to American-Marietta, a producer of aggregates and other construction materials (now Martin-Marietta), in 1959, Gentleman, who knew he had to increase revenues or be out of a job, began looking for other opportunities.[27]

Even though prospects at MCI were looking up and the firm was now at the break-even point, Gentleman resigned in early 1960 to start his own business. Initially Rudy suggested Fred become full-time general manager of MCI. Fred liked the idea, but after some more thought, Rudy reconsidered. Instead, he decided to bring in an experienced manager for MCI. Jack Downing was hired at the end of the year, and Fred was assigned to work full-time as an understudy for Downing while being relieved of the rest of his duties.[28]

As this situation simmered, Rudy had entered another business through acquisition. While the Weitz Company was building a

Davenport facility for Ralston Purina (now part of Nestlé) during the economic slowdown of 1958, Rudy visited its headquarters in Saint Louis hoping to drum up more work. Here he heard that domestic opportunities for construction in the grain processing and storage field were relatively flat, but Ralston Purina officials were bullish about such prospects overseas. And here he also learned about Jones-Hettelsater Engineers, a respected Kansas City design and construction firm specializing in such work. The contractor had run into financial trouble two years earlier when an elevator it recently had erected for the Glidden Company in Chicago failed, dumping fifty thousand bushels of wheat into the Calumet River. Glidden sued for loss and damages, and company owner Anton R. "A. R." Hettelsater promised to make good, although it was unlikely his business could survive without combining with someone else.[29]

Rudy was intrigued. Don English, head engineer at Ralston Purina, put him in touch with Hettelsater. The two talked; both were interested in merging, but Hettelsater and his attorneys wanted the Glidden affair settled before going forward, and negotiations broke off in November 1958.[30]

A year later, however, once Jones-Hettelsater's insurance company was found liable for a portion of the Glidden elevator damages, Hettelsater called to see if Rudy were still interested in merging. He was, and within a month, in December 1959, the Weitz Company bought the operation. It was renamed Weitz-Hettelsater Engineers (W-H) but remained based in Kansas City and was operated as a semiautonomous division. Key employees such as Henry Heckman and Ross Jay were retained, and A. R. Hettelsater stayed on as the director of engineering.[31]

The acquisition gave the Weitz Company a firm that had been engineering, designing, and building agribusiness processing plants and bulk elevator storage facilities across the nation since 1920. Although Rudy planned to continue seeking such work domestically, his earlier conversation with Ralston Purina officials about overseas jobs in the field stuck in his head, and shortly after the purchase, he headed to Washington, DC, to investigate. Through contacts, he arranged meetings with administrators in the Foreign Agricultural Service division of the US Department of Agriculture as well as the International Cooperation Administration, a US State Department organization that provided nonmilitary aid. They reinforced what he had learned earlier: there was a "great need" for grain elevators and processing plants in developing countries, particularly in South America as well as in Lebanon, Egypt, Pakistan, and India. This was all Rudy needed to hear; he read up on the subject, met with people in the grain and elevator business, and in the spring of 1960, he traveled to Washington, DC, and New York before heading to Cairo, Egypt; Karachi, Pakistan; and New Delhi and Calcutta, India, to introduce the company and solicit business. This would be the first of several overseas trips he would take on an annual basis throughout the decade while he focused more and more heavily on Weitz-Hettelsater operations.[32]

As Rudy peddled W-H's construction and design capabilities, he also began offering other services that were of particular interest to developing nations. These included economic research and project feasibility studies, assistance in the selection of contractors and overseeing project construction, and a management and training program to prepare clients to manage and operate storage and processing facilities. Meanwhile, W-H was busy with jobs at home, especially important because the recession of 1960–61 had slowed construction work for parent company Weitz, which only completed one project in the two-year period. By contrast, W-H won a $2.5 million elevator project in Long Beach, California, in the spring of 1960, and by that fall, it was working on seven other projects, including feed mills in Portland, Oregon, and Baltimore, Maryland, a cement terminal in Waco, Texas, and a Pillsbury facility in Los Angeles. As a result of these work patterns and because of Rudy's belief in its overseas potential, Weitz-Hettelsater's staff grew, and Bill Folk, the executive engineer for General Mills, was brought in to run its engineering and design departments. Some managers were transferred from the Weitz Company in Des Moines to the Kansas City unit, including chief estimator Norm Hall and engineering estimator Jim Morson.[33]

Rudy's interest in developing overseas work coincided with a shift in the direction for US economic aid to developing nations. Immediately after World War II, the United States provided billions of dollars in assistance to Europe and Japan in an effort to rebuild their economies and create a bulwark against the spread of communism. But as the 1950s progressed, the threat of communism appeared more prevalent in the developing world, and US economic aid began targeting countries in Asia, Africa, the Middle East, and Central and South America. However, the bureaucracy was complicated and aid flowed through a number of different and sometimes competing agencies.

Shortly after John F. Kennedy became president in 1961, he streamlined the foreign aid operation by signing the Foreign Assistance Act. This called for the creation of a single organization to coordinate foreign assistance. With this authority, Kennedy established the Agency for International Development, which "assumed responsibility for the disbursement of capital and technical assistance to developing nations." It was this agency, along with the World Bank, that would fund much of Weitz-Hettelsater's overseas contracts.[34]

Egypt soon became Rudy's focus, when its government began considering a multimillion-dollar grain storage and distribution system. The country was becoming increasingly dependent on US wheat, which was a major portion of America's economic aid package. Such shipments were authorized under the Agricultural Trade Development and Assistance Act of 1954, commonly called Food for Peace, or Public Law 480 (PL-480), and accounted for 24 percent of Egyptian grain imports in 1959 and 66 percent the following year.[35]

Unfortunately, the lack of modern storage elevators meant that as much as 128,000 tons of wheat per year was lost to spoilage or other causes. In 1961, Rudy's efforts started paying off when the state-run General Egyptian Organization of Silos and Storage retained Weitz-Hettelsater to do a feasibility study for the elevator project. In 1962, USAID approved a $17 million loan for part of a $42 million system of grain elevators and warehouses, and Weitz-Hettelsater won the contract for the engineering and design work. As hiring was ramped up for the job, the firm also received contracts for project feasibility studies in Syria and Brazil, and the future for the Weitz Company's new division looked bright.[36]

Fred, however, did not see his future at the company as bright. His first few years there had been rocky as he and his father never quite found a workable relationship. Both understood there were difficulties, with Rudy noting in his journal in the spring of 1960 that the two had "spent a good deal of time talking over our personal relationship and attempted to put it on a more objective basis." Conflicts with his father, however, seemed to disappear once Fred started working full-time under Downing at MCI in early 1961, because he and Rudy had much less contact with one another. Nonetheless, Fred was increasingly unhappy in his position at MCI;

he was poorly paid and did not see an opportunity for moving up in the Weitz Company anytime soon. Interestingly, although Fred was apparently unaware of it, Rudy discussed moving his son to Kansas City to work as treasurer for the growing Weitz-Hettelsater business that April, but Downing told Rudy he "would hate to lose Fred," and later explained that he thought Fred "ought to be left… [at MCI] another year or two before he proceeded on to other things." Rudy agreed and made no changes.[37]

By the fall, Fred was "fed up" with his situation and felt he "should leave the company for a while and demonstrate his ability on his own." This troubled Rudy. Although he had been unable to find a place for his son and was well aware that their work rapport had often been contentious, he remained committed to passing the mantel on to Fred and worked to keep him at the firm. In October, Rudy delayed Fred's departure by moving him from MCI to the company office downtown for an operational review of all firm operations. Meanwhile, sixty-eight-year-old president and general manager Leonard Howell decided to retire at the end of the year. This opened a potential managerial slot for Fred, as Rudy and Joe Batten, a management consultant with whom Rudy worked, considered "how best to fit him in" the firm's hierarchy.[38]

Clearly Rudy realized that only a position of authority would keep Fred, and naming him general manager in Des Moines would fill a current need and provide good training for the eventual company presidency. By January 1962, Rudy believed his son was "willing to stay if we can put together a program on paper." Other alternatives for Fred included making him a Weitz-Hettelsater project manager and sending him overseas (probably to the Middle East) or moving him to Kansas City where he would serve as the W-H engineering manager. In March, all agreed on the Des

Moines option; Fred became the company vice president and general manager with decision-making responsibility when Rudy was out of town. The following year, he was promoted to the presidency, his father remained chairman, and for the next ten years, Fred essentially supervised the firm's domestic endeavors while Rudy concentrated on W-H's international efforts.[39]

Initially the new vice president and then president did not have much work to oversee. Recovery from the recession at the beginning of the decade had been slow, and the Des Moines construction firm struggled along with three or four projects a year until mid-decade. A turnaround was clear in 1966, when the company built additions for Delavan Manufacturing, Firestone, Massey Ferguson, which had taken over the Solar Aircraft Plant, John Deere, which had taken over the Des Moines Ordnance Plant, as well as erecting a major addition to the Ames Municipal Power Plant. The Weitz Company remained busy over the next few years. Annual volume was in the $12 million range and included, for instance, construction for the Maytag Company in Newton as well as married student housing and a major addition to the Parks Library at Iowa State University in Ames.[40]

In Des Moines, the company was very active, erecting Herbert Hoover High School, another addition for Des Moines's Firestone plant, and the I. M. Pei addition to the Des Moines Art Center. It also partnered with real estate developer Allen Block of Kansas City, bought some land in the city's urban renewal district along Second Avenue, and erected the River Hills theater complex. Other work included building the Allied Mutual Insurance Building, a new $7 million United States Post Office, a Holiday Inn on Merle Hay Road (now a Ramada Inn), the twelve-story addition to Northwest Bell's (now Century Link) facilities downtown, a condominium project in Southern Hills on the city's southwest side, a new headquarters for West Des Moines State Bank (now West Bank) in West Des Moines, and, just to the north of Des Moines, Big Creek Dam.[41]

As work picked up, two other changes took place. First, Heinrich began toying with the idea of selling his stake in the firm shortly after it became clear that his sons were not going to pursue a career with the company. By 1966, Heinrich was certain he wished to do so, and Rudy decided it was a good idea, especially because he expected his brother to retire in several years—Heinrich did so in early 1972, although he remained active on the company board. Thus attorney Donald "Don" Brown worked out the details of stock redemption that summer of 1966, and when the deal was completed, Rudy and Sally—and to a much lesser extent sons Fred and Steve, who had been gifted a few shares in the late 1950s—owned all the voting stock of the company. That same year, Fred and Rudy decided to move company headquarters instead of renovating its current space in the dated Fleming Building. Likely encouraged by John Ruan, the majority owner of Bankers Trust, where Rudy served on the board, in 1967 the Weitz Company set up shop at Sixth and Locust Streets in the newer addition to the Bankers Trust Building, which the Weitz Company had built in 1959.[42]

More significant than these changes, however, was a new direction for the company, unexpectedly begun in 1962. That spring, Dr. Kenneth Berg, a Presbyterian minister from Lee's Summit, Missouri, came to see Rudy and Fred. In addition to pastoring his flock, the reverend had become an advocate for what he called "life care retirement communities" and wished to discuss building one in Des Moines with the Weitzes.

These facilities, now generally referred to as continuing care retirement communities (CCRCs), provide housing, social activities, and increased levels of health/medical care as residents' needs change as they age. Berg's interest in such retirement homes put him in the early stages of a growing movement that was taking place across the nation. By the 1950s, there were an increasing number of retirees with pensions, giving a larger number of seniors the financial means of entering CCRCs. At the same time, the country was experiencing a religious revival: from 1940 to 1960 church membership jumped from 49 to 69 percent, and a number of clergy were becoming concerned about the needs of their elderly. Led by churches and nonprofits, groups began creating CCRCs. Some early ones were established in Oregon in the 1950s, with the United Methodists sponsoring Willamette View Manor in Portland, while in Medford, Rogue Valley Manor was jointly established by the Episcopal, Presbyterian, and Methodist churches. Meanwhile, in Ojai, California, the National Retired Teachers Association founded Grey Gables as a CCRC in 1954. Such efforts were given an additional boost in 1959 with the National Housing Act, providing federal mortgage insurance for the building of housing for the elderly.[43]

Berg became involved just as the CCRC concept was beginning to take off in the Midwest. While serving a church in Ottumwa, Iowa, during the 1950s, the entrepreneurial minister started a variety of side ventures in finance, construction, and development. When he left Ottumwa in 1960 to serve two small churches in Walnut Springs and Spruce, Missouri, his background in construction and the new idea of CCRCs sparked his interest in the retirement home business. He began reading up on the subject and visiting retirement communities in Davenport, San Francisco, and Topeka. The following year, when he took over the First Presbyterian Church in Lee's Summit, a suburb of Kansas City, Missouri, he began working with the Temple Baptist Church in Kansas City and founded the nonprofit Temple Foundation, established to develop Temple Towers, a high-rise retirement home in that city.[44]

Berg was a promoter, and with this project still on the drawing board, he began thinking about establishing other retirement communities. He next looked to Des Moines, a city he knew because he had been raised in Boone, a small town fifty miles northwest of the capital, and had attended Drake University. Here Berg had been impressed with Wesley Acres, one of the only retirement facilities in Des Moines, then located in the Chamberlain mansion on Grand Avenue, and had become acquainted with its administrator, George Dimmitt. Dimmitt told him that while mainline denominations were involved in retirement homes, evangelical churches had not shown much interest. Berg took this as a suggestion and began selling the idea for such a community to the evangelical leaders throughout the city. Soon he had optioned some land on the east side of Des Moines, asked architects Brooks-Borg to do some preliminary drawings, and put together a local sponsor group—Evangelical Retirement Homes Inc.—consisting largely of evangelical churches throughout the city. Berg envisioned a complex of one hundred units, most situated in a large, two-story building, which would also include a nursing home, while some residents could reside in detached duplexes or in four-family units also on the grounds.[45]

Berg had most of the pieces in place. Residents would be charged a $7,500 entrance fee, and he planned to begin selling subscription commitments before the complex was completed. Furthermore, Des Moines Savings & Loan had agreed to give Evangelical Retirement Homes a permanent mortgage loan for the building once it was completed, but the bank was not willing to provide Berg a construction loan. A bank officer suggested the minister work with a local contractor. Berg talked with architect Joe Borg, who knew business was slow at the Weitz Company, and Borg arranged for the pastor to meet Rudy and Fred in April 1962. The Weitzes were intrigued with Berg's pitch and his concept of a life care retirement community, which would have no serious competition in Des Moines. After some research, they were willing to gamble on the project. Fred worked out the deal: the Weitz Company would build the facility using its own credit, and once it was completed and after residents had moved in and their entrance fees had been collected, the sponsoring Evangelical Retirement Homes would take out a mortgage and pay the Weitz Company for the construction.[46]

In the midst of the deal, Berg lost the option on the land, and the project was relocated to the intersection of Hubbell and Guthrie Avenues, where the Weitz Company erected the eastside complex in 1962 and, as planned, sold it to the nonprofit sponsor organization. Both Fred and Rudy were pleased with the result, and even before Valley View Village was completed, Fred was busy working with Berg on a number of other possible retirement community projects—in Kansas City (Temple Towers and one in Lenexa, Kansas) and Saint Louis, Missouri; Pompano Beach, Florida; and another in Des Moines. A partnership rapidly developed. Berg the salesman arranged local sponsors, usually consisting of evangelical and interdenominational ministers, found the land, generally close to shopping, transportation, churches, and other social amenities, and sold subscriptions to retirees, which guaranteed future residents apartments in the retirement complexes once they were completed. For this work, the Weitz Company initially paid him a monthly fee plus a commission and later solely a commission on the contracted price of each property while it handled the legal and financial matters involved and managed construction of the facilities, before selling them to the sponsoring body.[47]

Fred spent an increasing amount of time on retirement homes over the next few years. Some projects did not pan out: plans for the Saint Louis complex, for example, never got off the ground, and because subscription sales were slow both at Temple Towers and at what eventually became the Baptist Village Retirement Center in Pompano Beach, the Weitz Company bowed out of these ventures. But most went forward. Following Valley View, Fred and Berg completed Lakeview Village in Lenexa, Kansas, and Calvin Manor in Des Moines in 1964, and by then they were ironing out details for Ridgecrest Village in Davenport, which was built two years later. Amid these projects and the increased building in Des Moines, Fred needed help, and in June 1965, he lured structural engineer John Hart, a partner at Brooks-Borg, to serve as the company's manager of construction. Hart soon became Fred's right-hand man in Des Moines, and he was named a company vice president the next year.[48]

Three more retirement communities followed from 1967 through 1970, with the Weitz Company building two in Nebraska—Eastmont Manor in Lincoln and Skyline Manor in Omaha—as well as Sunny Acres Villa in Denver, Colorado. The complexes varied in size and style from low-rise buildings on a large campus to high-rise towers on smaller plots of land, but the process of developing and selling them remained the same. As business picked up for the firm in the Des Moines area by the mid-1960s, retirement home construction was becoming an important niche for the company.[49]

Unfortunately, as the situation for the firm improved domestically, it took a turn for the worse overseas, when the huge Egyptian project was suddenly called off. The grain storage facilities that Weitz-Hettelsater was designing for Egypt were to be financed by a USAID loan as part of the Kennedy administration's effort to improve relations with President Gamal 'Abd al-Nasser, which had soured during the Suez Crisis in 1957. Eisenhower had tried rebuilding ties with shipments of wheat to Egypt in the last years of the decade, and Kennedy built on these efforts. Although Nasser wanted US aid, he also sought aid from the Soviet Union and tried walking an independent line. But in 1964, his public statements were becoming increasing anti-American. Then, after confirmation that Nasser was aiding rebels fighting against the western-backed regime in the Belgian Congo (today the Democratic Republic of the Congo), the downing of a private US plane over Egypt, and the burning of the US Embassy library by a Cairo mob, President Lyndon Johnson and Congress had had enough, and the USAID grain storage project for Egypt was canceled.[50]

Weitz-Hettelsater was eventually paid for the design work it had done, but the loss of the job was a blow for the company, which had been slated to supervise the massive construction project. Still, Rudy remained sanguine about W-H's prospects, and he, as well as W-H staffers including chief engineer Folk, overseas supervisor Vahe Melkonian, and construction supervisor John Heimovics, were actively traveling the globe seeking work. In the midst of these trips, most to developing countries often in volatile areas, a Central Intelligence Agency (CIA) officer paid Rudy a visit in 1965, asking to interview W-H employees when they returned from overseas and to see any reports "that might be valuable to their files." Rudy was annoyed to discover that the CIA had been "consulting" with Folk since the engineer's arrival at W-H in 1960—a fact Folk had only recently revealed to Rudy—and while he wished to cooperate, he explained that he also felt the company owed "some professional protection" to its clients and would not "jeopardize relations between ourselves and our clients." The journal entry about the CIA visit concluded with Rudy deciding to turn over any report the agency could obtain from the USAID or other similar government office.[51]

Despite Rudy's focus overseas, W-H was more active in the United States than abroad. During the last half of the 1960s, the company did work for Continental Grain in Saint Louis and New Orleans, General Mills in Kansas City, Mid-States Terminals in Toledo, Ohio, Great Western Malting in Los Angeles, and Caribe Mills in Puerto Rico, as well as a job in Denver, erecting the concrete core for the twenty-six-story Colorado State Bank Building. But by far the largest undertaking was a huge grain export elevator for Farmers Export Company, a group of seven grain cooperatives, in Ama, Louisiana, located on the Mississippi River about twenty miles west of New Orleans. The $14 million design and build project was so big that W-H brought in two partners, W. A. Klinger of Sioux City and Barnard and Burk Industrial Corporation, a Baton Rouge firm. Profits were shared equally between the three, except that W-H received an extra 10 percent share because it also provided construction supervision.[52]

This success notwithstanding, Rudy continued concentrating on projects abroad. His travel, and that of other W-H staffers, resulted in a number of additional feasibility studies, as W-H examined the possibilities of grain storage and/or processing facilities in the Philippines, Colombia, Argentina, Honduras, Saudi Arabia, and the Entente Council of West Africa—an economic development group made up of Dahomey (now Benin), Côte d'Ivoire, Niger, Upper Volta (now Burkina Faso), and Togo. Unfortunately, none of these expensive and time-consuming studies led to further work. The company also made a significant effort to win a USAID rice drying and storage complex in Vietnam, but the 1968 project went to another contractor.[53]

Weitz-Hettelsater did land a few more jobs, however. The most important was in East Pakistan (now Bangladesh), where the World Bank financed the development of four large grain storage elevators located in Chittagong, Narayanganj, Santahar, and Ashuganj. The firm was on the job from start to finish, doing the feasibility study, the initial design work, hiring and supervising the construction—Swedish company Skanska for the civil engineering and the German firm Miag-Buhler responsible for the mechanical and electrical work—and providing training in the operation and management of the sites. As the project wound down in 1971, it appeared that the CIA's interest in where W-H operated was well founded; company engineer Bill Duane was in Dhaka, East Pakistan, when the Bangladesh Liberation War began and was one of a number of foreigners evacuated from what became the Bangladesh capital by the British Royal Air Force. More dramatic than Duane's exit, however, was the impact the new grain storage facilities had on Bangladesh, which, according to the *Des Moines Register*, were "credited with helping to avoid famine during the chaotic period following Bangladesh liberation."[54]

Weitz-Hettelsater followed this job with smaller ones in Nicaragua and Guyana, but by this time Rudy and Fred had begun reevaluating its future. There was no backlog of domestic work, and operating overseas was not proving very profitable. At the same time, Rudy was starting to slow down; the heavy international travel schedule he maintained for W-H was becoming much less appealing. As if symbolic of this shift in attitude, the sixty-nine-year-old spent the winters of 1970 and 1971 with Sally in La Jolla, a wealthy seaside community just north of San Diego in Southern California. Although he kept in close touch with his son and managers in Des Moines, Kansas City, and overseas, this marked the first time Rudy had spent extended time away from the office focusing largely on leisure activities.[55]

As early as 1968, Rudy, Fred, and Hart had considered operating W-H without a Kansas City branch manager, with overseas operations overseen by Fred and its domestic jobs by Hart. With work continuing to slow, Fred sent Hart down to Kansas City to see what could be done. He reorganized the office, let some people go, and sent estimator Bill Bontrager to Des Moines, where the office was busy. Bontrager was happy with the transfer, because he "could see the writing on the wall," and believed W-H's days were numbered. After Hart's restructuring, W-H was indeed without a branch manager, and unless local jobs picked up, there were no plans to replace the position. The three were also discussing whether or not the firm's engineering operation should be emphasized and if they could consolidate all construction operations in Des Moines. But by the end of the year, they were also thinking about selling the firm or merging it with another outfit.[56]

While these discussions were taking place, W-H continued its engineering oversight work of a USAID project for rice drying and storage facilities in Georgetown, Guyana. The firm became the third engineering consultant on the job when Nance Engineering Company, which had replaced the original company, ran into financial trouble and withdrew from the venture. Pemar International—a subsidiary of Houston-based conglomerate International Systems & Controls (ISC) since 1968—was the contractor in Guyana as well as in Nicaragua, where W-H was overseeing its building of ninety farm storage centers. As both ventures moved forward, Fred put feelers out about selling W-H, and ISC expressed interest. In September 1972, Fred and Rudy met with Gordon Bing, ISC vice president of acquisitions and divestments, and the deal was concluded that November. The Weitz Company, however, took over the engineering consulting work in both Nicaragua and Guyana since ISC now controlled both Pemar and W-H, and oversight by a firm independent of the contractor was required on USAID projects.[57]

Closing the doors on its Kansas City-based business was not the only change taking place at the Weitz Company. Rudy and Fred had long been concerned about Midwest Concrete Industries, which had never lived up to expectations. Although it was getting jobs manufacturing precast panels for structures throughout the Midwest and by 1966 its volume had exceeded the break-even point for three years, quality control and profit margins remained a problem. The two considered selling the company, and late that year an offer came from Greg Gentleman and two partners. Gentleman was the former manager of MCI, who had left in 1960 to start his own company as a manufacturer's representative; the following year, he bought a controlling interest in Swanson Sales, renaming it Swanson Gentleman Inc., which represented architectural products. He had remained interested in MCI because it was one of his clients, and he and his partners now offered to manage MCI for a share of the profits. But the Weitzes were evidently holding out to sell the business, and no deal resulted.[58]

Nothing materialized over the next few years, but by the fall of 1971, as Fred and Rudy were considering selling W-H, they refocused their efforts to get out of the precast concrete business as well. Iowa Prestress Concrete Company and Jim Hoak of the

Wheeler division of St. Regis Paper Company in West Des Moines had expressed interest, but talks with both came to naught. The issue sat on the back burner for three more years, until original suitor Greg Gentleman came back into the picture and bought MCI in 1974.[59]

While Rudy and Fred were narrowing the firm's focus, they were also refining the company's involvement in the retirement home business. Up to this point, the Weitz Company had served only as the contractor, building turnkey retirement complexes and selling them to the sponsoring bodies Berg had established. At the same time, the company's working relationship with the minister was rather informal. After nearly a decade of building such complexes, Fred considered becoming more involved in the business. Continuing care retirement communities were still relatively new, and Fred remembered thinking, "Gee, there's a real need for these, [and] old people are living happier because of these." Just as important, he recalled, "the market was wide open." With the possibility of developing a real profit center, Fred created Christian Home Services Inc. (CHSI), in May 1971, a corporation devoted "to plan, market, design, construct, and manage retirement facilities."[60]

The company moniker was a nod to Berg, who wanted the word "Christian" incorporated into the firm's name. The Weitz Company and Berg each owned 50 percent of the new business, which was based in Des Moines at the Weitz Company office. Fred served as chairman and CEO, Berg was president, but because he undertook many independent ventures—which would ultimately prove to be a problem—he was not involved in day-to-day issues, and Larry Laird, a manager who had worked with Berg as an administrator of retirement communities the minister had established in Iowa City and Waterloo, Iowa, and Jackson, Michigan, was brought in as vice president.[61]

Once established, Fred thought there might be economies in developing a standardized design for retirement communities, similar to what Holiday Inn did for its motels, and CHSI retained Engelbrecht, Rice, and Griffin Architects to create such a modular plan for low-rise complexes. But before this model was tried, CHSI developed a retirement facility in Santa Fe, New Mexico, in 1971 by converting an apartment building into El Castillo Retirement Center, and the next year, the Weitz Company completed Inter-City Christian Manor in Allen Park, a suburb of Detroit, Michigan. This latter complex was developed and built by the Weitz Company, but it was begun prior to the creation of CHSI, which was not involved in the project. In 1973, CHSI developed Friendship Village Greater Milwaukee.[62]

Meanwhile, shortly after the nascent company had been created, Berg took matters into his own hands in 1971, and without talking to Fred, he contacted the sponsors of Heather Manor, a downtown Des Moines retirement community owned by the Iowa State Education Association, and convinced them to hire CHSI to manage the facility. Not really prepared to manage yet, CHSI scrambled to employ someone for the job, settling on Charles Godfrey, Fred's uncle, whose only relevant experience was managing the Weitz Company-owned apartments Wakonda Village and University Terrace before both were sold in the early 1960s. Actually, because the retirement community business was still new, finding qualified administrators to manage complexes would remain a challenge for CHSI.[63]

In late 1972, just as this new corporation was getting started, Rudy was diagnosed with pancreatic cancer. The cancer went undetected in its early stages and had advanced to the point that the prognosis was poor; doctors did not recommend any treatment options. Rudy may have handled this news better than most, for he was a Christian Scientist, and although the church ultimately left health care decisions up to each individual, prayer was considered the first recourse, and he was not faced with the decision of whether or not to accept medical intervention. Although his mother had also been a Christian Scientist, Rudy was not raised in this church, and he and his wife, Sally, had come to the religion in the early 1950s. They were, according to son Steve, "fairly practical Christian Scientists" who continued drinking alcohol socially but "did very much believe in the basic tenets of the religion and read their lessons and went to church." These doctrines of the church, especially of God's goodness, prayer, positive thinking, and self-help gave Rudy a good attitude during the last eighteen months of his life.[64]

He maintained his regular work schedule and went to the office daily as long as possible, but he soon dispensed with his journal—a detailed record of his business activities and thinking, which he began keeping during his years at the Pentagon. His last journal entry was in January 1973, certainly suggestive of a change in priorities. Rudy gradually grew weaker and was eventually largely confined to his home, a luxury condominium building on Grand Avenue where he and Sally had lived since the late 1960s, near the house the couple had built years earlier on Fifty-Sixth Street. It was here that the seventy-three-year-old Weitz Company chairman died on May 26, 1974.[65]

At his passing, the *Des Moines Tribune* wrote of Rudy's significance. Although the editorial noted his business activity, it emphasized his contributions to the community through the Des Moines Chamber of Commerce, the Greater Des Moines Committee, and his service on behalf of nonprofit groups like Community Chest (now United Way). It was for these efforts, the paper noted, "that Mr. Weitz will best be remembered here."[66]

Rudy would certainly have been proud of his involvement in the community, but he would have been prouder still of his work at the family company, where he had labored for fifty years. It was Rudy who brought the firm back from receivership and gradually restored it to profitability. He then built the business and expanded into new areas. And it was Rudy who had groomed Fred, a fourth-generation family member, to take over the company. When Fred started at the firm, he and Rudy found the father-son dynamic within the workplace difficult, and it took several years for the two to negotiate a solution, with Rudy ultimately devoting his energy to overseas projects and Fred supervising domestic construction. The arrangement worked, and the company grew, but not as either expected. Areas where Rudy and Fred consciously expanded—MCI and Weitz-Hettelsater—failed to meet expectations and were eventually abandoned, but it looked like the retirement community business, which the Weitz Company had entered serendipitously, could become a real growth engine.

Fred's long apprenticeship and then partnership with his father was over. The ship was now in his hands, and the forty-five-year-old executive was eager to put his imprint on the refocused Weitz Company, building on its long heritage and moving into new areas.

Chapter Eight

REIMAGINING WEITZ

Much as his grandfather and father had done, Fred Weitz remade the company once he took charge. Construction remained at its core, but the retirement community component grew in importance, developing into an industry leader. It was this division that introduced the Weitz Company to new markets and led the construction firm to establish branch offices in the Sun Belt. Indeed, Fred once called the company "opportunist" as it aggressively went after prospects outside Des Moines and Iowa. His was a growth-oriented strategy, seizing prospects for expansion that included creating a nonunion shop to go after jobs outside the central Iowa market, setting up a branch office in Lexington, Massachusetts, and buying Denver-based Al Cohen Construction, which increased the size of the Weitz Company building business by over half.[1]

Despite this orientation, Fred kept the firm grounded in Des Moines, and much like his father, he was active on a variety of local boards and community foundations, including a stint as head of the Greater Des Moines Chamber (now the Greater Des Moines Partnership). Likewise, the Des Moines influence remained strong as Fred created a new corporation to oversee the firm's increasingly diverse operations and recruited strong, local, nonfamily board members to bring expertise and an outside perspective to the company.

All of these changes paled in comparison, however, with Fred's decision to open ownership of the company to nonfamily employees. This started in the late 1970s as an incentive to keep key managers at the firm. But the move began a process that was much more groundbreaking. As the fourth-generation Weitz to run the company, Fred worried about the future. Even though at that point he had four children, he reasoned, "We couldn't depend on the family to have more and more generations coming along who wanted to join the business and who had the talents necessary to provide management of a top notch and expanding firm." While the stock purchase program was initially motivated by the need to retain high-quality managers, it clearly opened up the possibility of a Weitz Company not controlled by the Weitz family.[2]

Although Fred had been overseeing the domestic side of operations for some time and managed more and more of the business as Rudy began slowing down, it remained clear that his aging father was still the company's chief executive. While Fred and Rudy's work relationship had improved since the early 1960s, Fred continued to find it challenging. "To work for your father," he once recalled, "is not always the easiest thing in the world." By the early 1970s, Glenn DeStigter, then a project manager, and Jack Hall, then the vice president in charge of Des Moines construction operations, noted that employees were "scared" of Rudy and saw him as imperious. Jerry Gosselink, another young project manager at the time, remembered hearing Rudy and Fred get into serious arguments. These staffers sympathized with Fred and saw the difficulties he faced working with his father. Hall remembered Fred telling him, somewhat facetiously, "My brother was the smarter of the two of us; he didn't get involved in the family business."[3]

Regardless of some ongoing father-son issues, Fred relished work, and like many other successful business leaders, he explained, "I get a great deal of pleasure out of it. I enjoy it." The *Des Moines Tribune* reported that Fred "plunges into his job...with an eye for detail and a mathematician's precision." This was exactly what he did when his father died in 1974; the newly minted CEO began rethinking the company. Changes, in fact, had already started, as the firm had recently disposed of Weitz-Hettelsater, its division responsible for overseas work, sold Midwest Concrete, its exposed aggregate panel business, and moved into the management and development of retirement communities by launching Christian Home Services.[4]

Soft-spoken but serious, Fred looked very much like the earlier generations of Weitz men who had preceded him in the post. He was tall and slender; his oval face and angular features were framed by a prominent pair of glasses; bushy eyebrows sat atop intense blue eyes, and he was balding. Once describing himself as a "fairly colorless person," Fred was extremely intelligent and analytical by nature. He had a wry sense of humor, and while the *Des Moines Tribune* noted he had "a warm and engaging personality," it was often hidden, the paper continued, by a "hard veneer." He did not often engage in small talk, but was generally more interested in getting to the bottom line of a conversation.[5]

Charles Webb, executive vice president of the Des Moines Chamber of Commerce, explained, "I think people are a little intimated by Fred. He kind of cuts to the quick." A number of associates were well aware of Fred's "penetrating stare," which he occasionally directed at those who aggravated or upset him. According to local journalist Gregory Goaley, the look was similar to "the way Clint Eastwood glares at a nasty villain."[6]

Ultimately Fred saw himself as "more of an organization man than an entrepreneur," and he proved a strong and effective leader who cared deeply about the company. He was a builder determined to grow the firm, explore new ideas, and develop managerial structures that would bolster the operations.[7]

He began by creating a new holding company and establishing a strong board of directors. Although his father had relied on advice from various consultants, particularly Des Moines's Joe Batten, early on, and had added attorney Arthur Davis to the company board, Rudy had not used board members for serious discussion. Fred chose to do so. In March 1975, Weitz Brothers Inc. was established. Original incorporators/directors were Fred, his uncle Heinrich, Davis, James Swab, a management expert who worked with Batten, and Fred's younger brother Steve, who had become more involved in the Weitz Company by attending board meetings after Rudy fell ill. He joined that board in 1974.[8]

Now that Rudy was dead, Fred, Steve, and their mother, Sally, held all of the firm's voting shares, and Fred wanted his brother familiar with the decision-making process in all Weitz operations. Soon Swab resigned, and Fred invited two other Des Moines business leaders whose Iowa roots and elite eastern education mirrored his own. First was Tom Urban, an acquaintance of Fred's who would grow to be one of his closest friends. Urban was born and raised in Des Moines but received a BA and an MBA from Harvard and was at that time vice president of Pioneer Hi-Bred International. The other was Marvin Mazie, a Sioux City native with undergraduate and law degrees from Harvard as well. He was then serving as vice president and treasurer of Dial Finance (today part of Wells Fargo). Together with Davis, these two provided valuable input at board meetings. The board would remain unchanged until Heinrich died in 1981; he was not replaced until 1987, when Fred brought Fred Hubbell—another bright Des Moines business figure educated on the East Coast who at the time was the president of Equitable of Iowa—on to the Weitz board.[9]

The holding company, which would be renamed The Weitz Corporation in 1983, and its strong board were only the beginning of the transformation. Fred had taken over the company during the recession of the mid-1970s, and as a result, construction jobs had dried up, so much so that in November 1974 he reported to the board that the outlook for the conventional construction business in the Des Moines area was "miserable." A little over a year later, the situation remained grim, as Fred explained in the in-house newsletter *Building*: "Nineteen seventy-five is behind us, thank goodness! In terms of new business volume, 1975 was our worst year in a long time." Not surprisingly, the economic trough prompted more change at the Weitz Company. A few years earlier, in 1972, vice president John Hart had suggested the company consider establishing a nonunion shop that could compete for jobs outside central Iowa, where the union contracts remained dominant. The idea did not initially get any traction, but two years later, Fred asked Glenn DeStigter, who had started at Weitz in 1968 and was then a project manager, to investigate. DeStigter reported there was real potential for the operation, company studies confirmed his findings, and Jack Hall, who was now the vice president after replacing Hart in the summer of 1972, was supportive. Fred agreed, and the subsidiary Vulcan Construction Company was born in 1975.[10]

DeStigter was put in charge of Vulcan, which Hall believed "broadened the company's horizons." As had been hoped, Vulcan began getting nonunion jobs outside the metropolitan Des Moines area. Initial work included a Union Carbide addition in Centerville, a small Iowa town ninety miles southeast of Des Moines, and a contract with Vega Industries, maker of the Heatilator fireplace insert, in Fairfield, another small town 110 miles southeast of the capital city. Bigger jobs followed, including a new music education building at Iowa State University, an expansion of the Sheaffer factory (a maker of pens, now part of the French firm Société Bic) in Fort Madison, and a building for Vanmark Corporation, which manufactured food-handling equipment, in Creston, seventy miles southwest of Des Moines.[11]

Once Vulcan was established, Fred decided greater effort was needed to market the company and "tell our story to customers and other outsiders." In response, he created a marketing department headed by Richard "Dick" Oggero. A people person who excelled at schmoozing and making deals, Oggero was a good selection. He had been with the firm since 1967, working as a safety engineer and then moving through the ranks on the insurance and real estate side. In his new capacity, Oggero spent much of his time calling on past and potential customers and architects to win more jobs. To assist in this endeavor and drum up business, he also developed a new company publication. Called *The Builder*, the glossy pamphlet was produced twice a year and loaded with photographs of current and recently completed projects. It was sent to architects, customers, and suppliers as well as in-house staff, who also still received the company's internal, more frequently published newsletter, *Building*.[12]

This promotional effort, combined with an economy that gradually picked up and the continuing revival of downtown Des Moines, led to more work. Significant Weitz Corporation jobs in the last half of the 1970s included physical education buildings at both Simpson College, twelve miles south of Des Moines in

Indianola, and Drake University; several buildings in West Des Moines, including a manufacturing and office facility for Windsor Windows, an office building for IMT Insurance, and the Westridge III and Blue Creek office buildings; and the Lutheran Park Apartments and Stonecrest Retirement Home in Des Moines. Two other projects involved Fred and the firm in the downtown's ongoing rejuvenation, which was finally picking up steam.[13]

Des Moines's core had been losing population to the growing suburbs, with retailers and businesses soon following. Dated and dilapidated buildings remained, a growing number of them empty, and, according to Bill Knapp, founder and owner of Iowa Realty, the state's largest real estate firm, by the late-1960s, "Downtown was really kind of a disaster." But a turnaround was in the works. An urban renewal project was underway along the Des Moines River that already included a new US Post Office and south of that, where the Wells Fargo Arena now stands, was the River Hills Cinema. Both of these were built by the Weitz Corporation, with the theater developed by Weitz and partner Allen Block out of Kansas City. Other office and retail buildings went up in downtown as well, including the new federal building and the United Central Bank high-rise in 1967, followed by a J. C. Penney store and the new home office of Employers Mutual, which was also built by the Weitz Company in 1971.[14]

Redevelopment got another big boost in 1973, when businessman John Ruan announced the construction of his thirty-six-story Ruan Center, which would be the headquarters for his trucking firm as well as his bank, Bankers Trust. The tower was erected on the western half of the block bounded by Grand and Sixth Avenues and Locust and Seventh Streets. Original plans called for taking down the old Bankers Trust Building and its annex at Sixth Avenue and Locust, where the Weitz Company was located.[15]

Although the Bankers Trust Building would stand for several more years, the Weitz Company needed more room, and Fred decided the time was right to look for new office space. At the same time, Allen Block, Fred's partner in their urban renewal area development projects, suggested that together they build another office building near their River Hills theater complex and the IBM Building they had recently erected at Crocker Street and Second Avenue, for use by the Weitz Company and other tenants. Fred agreed, and his firm built the three-story office structure, which opened in March 1976. The Weitz Company, Vulcan, Christian Home Services, and Village Distributors—a subsidiary established to supply materials for retirement complexes under construction—occupied the third floor. The following decade, Block wanted out of the joint venture. The IBM Building was sold, but the Weitz Company bought Block's interest in the Weitz Building and the theater complex. The 1987 acquisition gave the firm more space for present and future growth and cost the company just over $2 million.[16]

Meanwhile, as the Ruan Center starting rising, city leaders focused on replacing the rundown KRNT Theater, downtown's 3,000-seat auditorium, with a new complex that would include a 2,500-seat performing arts theater, a convention center, a hotel, and a large, open-air plaza to be located between Grand Avenue and Walnut Street and Second Avenue and Fourth Street. But when the $22 million urban renewal bond issue to fund the facilities went before the public in the fall of 1973, it did not receive the 60 percent majority required for passage. With public funding unavailable, plans were reconsidered and downsized; the hotel and convention center components were scrapped, leaving the new civic center to include the theater and outdoor plaza. Mayor Dick Olson convinced Des Moines officials to donate the land for the project if private money to build it could be found. The fundraising effort was launched in 1975. It was headed by John Fitzgibbon, president of Iowa-Des Moines National Bank, and David Kruidenier, CEO of the Des Moines Register and Tribune Company, and in just three months, they raised more than $9.5 million.[17]

With the land donated and funds pledged, the Civic Center of Greater Des Moines and Nollen Plaza went out for bid. The Weitz Company won the contract in December 1976, and the theater and public space with its park and reflecting pool were completed in 1979. Like his father, Fred was not only a beneficiary of the building and rebuilding of the city's core, he became actively involved in the community and in shaping the downtown. His move beyond the confines of the company began with him serving on a growing number of boards, beginning in 1969, when he became a trustee for Simpson College—although at the time, Rudy made it clear that Grinnell College was to receive the family's primary support. The following year, he was invited to join the boards of Valley Bank and Trust Company and the Master Builders of Iowa, continuing a long family tradition at both institutions. These were followed by other appointments, including positions on the boards of the Des Moines Construction Council, Des Moines Savings & Loan, Bankers Life (now the Principal Financial Group), and Pioneer Hi-Bred International.[18]

Two other organizations, the Greater Des Moines Chamber of Commerce and the Des Moines Development Corporation, played an even greater role in drawing Fred into activities downtown. Fred had long participated in the chamber and began serving on its board in the early 1970s. At the end of the decade, he was elected president, beginning his annual term in January 1980. Once selected, Fred and his father, who had been the chamber president in 1956, became the third father-son duo to each serve as the group's top elected official. As he did with all tasks, Fred immersed himself in the job, and a chamber staff member believed he was "one of the hardest-working presidents we've had in a long time." Fred focused on expanding the chamber's horizons by reaching out to groups not ordinarily involved in its activities, including small businesses, suburban organizations, government bodies, and nonprofits. Fred also worked on strengthening the chamber's Des Moines Convention and Visitors Bureau, and under his leadership, the chamber continued pushing for a new convention center connected to the burgeoning skywalk system and close to hotels and restaurants instead of adding on to the existing Veterans Memorial Auditorium. The chamber even funded a market study that Fred believed would support the move for such an addition.[19]

A new convention center was also a priority of the Des Moines Development Corporation (DMDC), the other key downtown group, which also occupied Fred's time. Although it had been founded in 1961 as the financial committee of the chamber, its role proved unimportant until it was reorganized in 1978. The revamped DMDC remained a nonprofit affiliate of the Greater Des Moines Chamber and saw itself as a "catalyst" to economic development in the metropolitan area, especially downtown. Because decisions were often needed quickly and the group required significant operating funds, only CEOs could join, and annual dues were considerable— varying from $10,000 to $50,000, depending on company size. The DMDC had no paid staff, but it was capably led by Robert Houser, president and CEO of Bankers Life, who volunteered for the job. Besides Houser, there were seventeen other original members, including leading business figures such as Fitzgibbon, Kruidenier, and Ruan; attorney Arthur Davis; James Hubbell Jr., president of the Equitable of Iowa; Robert Burnett, president of Meredith; Bill Knapp, owner of Iowa Realty and a leading developer; Robb Kelley, CEO of Employers Mutual; and Fred.[20]

By spring 1981, the chamber's convention center study was completed, confirming Fred's belief that it would justify a new facility. At that point, Ruan took the lead, pushing for the center while the *Register* and *Tribune* threw their editorial support behind the project and the DMDC pledged to donate land for the center—located along the west side of Fifth Avenue between Grand Avenue to the south and Keosauqua—and cover a portion of the projected annual deficits the convention center would run. These efforts paid off, and the business community persuaded the city to build the Des Moines Convention Center, which opened in 1986. Eventually taken over by the county and renamed the Polk County Convention Complex, the center was ultimately superseded by the Iowa Events Center and is currently being remodeled as downtown's new Wellmark YMCA.[21]

Fred's involvement with the downtown area also made him aware of the city center's housing shortage, so it was no surprise that the Weitz Company joined a Bill Knapp-led consortium of twenty-six local businesses to develop a downtown apartment complex in the summer of 1981. The group proposed Civic Center Court—a $3.8 million facility of 141 medium-priced garden-style apartments designed for people who worked downtown—to be located on the block of land north of the completed Civic Center of Greater Des Moines, bounded by Second Avenue and Third Street. And Fred showed his softer, more compassionate side when, after the plans were approved, he announced that his firm would build the complex "at no profit to the company."[22]

However, even as Fred became more active in these areas, there was no doubt that his focus remained on his companies. Besides working to expand the construction business, he also oversaw the growth and evolution of Christian Home Services Inc., the retirement community operation, which was becoming increasingly important. Suggestive of this significance were volume numbers for Weitz Company construction projects in the midst of the recession. In 1973, for example, construction involving CHSI projects generated $8.1 million in volume, while other jobs accounted for roughly $7.4 million. This was not always the case, of course, and some years, regular construction accounted for more volume than CHSI work, but it was clear that such developments were significant to the company's bottom line. However, it was also clear by the mid-1970s that some changes at CHSI were necessary. The biggest issue may have been partner Kenneth Berg. Although he had led Weitz into the profitable retirement home business, he had been a challenge from the beginning.[23]

When Fred established CHSI with Berg in 1971, the two agreed that neither would work independently of the other in the retirement home industry. But Berg paid little attention to the arrangement, and acting through his own firm, Christian Services Inc., he began expanding his John Knox Village, a retirement facility in Lees Summit, Missouri, into what became the largest continuing care retirement community in the country. Soon he was working on other John Knox Villages, including complexes in Lubbock, Texas; Higginsville and Waynesville, Missouri; and Pompano Beach, Florida. Two years into the partnership, Fred began considering parting ways with Berg but was concerned that CHSI would then likely lose access to long-term mortgage loans from Prudential, which Berg had arranged, as well as Harvey Beck, CHSI's sales manager, who had worked with Berg previously. Beck would likely stay with the minister and would be difficult to replace.[24]

By spring 1976, Fred had had enough. He opened negotiations with Berg, either to buy him out or sell him the Weitz Company's share of the business. A deal was consummated that summer, with Weitz acquiring Berg's interest in the company. It was not cheap. Subsidiary Weitz Properties purchased Berg's stock for the book value of $106,000, and CHSI paid him his fees for several ongoing projects as well as buying notes due Berg from their Vista Grande Villa project in Jackson, Michigan. All told, Berg received $838,000. The agreement included a five-year noncompete clause, barring either party from building a project within twenty-five miles of one being developed by the other, and required Christian Home Services to change its name because of its similarity to Berg's firm, Christian Services.[25]

The Weitz Company's move away from Berg was fortuitous, as the minister, who often oversold ideas and plans, was soon entangled in a slew of legal difficulties. From the late 1970s into the 1980s, he faced several civil lawsuits, ran afoul of the Internal Revenue Service, and was convicted of a federal fraud charge resulting in prison time. These problems destroyed his retirement community empire.[26]

As Berg's troubles mounted, the Weitz Company moved ahead in the senior living business. Now a wholly owned subsidiary, CHSI was renamed Life Care Services (LCS) in 1976, and later that year, the company trademarked the term "life-care" to describe its "comprehensive approach to retirement living," which "permit[ted] each resident to maintain the style of life to which he or she has become accustomed without having to worry about certain financial or health concerns, and without having to perform troublesome routine tasks associated with household maintenance." In LCS complexes, seniors enjoyed private residences, meals were available in a community dining room, and services such as housekeeping, laundry, transportation, repairs, and security were provided. Equally as important, each campus had a skilled nursing facility on site and furnished "emergency, recuperative, and long-term care."[27]

Meanwhile, as expected, Harvey Beck left to work for Christian Services, and with Berg out of the picture, loans for LCS projects from Prudential were no longer available. These were not major problems, however. Larry Laird replaced Beck with H. B. "Skip" Kedney, who proved adept at marketing and sales, and although Fred and his wife, Emily, had to provide their personal guarantee for construction loans for all LCS projects, Fred and later Oggero eventually found other sources of funding.[28]

Life Care Services continued developing retirement communities at a brisk pace, providing a lot of construction business for the Weitz Company. It completed three projects in 1975, two each in 1977 and 1978, and four in 1979. To facilitate the process and keep up with demand, Fred hired Stan Thurston as LCS's first director of development in 1977. Prior to this, development details had been handled by Oggero and others at the Weitz Company. Thurston possessed the perfect background for the job: a degree in architecture from Iowa State University, an MBA from the Harvard Business School, and experience at Cadillac Fairview Corporation, one of North America's largest developers and owners of commercial real estate. He would eventually go on to become the president and CEO of LCS, but that was well down the road.[29]

Most of these projects in the mid-1970s began with the standardized modular design of low-rise apartment complexes, which Fred had the architectural firm of Engelbrecht, Rice, and Griffin develop. He had hoped the model would provide economies to developing new retirement projects, and initially it appeared to be working. Communities that employed the scheme included Carolina Village in Hendersonville, North Carolina (1974); Friendship Village, Dayton, Ohio (1974); Friendship Village, Kalamazoo, Michigan (1975); Friendship Village of West County, Chesterfield, Missouri (1975); Friendship Village, Columbus, Ohio (1978); and Friendship Village of Dublin, a suburb of Columbus, Ohio, (1981).[30]

However, once LCS took over the development role from the construction company, regard for the standardized design for retirement complexes dimmed. Shortly after Thurston started at LCS, he hired Peter Taggart, whose background in market research and real estate led the subsidiary to reconsider how sites for retirement communities were selected. When the Weitz Company handled development, it usually sought large, flat pieces of land, which simplified the construction process and were conducive to the low-rise modular buildings in its standard plan. Taggart and LCS began looking at potential markets more carefully, analyzing census data, income, home ownership rates, and demographic and economic trends to determine where facilities should best be located. Focus groups also revealed that more affluent seniors wanted larger apartments and more amenities. These did not easily fit within the Engelbrecht, Rice, and Griffin model. Thus, by the end of the decade, projects such as the Whitney Center in Hamden, Connecticut, jettisoned the standard design and were built to fit the site and the desires of the incoming residents. As this development was going up, Fred and Thurston decided the cookie-cutter approach

217

would not work for LCS. The standardized model was scrapped, and from the early 1980s on, each of the company's retirement communities was designed from scratch.[31]

Except for this issue, development moved along relatively smoothly, assisted by an innovation Fred devised: the creation of Life Care Retirement Communities Inc. (LCRC), a single board designed to oversee a number of retirement communities. For years, the Weitz Company and CHSI had gone through the time-consuming and repetitive process of setting up individual not-for-profit sponsoring boards, initially church related, but later community based, to own and oversee each retirement community. This required a lot of time educating each group about the business and attending many different board meetings. Instead, Fred thought, economies of scale could be achieved by establishing a single, not-for-profit board for this purpose. Thus, LCRC was born in 1976. For directors, Fred recruited bright, knowledgeable figures with experience in the field, and to encourage them to take the job seriously, they received modest directors' fees.[32]

The initial LCRC board consisted of finance executive Thomas Haeussler from Columbus, Ohio; banker Donald Koessel from Minneapolis; Presbyterian minister Donald McNair from Saint Louis; retired Iowa Blue Cross Blue Shield president Fredric P. G. Lattner from Des Moines; and commercial loan executive Jim Smith, also from Des Moines. The first project the Weitz Company, LCS, and LCRC worked on together was a new Friendship Village in Bloomington, Minnesota. It was built by the Weitz Company, designed and managed by LCS, and owned by LCRC. Local boards were still employed while LCRC became more familiar with the industry, but gradually it assumed ownership of more and more LCS developed projects.[33]

One problem that nagged CHSI and then LCS throughout its early years involved overseeing its senior living complexes. Because the industry was relatively new, finding experienced and/or trained people to manage the facilities the company developed proved difficult. Early on, Fred recalled, the company had made some poor choices for facility administrators, a few of whom turned out to be dishonest or unprepared for the task. Maybe the most embarrassing incident occurred at Friendship Village of Schaumburg, Illinois, in 1977, when it was discovered that Henry Gully, its LCS administrator, had previous managed two nursing homes that were both closed by regulators during his tenure because of the poor service and unsanitary conditions. At the same time, Gully had been charged with stealing equipment from one of the nursing homes and writing bad checks. Court action against Gully was pending when he was terminated.[34]

This difficulty in finding qualified administrators led Fred and Laird to consider hiring an outside firm to provide management services for LCS projects. The idea was soon dropped, however, when Laird and operations manager Phil Roberts saw successes in their "administrator-in-training" program. This was essentially an apprenticeship program that placed a trainee under the wing of an experienced administrator for two years before placing the newly minted manager in charge of a complex of his own. By the end of the decade, LCS had developed a stronger core of administrators for its facilities and finally felt comfortable doing what had long been intended: offering management services to complexes beyond those that LCS developed.[35]

To this point, the only such facility the company managed was Heather Manor, which, as discussed in the last chapter, was a situation where Kenneth Berg had jumped the gun and offered services

CHSI was not truly prepared to provide. Now, however, the firm had the capability and began soliciting management business from non-LCS-developed projects. The first contracts it obtained in this area were with Westminster Manor of Austin, Texas, in 1979; Greenwood Village South in Greenwood, Indiana, and Marquette Manor in Indianapolis, Indiana, in 1981; and then Thomas House in Washington, DC, the following year.[36]

At the same time, LCS was taking the Weitz Company in another new direction. The planning and then building of retirement centers in growing Sunbelt communities led Fred to consider branch offices outside the confines of the state. He understood there was a "limit to what we can do here in Iowa, because Iowa's economy is stable at best, and so if we're going to continue to have growth within our organization, we needed to go someplace else." The company's first satellite office was in Arizona, where it was building a Friendship Village in Tempe, a Phoenix suburb. The complex opened in 1980, and that same year, after investigating the local economy and its construction sector, the Weitz Company established a branch in Tempe. The following year, its Vulcan subsidiary set up an office in West Palm Beach, just to the north of where it had completed the Abbey Delray retirement community in Delray Beach, Florida.[37]

Fred's strategy in Tempe and West Palm Beach called for each branch to act as a "local" contractor by creating a presence in the area, marketing locally, and striving to develop ties within the community. The approach worked; the Tempe office rapidly established a "good reputation" and soon had work, erecting an office building for Communications Consultants Inc., a warehouse for Searle Pharmaceutical Company, a manufacturing plant and office for Sonee Heat Treatment, and the Westcourt Hotel. The Vulcan operation in West Palm Beach initially had some trouble getting contracts, but won a big job in 1981, building a luxury shopping center in Manalapan, just south of West Palm Beach. Work picked up after that, and both offices would expand, becoming important components of the Weitz Corporation.[38]

All of these activities were suggestive of Fred's intent, as he would later recall, of wanting "to build a powerhouse of a company." Growth had certainly occurred since he became president in 1963, when the firm employed about fifty people, to 1980, when roughly two hundred people worked for the corporation.[39]

But in the midst of this expansion, Fred became increasingly concerned about retaining and attracting talented people to the fold. Over the years, he had seen important managers, such as Harold Carlson and Buell Rocky, leave to set up their own companies or join firms that offered them stock. Consequently, shortly after he had control of the firm, Fred decided that key staff members needed "a piece of the action" because it was relatively easy for good people in the construction business to go off on their own. The move broke with tradition and opened company ownership to important personnel.[40]

In the spring of 1977, he and the board initially offered stock to vice president Jack Hall, treasurer and chief financial officer Roscoe Paulson, and four other top managers who would all be named vice presidents in 1979: Glenn DeStigter, Jerry Gosselink, Dick Oggero, and construction manager Michael Carlstrom. A month later, estimator Bill Bontrager, also named a vice president in 1979, and Larry Laird of LCS, were offered stock as well. Originally, all were sold shares in the subsidiaries, the Weitz Company, Village Distributors, and Vulcan, except Laird, who was sold stock in LCS, and all were given three years to pay off the balance at 7 percent interest, which was below market rate at the time. Two years later, Skip Kedney, Phil Roberts, and Stan Thurston were offered stock in LCS, and by 1980, nineteen employees owned nearly 20 percent of the corporation.[41]

But Fred's plan was much more revolutionary than merely providing top officials an ownership stake. The forty-nine-year-old had begun considering the fate of the company, and he saw the stock sale as the first step in a process of securing the future of the Weitz firm and keeping it in Des Moines. Although he and Emily had four children—by 1977, Alice Cary was eighteen years old, Frederick "Fritz" Booton was seventeen, Ankeney "Ann" was fifteen, and Sarah Stevenson was thirteen years old—it was too early to determine whether any of them would want to make a career working for the Weitz Company. Ann would later write a history of the family and firm, while Fritz would join the Weitz Company and work his way up to assistant superintendent on construction sites in Boston and Phoenix and later a superintendent in preconstruction.[42]

So Fred continued holding open the possibility that the fifth generation would play a significant role in the business, although he recognized the likelihood that there might be a Weitz Corporation without Weitz ownership or involvement. In place of family members running the firm, he imagined the Weitz name and company continuing under the watchful eye of an experienced team of owner-managers steeped in the traditions and values of the enterprise.[43]

As Fred thought about the future, he and his managers negotiated the difficult economy of the late 1970s and early 1980s, which saw the annual inflation rate move from single to double digits, while home mortgage interest rates jumped from 9.6 percent to 16.6 percent. Amid this continuing uncertainty, the Weitz Company experienced the ups and downs of the construction industry, depending on the particular conditions of the markets where it was operating. Although its revenues bounced up and down over the course of the troubled economy, Fred noted that the firm had "done very well during the slump," and recalled it "maintained pretty good volume right on through." In 1978, the firm's building volume stood at $60 million, ranking it 218th among contractors nationally. The next year its business dropped by roughly 10 percent, but two years later, volume shot up to $106 million, and its ranking jumped to 187th. In 1982, however, construction volume plunged again, dropping to $55 million and pushing its national ranking down to 284th.[44]

Life Care Services was experiencing problems as well. High interest rates hit the housing market hard, making it tough for prospective residents to sell their homes before buying into an LCS retirement community. As inflation pushed the cost of living higher, retirees on fixed incomes thought twice before making such a commitment. These factors slowed sales at recently opened LCS retirement communities and concerned Fred, Laird, and Thurston. Company managers soon agreed that financial inducements were needed to stimulate sales, particularly in Friendship Villages in Bloomington, Minnesota, and Tempe, Arizona, and Florida's Abbey Delray in Delray Beach and The Waterford in Juno Beach. Special deals that encouraged seniors to buy into these facilities included guarantees of sales contracts or buy-downs on high interest rates. Such offers and the economic rebound in 1983 turned the tide, and the complexes eventually filled up.[45]

The building of Des Moines's $48 million eight-story Capital Square complex heralded the beginning of good times for the Weitz Company and was another step forward in the downtown's renaissance. Located immediately west of the new Nollen Plaza (now Cowles Commons) and the civic center, between Locust and

Walnut and Fourth and Fifth Streets, the gleaming office and retail facility was hailed by the *Des Moines Register* as "the city's newest downtown showplace." Once again the Des Moines Development Corporation played a significant role, buying the run-down structures of the Ward Block, so called because of the empty Montgomery Ward building situated on the north side of the parcel, and selling it to the city at cost. After the city solicited bids, it upset some in the Des Moines business community by selecting Chicago-based Draper and Kramer, the only out-of-state developer in competition for the project. But the local Weitz Company was picked as the building contractor. Construction began in April 1981 and was finished two years later.[46]

Other significant work in the rebuilding of downtown soon followed. The Weitz Company erected Hub Tower, a new twenty-five-story office building, and the adjacent Kaleidoscope at the Hub Mall at Walnut and Seventh Streets in 1985, and two years later, it completed the new State Historical Building. It also participated in Drake neighborhood rehabilitation in the last half of the decade. As an investor in Civic Center Court Inc., the firm was part of the group that developed the Old Main Apartments, a four-building complex located between Twenty-Third and Twenty-Fourth Streets and University and Carpenter Avenues, as well as Drake Court and Drake Pointe, two smaller apartments in the neighborhood. The company also built the Drake University Inn, bounded by Twenty-Fourth and Twenty-Fifth Streets south of University Avenue, and the Drake Legal Clinic, just north of the motel. At the same time, business was picking up across the country, and the Weitz Company's divisions in Phoenix and West Palm Beach, now operating under the Weitz name, as well as its national division, run by DeStigter out of Des Moines, all enjoyed much more work.[47]

Besides the economic turnaround, the company experienced some major changes in the mid-1980s. There were three significant personnel changes. In December 1984, Fred announced that he had hired current Des Moines city manager Richard "Rich" Wilkey. Wilkey had served in that position for ten years and had been an important figure in the downtown renaissance. He started at Weitz the following February as vice president of administration and finance, and Fred saw the appointment as a "terrific opportunity for us to add strength to our operations." It was an unusual move for the company, which usually promoted people from within, but it was not without precedent: Rudy, for example, had hired former Des Moines city manager Leonard Howell in the late 1950s to serve initially as the firm's vice president and general manager.[48]

Early in Wilkey's tenure, he became involved in a special project: in February 1985, developer Kenny Grandquist, who had been granted a license to build a horse racing track, retained the Weitz Company to construct what would become Prairie Meadows. Unfortunately, Grandquist could not sell the $40 million in revenue bonds required to finance the complex, and in July 1986 he gave up. The license was reissued to a nonprofit group called the Racing Association of Central Iowa, headed by Rich Wilkey, who had been a major advocate of the project while city manager. Fred gave his vice president the go-ahead to focus on bringing the track to reality. Wilkey worked quickly and, using his connections throughout the community, pieced together a public-private partnership for the track. The $40 million in bonds were guaranteed by the Polk County supervisors, which made the taxpayers liable if the track failed, and thus made purchase of the bonds much more appealing. The Des Moines Development Corporation agreed to lend the track $4 million, and the nonprofit established to manage the track raised several million more from the private sector. With the project rejuvenated, the Weitz Company was awarded the job to build the $30 million track.[49]

This time, however, the Weitz Company's winning of the bid raised some eyebrows because Wilkey was the prime mover of the track project and was employed by the company that received the contract. Fred understood the appearance of impropriety and realized that there might be some "justification to be skeptical about the contract," but recalled that the company never had a sense that it was guaranteed the job.[50]

Lloyd Clarke, a member of the building committee, explained that Weitz was selected because the company "understood the overall project" and had a record of completing large projects on time and within budget. The other bid was a joint proposal from Des Moines firm Ringland, Johnson, Crowley, who would be responsible for only 30 percent of the work, and the New Jersey-based Gilbane Building Company. This proved another reason the job went to the Weitz Company, as the building committee was interested in keeping the track an all-Iowa project. Meanwhile, although Orville Crowley was disappointed that his bid was not selected, the *Des Moines Register* noted that he felt his company "got a fair hearing."[51]

As Wilkey was resuscitating the track project, two other company executives left the firm. Jack Hall, the executive vice president, was having personal and family problems and left the Des Moines office for Florida in 1984 to beef up the Palm Beach operation, but Hall eventually resigned from the company later that decade. Jim Koepnick, who had been running the Palm Beach office, remained there, and Glenn DeStigter replaced Hall overseeing company construction operations. Meanwhile, Larry Laird, LCS's executive vice president, resigned to take a position with businessman Oswald

Mutz of Indianapolis, who was getting into the retirement home industry. Actually, Mutz had talked to Fred about buying LCS, but when Fred would not sell, Mutz lured Laird away. This led to a restructuring at the subsidiary, with Wilkey being named president and chief operating officer, vice president Stan Thurston moving from head of development to operations, and development being taken over by Steve Hoover and Bill Klemme.[52]

These changes occurred while LCS was growing. Development of new communities had always been the company's bread and butter and led the way, especially as the economy rebounded. The firm had opened only two facilities in 1980, but opened four the following year and three in 1982. Three more were ready in 1986, one in 1987, and six in 1988. From 1982 to 1987, this construction averaged $50 million in annual volume for the Weitz Company. Operations grew too, with LCS managing the facilities it built, but also taking over management responsibilities of several facilities that had struggled under other firms. And by 1986, operations eclipsed development for the first time, with it contributing $2.25 million to the corporation, while development accounted for $2 million. The following year, LCS was one of the nation's largest life-care retirement community providers, managing thirty-one retirement communities in seventeen states; nineteen had been Weitz Company projects, while twelve were complexes taken over by LCS.[53]

As had happened earlier in the decade, one of these LCS projects led the Weitz Company to open another regional division. In 1983, the firm broke ground on North Hill, a retirement community in Needham, a suburb of Boston, Massachusetts. While working on the complex, the Weitz Company landed a $7.5 million job in Lexington, a suburb northeast of Boston. Soon it was competing for another sizable job in the area, and with that, Fred decided to establish a branch office in Lexington in 1985. It won a few large contracts, including the Greenleaf Woods fitness center and office complex and the Sheraton Harborside Hotel and condominiums, both in Portsmouth, New Hampshire, sixty miles north of Boston. However, the savings and loan crisis—commonly referred to as the S&L crisis—hit the region's construction industry especially hard, and Fred explained that "business began to falter" shortly after the Weitz Company set up shop there, "and it wasn't profitable for us." Consequently, after only four years, the company closed this New England office and pulled out of the region in 1989.[54]

Despite this misstep in Boston, another change was afoot. Fred and top LCS officials Larry Laird and Stan Thurston considered altering their model and building for-profit retirement communities, which the firm would own and operate. To date, the Weitz Company and LCS were assuming all the development risk and then turning over completed complexes to nonprofit owners. If the company owned the facilities it built and managed, greater profits could be realized.[55]

All agreed on the new strategy, and in the mid-1980s, LCS began developing its first for-profit communities—Village on the Green in Orlando and Harbour's Edge in Delray Beach, Florida, where it owned 50 percent of the project. But a change in the tax code gave the company pause. New federal regulations called for taxing residents on the entrance fees they paid to for-profit continuing care resident communities, and LCS was concerned about the legislation's negative impact. Therefore, while these two Florida facilities were under construction, Life Care Services leased them to the nonprofit LCRC, which operated the complexes, and residents avoided the tax. Soon, however, LCS decided to go forward with for-profit communities regardless of the tax, and over the next eight years, it established Sandhill Cove in Palm City, Florida; Essex Meadows in Essex, Connecticut; and North Oaks and Blakehurst, both in suburbs of Baltimore, Maryland. All these projects proved successful, and the firm continued planning more for-profit centers.[56]

Meanwhile, there were two other significant changes. The first dovetailed with Fred's interest in growing the company. Although he was not looking to expand through acquisition, he was open to the possibility, and such an opportunity presented itself in early 1986. Hugh Rice, a manager at FMI, a leading consulting firm and investment banking house for contractors, contacted Fred, telling him that Al Cohen, owner of the Denver-based construction company of the same name was looking to retire and sell out. Rice knew the Weitz Company because he had done annual stock valuations for the firm ever since Fred started selling stock to key employees, and he thought the two firms would fit together well. Fred was intrigued, and in March he traveled to Denver to get acquainted with Cohen and his operation. When he liked what he saw, he hired Des Moines management consultant Roy Park to do more digging into the company.[57]

Through his contact and Park's findings, Fred was struck by the similarities of the two companies and their values. He noted that when Weitz Company officials visited with Cohen employees, "It was like we were talking with people from our own organization." This shared culture, obtaining Cohen's expertise in high-rise buildings—most Weitz projects were under ten stories—and access to its markets in Denver and Los Angeles were appealing. Fred had Wilkey negotiate the deal, which was consummated in August 1986 with the Weitz Company, the nation's 109th largest contractor, acquiring Cohen Construction, the 186th largest builder.

The purchase vaulted the Weitz Company into the nation's top one hundred contractors when in the spring of 1987 it was ranked ninety-fourth by *Engineering News-Record*, with a building volume of $216 million. It also garnered the company some unusual press when Fox Plaza in Los Angeles, a thirty-four-story tower Cohen had started in 1985 and completed under Weitz in 1987, was prominently featured as the fictional Nakatomi Plaza in *Die Hard*, the Hollywood blockbuster film of the following year.[58]

Much as Fred had expected, the cultures of the two companies meshed well together, and it was soon clear the purchase brought a talented pool of personnel into the Weitz Company, including, for example, Leonard "Len" Martling, the firm's current president and CEO. And while Fred and his management team were well aware that Denver's market was more volatile than the relatively stable one in Des Moines, it took some time to get used to the cyclical nature of the market in the Colorado capital. The company indeed enjoyed outstanding years during booms in the Denver economy, but it struggled through tough times during stagnant periods.[59]

Besides buying Cohen, the other significant move in the mid-1980s was the creation of the employee stock ownership plan, or ESOP. Fred had been thinking about this for some time, as he remained intent on increasing his employees' stake in the business. Although he found the Weitzes' multigenerational ownership of the company "historically interesting" and thought it would be satisfying to "carry on the family business," Fred strongly believed that "the thing you have to guard against is having a sentimental point of view that ends up in making dumb decisions." Most important, he noted, "You don't want to run the thing into the ground just to carry on a tradition." More analysis of the situation led Fred to conclude he "would rather run a business where we share ownership of the company, and thereby we can attract the kind of people we want and keep them." To open up more stock to employees, the company's profit-sharing plan was converted into an ESOP in 1985, and after a year of service, employees became shareholders through the company's retirement plan.[60]

Fritz Weitz was now working for the company on the LCS facility being built in Boston, and although Fred was still unclear about his son's future, explaining in 1985, "Where he ends up remains to be seen," he realized the twenty-five-year-old would not be his immediate successor in any event. Instead, he imagined being followed by "one of the folks around [the Weitz Corp. office] that are here now working." It was in this vein that the ESOP was created; in concert with Fred's belief that a current top manager would one day succeed him as company CEO, he was now leaning toward the firm eventually becoming employee-owned. Such an operation, he believed, would carry on the Weitz name and company traditions, and he saw the ESOP as the vehicle through which this could ultimately be accomplished.[61]

By early 1990, however, it was clear that one manager was no longer a possibility for the top job at the firm. Originally Wilkey had been "seen as a possible successor to Fred Weitz," according to the *Des Moines Register*, but he announced his resignation that January. Wilkey explained simply, "My situation [at Weitz] has not developed as anticipated."[62]

Fred had been impressed with Wilkey's deal making and leadership of downtown development while at the city and expected him "to be a guy that could help us move forward." Although he had some successes at the company, especially in arranging deals such as putting together the plan that made Prairie Meadows possible, which resulted in a big Weitz Company contract, or in negotiating the Al Cohen purchase, his lack of background in either the construction or retirement facility business made his position at the company difficult. Moreover, Fred recalled, he had not set the stage well for the former city manager. His failure to delineate Wilkey's role in the company with current managers caused confusion and resentment, especially because of the firm's tradition of promoting from within, and as an outsider, Wilkey was never really accepted in the managerial structure. After several years, Fred and Wilkey both realized the position was untenable; Fred provided him a generous severance package, and Wilkey resigned.[63]

At the same time, Fred was recognized as one of the city's foremost leaders. In January 1990, the *Des Moines Register* ran the results of its second "The Powers That Be" poll—the first was conducted in 1976—which asked prominent area business and civic leaders to identify the city's most influential figures. Fred was ranked seventh, tied with Fred Hubbell, president of the Equitable of Iowa Companies and a board member at Weitz. Ahead of him were Bill Knapp, named the city's most powerful; followed by John Ruan, who was the most powerful in the 1976 poll; David Hurd, president of the Principal Financial Group; Tom Urban, Fred's good friend, now chairman and president of Pioneer; Robert Houser, head of DMDC; and Marvin Pomerantz, chairman of Mid-America Group.[64]

Fred's interest and involvement in downtown Des Moines's restoration, often working with leaders who ranked above him on the list, and his management of the Weitz Company, which had erected a number of the city's landmarks, clearly led to his inclusion. But it was Fred's analytical ability that elicited comment. Arthur Davis, longtime Weitz Company attorney and board member, noted, "He has one of the great minds around," while

David Hurd explained, "He's an interesting blend of the pragmatic and visionary."[65]

The year Fred was named one of the city's most powerful coincided with his sixty-first birthday and the firm's 135th anniversary. Questions about the fate of the company upon his retirement were becoming more common. Fred brushed them aside, observing, "I'm still enjoying what I do—most of the time. I don't think anybody enjoys what they do all of the time. I'm not in any great sweat to get out of here." Yet, he admitted, "It's time for me to think about retiring....I don't think employees should be overly concerned, but, on the other hand, I understand that change produces anxiety. I want to produce an organization that will be strong and vital and continue to grow after I'm gone."[66]

Thus, over the next couple of years, Fred began laying the groundwork for his retirement, which also meant readying plans to transfer the company to employee shareholders. He had long been moving in this direction. In preparation, he hired FMI to craft the broad outlines of the move and started discussing the idea with attorney Don Brown and Randy Hamilton of KPMG, which handled the Weitz Corporation's accounting work. Fred also began talking with key people like Glenn DeStigter and Dick Oggero, the top managers/shareholders of the Weitz Company—the construction division of the Weitz Corporation—as well as Stan Thurston, the head of LCS, and Arthur Neis, the Weitz Corporation's treasurer and chief financial officer. DeStigter and Oggero were especially eager to get the ball rolling on the transfer and try their hand at leading the construction company.[67]

By early 1993, a broad framework of a deal had been worked out, and in the words of the *Des Moines Register*, "After 138 years and four generations of ownership, the Des Moines-based Weitz family is preparing to turn over ownership of the nation's for-ty-ninth largest building contracting firm [as well as one of the nation's largest developers and managers of retirement communi-ties] to employees." Details between the family and representatives for each of the units to be transferred still needed to be negotiated, but the die had been cast.[68]

The era of the family-owned and operated Weitz Corporation, which had grown from a one-man enterprise in the mid-nineteenth century to include one of the nation's leading contracting firms and retirement center businesses at the end of the twentieth century, was coming to a close. Just as Fred had wanted, he had built the enterprise into a "powerhouse" and major player on the national scene. Now he and the company were preparing for a new phase: the Weitz companies would go forward without Weitz family lead-ership or ownership.

WEITZ WITHOUT WEITZ

Fred Weitz was named to the Iowa Business Hall of Fame in 1995 for his long and successful career, growing and refashioning the Weitz Company into one of the nation's fifty largest contractors. That same year, he paved the way for an historic new era, finalizing the sale of the 140-year-old family-owned corporation. The reason for the deal was simple, he explained: "The family would rather see the company go on and be successful for the next 130 years than they would to try to hold the fort themselves." Ten years later, Fred could not have been happier with the results. By 2005, the construction firm's revenues had quadrupled, soaring from $250 million in 1994 to $1.1 billion. Fred was delighted, noting, "They have done a terrific job. It's just what I would have hoped." Life Care Services (LCS) also enjoyed success; by 2004 it owned thirteen senior living communities and managed 105 properties in twenty-nine states.[1]

Later in the decade, however, the situation changed. A recession that began in 2007 ushered in the worst financial crisis since the Great Depression of the 1930s and shook the economic landscape. Despite the slump, LCS continued doing well. Unfortunately, the same could not be said for the Weitz Company, as the turmoil created a number of problems that would ultimately lead to another sale of the construction firm.

But that was down the road. In the spring of 1993, when Fred announced his intention to transfer the Weitz companies to employees, he was optimistic about the upcoming divestiture. Details were still to be worked out, but the firms were in good hands; control would remain local, company names would live on, and the entrenched corporate cultures would continue. The management teams Fred had hired and honed would stay in place at the Weitz Company and Life Care Services, and both operations appeared headed down familiar paths.

Even amid the economic downturn early that decade, when the Weitz Company laid off 30 percent of its workforce and lost over $4 million in 1991, it remained in better shape than many other construction firms, working out of Des Moines and three major regional offices beyond Iowa— Phoenix, Denver, and West Palm Beach. As new commercial building slowed in those out-of-state markets, it moved into renovation and remodeling work; its biggest such projects included rehabilitating two famous historic hotels, The Breakers in Palm Beach, Florida, and the Arizona Biltmore in Phoenix. In Des Moines, a more stable market persisted, and the Weitz Company won several significant projects including the new Hy-Vee corporate headquarters in West Des Moines and the downtown Principal Financial Group's "Z" Building, so named because of its shape. The slowdown impacted LCS as well, reducing sales at its facilities, but the firm continued expanding, developing communities and obtaining additional management contracts.[2]

As negotiations between Fred and representatives from the construction group and Life Care Services went forward, two other Weitz executives realized their units did not fit neatly within the planned division of the corporation. First was Robert Bachman, a Weitz Company manager who had overseen its condominium and commercial projects in and around Bonita Springs on the southwest coast of Florida. A decade earlier, while the Weitz Company was building a retirement community in the area, Dick Oggero saw other opportunities, and under the name of Weitz Properties, he took the firm into the condominium and commercial development business in Naples, Florida. This led to other projects, including several in Bonita Springs, where the company also became involved in property management. Clearly the operation here was not suitable for LCS, nor was it viewed as appropriate for the construction group. At the same time, Bachman had moved his family to Florida and wished to remain there.[3]

He and Fred began discussing options, and the two soon hammered out a deal. Bachman would stay in Florida, and in exchange for the stock he held in the Weitz Corporation, he took over the development rights of the Oakwood condominium buildings in Bonita Bay, a planned community in Bonita Springs, which Weitz Properties had not yet completed. His new company was called the Weitz-Bachman Group (today known as WBG SW Florida Inc.) and also received a generous line of credit from the Weitz Corporation, allowing Bachman to complete the structures.[4]

At about the same time, Fred visited with James Brandl, head of the Weitz information technology department, about the future of the unit, which serviced both the construction company and LCS. Brandl, who years earlier taught computer science at Central College in Pella, had been hired to set up the computer system for LCS in 1981. Shortly thereafter, he did the same for the Weitz Company. He did not believe that dividing his technology group between the soon-to-be independent construction and retirement community companies made sense, largely because it would require the development of two separate systems with a lot of duplication.[5]

Instead, Brandl asked Fred if he could buy the group and provide computing services to both the new Weitz Company and LCS. "It was as if a light bulb went on in Fred's mind," Brandl remembered.[6]

"That might work, Jim," Fred replied, "but you're going to have to put the deal together, and you're going to have to have Life Care and Weitz be partners because you're going to need some of their money."[7]

Brandl immediately began working with Glenn DeStigter and Stan Thurston on spinning off the Weitz information technology (IT) unit into an independent entity. His thinking was that he and Steve Sikkink, his second in command, would become the largest shareholders of the firm, while the construction company and LCS would own smaller portions. By the spring of 1994 an agreement along those lines was finalized, creating the new company, Information Technology Group. In exchange for their Weitz Corporation stock, Brandl and Sikkink received 50 percent of the company stock—35 percent for Brandl, 15 percent for Sikkink—with the Weitz Company and LCS each retaining 25 percent of the business. With nine original employees, the freestanding operation would handle the IT needs of both the construction group and Life Care Services; when either decided to set up its own computer unit or contract with another provider, Brandl and Sikkink could buy its shares in the IT firm. In 2000, the firm changed its name to Alliance Technologies, and two years later, Brandl and Sikkink purchased the shares owned by Weitz and LCS.[8]

Over the next few years, the firm grew through acquisitions, and in 2008, Iowa Network Services, a local telecommunications company, purchased a majority stake in the business. Brandl retired that year, and Sikkink took over as CEO in 2011. Alliance

Technologies remains in downtown Des Moines and today employs over one hundred people.[9]

Finalizing the deal between Fred and employee representatives of the Weitz Company and LCS took more time, but the transaction was eventually completed in early 1995. The purchase price was set at $37.4 million. Fred and his family, who together owned roughly 60 percent of the enterprise, exchanged their interest in the company for several properties, stock, and notes receivable. The Weitzes took over the LCS retirement facilities of Essex Meadows in Essex, Connecticut; Sandhill Cove in Palm City, Florida; and the company's 50 percent stake in Harbour's Edge in Delray Beach, Florida. They also acquired the Weitz Building and the River Hills theater complex in Des Moines as well as commercial and residential properties the Weitz Corporation owned in Bonita Springs, Florida, and real estate in Las Vegas, Nevada. To oversee the assets, Fred established Essex Meadows Inc., a new corporate entity, which was based in Des Moines with an office in the Weitz Building. The family also received $2 million in redeemable senior preferred LCS stock as well as notes receivable from LCS in the amount of $2.8 million. Fred's son Fritz remained with the Weitz Company another eighteen months, leaving at the end of 1996. In 2002, he joined his father at Essex Meadows Inc.[10]

On the construction side, thirty-six employee shareholders exchanged their Weitz Corporation stock to become owners of the reorganized Weitz Company, with the largest shareholders being DeStigter, the president and CEO; Oggero, the company chairman; Gosselink, a vice president overseeing the Iowa and Florida operations; and Larry Mohr, who was head of the Arizona subsidiary. The employees of Life Care Services did the same, turning in their Weitz Corporation shares—as well as giving up properties and carrying debt—for stock in the newly independent entity headed by managers who were also large shareholders. Stan Thurston became president and CEO, Stephen Hoover and Ed Kenny, senior vice presidents, and Arthur Neis, treasurer and chief financial officer.[11]

Weitz general counsel David "Dave" Strutt believed Fred had been generous in the settlement. Indeed, Fred recalled, he had not been as "grabby" as he might have been. He agreed to less money for the companies than he probably could have gotten elsewhere because he felt the managers who had helped him build the businesses deserved a chance to own and run them. Moreover, he thought these new employee/owners would be more likely than others to carry on the Weitz name and traditions of Des Moines-based companies renowned for high quality and customer service. Over the next few years, Fred's expectations seemed more than realized.[12]

Under DeStigter and Oggero—and then just DeStigter, when Oggero retired in 2001 and DeStigter also became chairman—the Weitz Company surged ahead, riding an economy that rebounded from a recession early in the decade and took off in 1994. No longer part of a corporation that had been run for the good of all divisions, the new company only focused on growing and diversifying its construction business.

Shortly after the divestiture, Oggero signaled the importance of the company's regional market by announcing a partnership that brought together the state's largest construction firm with Iowa's largest grocer. In September 1995, Hy-Vee Weitz Construction LC was formed to be the "exclusive builder of $50 to $70 million a year in new construction for Hy-Vee." The joint venture proved successful for both firms and lasted over seventeen years, before Hy-Vee bought the Weitz Company's 50 percent ownership in March

2013. Over the course of the partnership, the business completed over two hundred projects in eight states, including warehouses and food processing facilities, new grocery stores, remodeling of existing stores, and gas stations.[13]

Actually, the Weitz Company had redoubled its efforts in the Des Moines construction market, where in the early 1990s it had slipped to the number two position behind contractor Taylor Ball—formerly Ringland Johnson Crowley; the partnership broke up when Jack Taylor and Darrell Ball went out on their own in 2001. The focus paid off, and over the next decade, the company won a number of major area projects. In West Des Moines, for example, it built the Norwest (now Wells Fargo) mortgage banking facility in the West Lakes development, and in a joint venture with Kansas City-based JE Dunn, it constructed the huge, $260 million Wells Fargo campus just south of the Jordan Creek Town Center. In the suburb of Urbandale, it erected the Deerfield Retirement Community, which was developed by LCS and owned by Life Care Retirement Communities (LCRC, now Lifespace Communities). Downtown, the Weitz Company continued its long tradition of building and remaking the community landscape. It put up the Wells Fargo Arena and Iowa Events Center in a joint venture with Turner Construction of New York, the new Des Moines Central Library, and in a back to the future moment, the contractor did the restoration work on the Hoyt Sherman Theater. The Weitz Company had originally built the facility for the Des Moines Women's Club when Alice Weitz, Fred's grandmother, headed the organization back in 1923. This time around, Fred chaired the capital campaign for Hoyt Sherman, raising the $5.5 million for the structure's renovation.[14]

Outside Des Moines, the firm had stepped up its activity as well, especially in the senior living facilities market. Weitz had been building such complexes since the early 1960s, but management now went after this business more vigorously. The strategy worked, bringing in a substantial number of jobs, and the Weitz Company would go on to become the nation's largest builder of these facilities.[15]

Expansion also took the company into new areas. In 1998, it created Weitz Golf International and partnered with golf great Jack Nicklaus to build golf courses and clubhouses around the country and eventually internationally. The following year, the firm bought Fairway Construction of California to secure business on the West Coast. Early projects of this subsidiary included The Bear's Club in North Palm Beach, Florida; Stone Eagle Golf Course in Palm Desert, California; and the Nicklaus Golf Club at Lion's Gate in Overland Park, Kansas.[16]

Besides the big push into golf, the company returned to industrial construction in 2000, with its purchase of Cedar Rapids-based Abell-Howe, a firm that had done a lot of work for enterprises such as Quaker Oats and ADM. It also added regional offices in Kansas City and Omaha. Then, shortly after its 2001 purchase of Norris Associates, a builder of multimillion-dollar executive homes in western Colorado, it added another office in Frisco, Colorado, hoping to capture the luxury home market in and around the resort community of Vail. More diversification followed. In 2006, the company purchased Watts Constructors, a California-based contractor specializing in military facilities in the Pacific.[17]

Signs of this growth were visible across the country where the Weitz Company was constructing new projects and buildings. Prominent examples included the senior living communities of Inverness Village in Tulsa, Oklahoma; Mary's Woods at Marylhurst in Lake Oswego, Oregon; golf complexes such as the Seven

Canyons Golf Course in Sedona, Arizona; the Hokuli'a Golf Course in Kailua-Kona, Hawaii; the Prado and Belvedere, two condominium towers in Denver, Colorado; the Gallup organization's Gallup University Riverfront Campus in Omaha, Nebraska; Casa Paloma Retail Center in Chandler, Arizona; and the Scripps Research Institute in Jupiter, Florida, which was built with partner DPR Construction.[18]

Such growth meant that the company soon required more space. The firm's corporate services group moved from the Weitz Building on Second Avenue to the Capital Square Building in 1997. Later, in January 2000, the operations units moved into a new Weitz Building constructed on the south side of Des Moines. A second wing was added to the new building in 2006, and corporate services moved to the facility at the end of 2009. Meanwhile, the Weitz family had sold the Second Avenue structure to LCS in 2000. The senior living business and Alliance Technologies had remained in the building until the following year, when LCS was forced to sell it to the county, which demolished the structure to make way for the Iowa Events Center, and both companies moved to Capital Square.[19]

However, there was a downside to this rapid expansion. The Weitz Company faced an increasing number of claims against it for issues ranging from poor workmanship and delays in project completion to payment defaults from developers. Such claims often postponed or reduced payments to the company, reducing working capital and liquidity. Yet continued good times masked the matter and diverted management from addressing it.[20]

Like the Weitz Company, LCS was also enjoying good years. But the large debt it owed Essex Meadows Inc. caused the firm to revise its strategy. Until it could pay off the two obligations, LCS focused on its fee-for-service businesses, such as maintaining and winning additional management contracts, and shied away from any new development projects. Guided by Stan Thurston, the firm paid the notes receivable and redeemed the preferred stock the Weitz family held by 1998, several years ahead of schedule. Then Life Care Services got back into the development of senior living communities and gradually expanded the number of facilities it owned, but the firm's approach changed. To avoid some risk and tying up a lot of capital, LCS sought and found a partner in Westminster Capital of Lake Forest, Illinois, to develop and own future facilities. The latest such project developed and owned by the partnership was Trillium Woods in Plymouth, Minnesota, a suburb west of downtown Minneapolis, which opened in the summer of 2015.[21]

When Thurston retired in 2006, Ed Kenny took over as chairman and CEO. The transition was seamless, and LCS navigated the down economy that hit at the end of the decade adeptly. By the end of 2014, the firm Fred started with Kenneth Berg in 1971 had grown to the third-largest operator of senior housing in the country, managing 119 properties and ranked twenty-fourth as an owner of such facilities, holding thirty-one communities.[22]

While the fortunes of LCS remained bright, those of the Weitz Company dimmed. During the middle of the decade, its future still appeared secure. By the time its revenues first topped $1 billion in 2004, DeStigter had decided that he would step down as CEO when he turned sixty-five in 2006. The board chose to hire internally, and after a lengthy process, it named chief financial officer Craig Damos president and CEO that June. DeStigter remained chairman. No significant changes were perceptible, and the company's upward trajectory continued unabated. In 2007, revenues rose to $1.47 billion, while locally, the firm won three big projects: Aviva's US headquarters (now Athene) and Methodist West Hospital in West Des Moines, and the new Wellmark headquarters in downtown Des Moines, just north of the Pappajohn Sculpture Park.[23]

The effects of the Great Recession were first felt across the nation in 2007 and 2008, but the Weitz Company was not initially impacted, largely because of its healthy backlog of jobs. Thus in 2008, the numbers still looked good, with revenues dipping just a hair to $1.43 billion; DeStigter stepped down as chairman and was replaced by Damos in that position.[24]

But then difficulties became apparent. As the backlog of jobs dried up, new ones were not replacing them. Claims against the company remained a concern, and the firm's federal contractor, Watts Constructors, was performing especially poorly, losing large sums of money. Weitz Company revenues in 2009 reflected these issues, falling to $1.08 billion, a 25 percent drop from the previous year. Layoffs and a corporate restructuring began, which would reduce the Weitz workforce from 1,500 to 750, and Damos initiated a lengthy strategic planning process.[25]

The layoffs compounded problems because the company's buy-sell stock agreement dictated that the company redeem shares of owner-employees who left the firm. Before the mass layoffs, employee shareholders had numbered over 250, and the large number of redemptions due forced the company to suspend these payments. These debts to former employee shareholders became liabilities on the firm's financial statements and decreased its equity, which troubled its banks and bonding firms. Unfortunately, more downsizing was required, which only made the situation worse. And revenues kept tumbling. In 2010 they declined to $716 million, a

50 percent drop from just two years earlier, setting off alarm bells for a number of people, including DeStigter. Although no longer chairman, he had remained on the board and stayed abreast of the company's situation. It was DeStigter who took action. The *Business Record* reported that he "had maneuvered for several months to muster board support to oust Damos."[26]

The board forced Damos to resign in June 2010 and replaced him with then chief operating officer Leonard "Len" Martling; DeStigter returned to the chairmanship. Martling worked to right the ship, eliminating a number of independent business divisions and again reorganizing management to reflect the company's smaller size. That fall, Martling contacted FMI Capital Advisors—the same consultant that had identified Al Cohen as a good acquisition for the firm and had assisted the family with the sale of the company to employees—to help the Weitz Company sell Watts Constructors. Unfortunately, FMI could not find a buyer for Watts, and 2011 proved a terrible year for Weitz. Revenues fell again, this time down to $682 million. Worse, for the first time since 1991, the company failed to show a profit, losing over $19 million.[27]

Then out of the blue, FMI executive Hugh Rice called Martling in March 2012, telling him that Orascom Construction Industries (OCI), then the largest publicly traded company in Egypt, was interested in partnering with the Weitz Company or possibly acquiring the Iowa-based contractor. Orascom was hoping to build an enormous fertilizer plant in Iowa and wanted to develop a relationship with a construction firm in the state. The Weitz Company had been recommended to OCI. Martling told Rice he would be happy to visit with Orascom officials, and a meeting took place the next month in Des Moines. Representatives from both firms discussed several options, including building the fertilizer plant as a joint venture, having Weitz act as a subcontractor for OCI, or OCI buying the entire Weitz Company operation. As the dialogue ensued, OCI executives became intrigued with the firm's Watts subsidiary. Orascom was a big defense contractor, but its focus was in the Middle East, and it saw Watts as a possible entrée into military work in the Pacific market. By July, OCI had decided to buy the Weitz Company and made an offer.[28]

The OCI bid had been unsolicited, but it was welcomed. As negotiations over details ensued, OCI also discussed an incentives package with state officials to build the fertilizer plant. The latter deal closed in September, when Iowa governor Terry Branstad announced that the state had upped its tax credits, forgivable loans, and other assistance to over $100 million to fend off an Illinois effort to land the facility. The $1.4 billion plant would be "the largest project in Iowa history" and would be built in Lee County, in the southeasternmost portion of the state. At the same news conference, Orascom announced its acquisition of the Weitz Company, which would build the fertilizer complex. Martling explained the move as good for Weitz, saying, "They love construction, as do we. They're looking to grow, as are we...And their reputation is what drives their business, as does ours."[29]

Although the Weitz Company had begun turning around prior to its sale, Mike Tousley, the firm's executive vice president in charge of Iowa and Nebraska operations, conceded it "would have taken us exponentially longer" to recover from the recession had the company not been taken over by OCI. Here he emphasized "Orascom's financial strength," which gave Weitz "the ability to play differently than we have in the past. We can take an equity interest; in the past, that is something Weitz couldn't do." Thus, the *Business Record* observed, combining with OCI "paid some immediate dividends for the Weitz book of business." For example, Weitz received the $80 million job to build Trillium Woods, the LCS-Westminster senior living facility in a Minneapolis suburb only when OCI offered to finance the project.[30]

In a broader perspective, OCI's purchase of the Weitz Company was part of the continuing consolidation of the construction industry, which had picked up steam late in the decade. From 2008 to 2012, the number of contractors across the country declined 19.6 percent. Some went out of business, some were bought by other American firms, and some, like Weitz, were acquired by foreign companies. Other examples of the latter include England's Balfour Beatty's 2009 purchases of RT Dooley of Charlotte, North Carolina, and Houston, Texas-based SpawMaxwell, or Sweden's Skanska's 2011 acquisition of Evansville, Indiana-based Industrial Contractors. And in Des Moines, the Weitz Company joined other historic and locally owned firms that had been swallowed up by out-of-state enterprises over the past thirty years. These included such iconic Iowa establishments as the Des Moines Register and Tribune Company, Pioneer Hi-Bred, the Equitable of Iowa, and Younkers.[31]

The sale saddened Fred. "I'm disappointed it's not going to be in employee hands," he told *Des Moines Register* business editor Lynn Hicks. "I had hoped it would continue longer than it has." If Fred was frustrated by the Orascom takeover of the construction company, he was happy to see the Weitz legacy living on at LCS and Alliance Technologies. Both remained locally owned, based in Des Moines, headed by people who came up through the ranks of the Weitz Corporation.[32]

Still, there were links to the past at the construction firm as well, suggesting the Weitz legacy survived there too. Day-to-day operations had not changed since the purchase. The Weitz

Company management team remained in place, and according to Dave Strutt, OCI is "very hands off" in regard to how the Des Moines-based subsidiary was run. The company had returned to profitability in 2012, and Martling predicted its revenues would again top $1 billion in 2015. Moreover, the Weitz Company preserved the corporate principles that had been stressed at the family-owned Weitz firm. To remind both employees and customers, the company's core values of "honesty and integrity, respect for people, performance with absolute reliability, long term perspective, and nurturing personal growth" are printed on the backside of its business cards.[33]

Few in Des Moines, however, noticed the changes at the Weitz Company. When central Iowans thought of the firm, they thought of construction, and much as the business had done over its long history, it was still shaping and reshaping greater Des Moines. Trucks and equipment emblazoned with the familiar Weitz logo continued moving across construction sites in central Iowa. Recent Weitz Company projects included the expansion of Iowa State University's Jack Trice Stadium and construction of a new wing for 1,800 workers at the already large Wells Fargo campus the Weitz Company had erected earlier in the Jordan Creek area of West Des Moines. It was also active in downtown Des Moines, rebuilding landmarks just a few blocks from where Charles Weitz started the business in 1855. Here the firm completed phase one of the redesigned Greater Des Moines Botanical Garden. More recently, it finished resculpting what was Nollen Plaza, the public square it originally built in the 1970s, into Cowles Commons, the new outdoor plaza that community leaders hope will serve as a gathering spot for generations to come.

Although this was not the future Fred had imagined for the company, he could take solace in continuities remaining at the firm. Founder Charles Weitz certainly would have been impressed. The tiny carpentry shop he had started in the small frontier town of Des Moines had endured and prospered as the city grew. First under his leadership, and then that of his sons, a grandson, and a great-grandson, the Weitz Company moved from being a central Iowa establishment to a nationally regarded contractor. And even though the Weitz family was no longer involved, Charles would have been proud that the Weitz Company was still moving dirt, pouring concrete, and building, especially in the city he had called home.

A NOTE ON SOURCES

Much of this book is based on privately held manuscript collections. Other important components of my research consisted of interviews and correspondence with Weitz family members and people who are or have been associated with LCS and the Weitz Company.

Manuscript Collections

Godfrey, Charles Jr. Papers. Private collection, Lathrup Village, Michigan.

Johnson, Elizabeth. Papers. Private collection, Des Moines, Iowa.

DeStigter, Glenn. Papers. Private collection, Ankeny, Iowa.

LCS Papers. Private collection, Des Moines, Iowa.

Weitz Company Papers. Private collection, Des Moines, Iowa.

Weitz, Fred. Private collection, Des Moines, Iowa.

Interviews and Correspondence with Author

Bachman, Robert. Telephone conversation with author, 30 October 2014.

Birocci, Linda. Correspondence with author, 11, 12 March 2014; 23 February 2015.

Bontrager, Bill. Interview by author, Cumming, Iowa, 6 May 2014.

Brandl, James. Telephone conversation with author, 31 October 2014.

Brown, Donald. Interview by author, West Des Moines, Iowa, 13 May 2014.

Brown, Phil. Interview by author, Des Moines, Iowa, 2 May 2013.

DeStigter, Glenn. Interviews by author, Des Moines, Iowa, 12 March, 2013; 30 July, 5 December 2014. Correspondence with author, 4 October, 8 December 2014.

Floyd, Chuck. Telephone conversation with author, 16 October 2014.

Gentleman, Julia. Telephone conversation with author, 6 June 2014.

Grieve, Lisa. Telephone conversation with author, 23 February 2015. Correspondence with author, 24 February 2015.

Godfrey, Charles Jr. Telephone conversation with author, 16 November 2013.

Gosselink, Jerry. Telephone conversation with author, 4 September 2014.

Hall, Jack. Telephone conversation with author, 30 July 2014.

Hamilton, Randall. Interview by author, Des Moines, Iowa, 16 October 2014.

Hinners, Joan. Correspondence with author, 4 December 2014.

Johnson, Elizabeth. Interview by author, Des Moines, Iowa, 3 September 2013.

Kenny, Edward. Interview by author, Des Moines, Iowa, 24 November 2014. Correspondence with author, 3 February 2015.

Laird, Larry. Telephone conversations with author, 1, 5 August 2014. Correspondence with author, 1 August 2014.

Larsen, Traci. Correspondence with author, 5 March 2014.

McClain, Tricia. Correspondence with author, 1, 2 December 2014.

Martling, Leonard. Interview by author, Des Moines, Iowa, 11 December 2014.

Mohr, Larry. Telephone conversation with author, 15 October 2014.

Neumann, Hal. Telephone conversation with author, 20 June 2014.

Sikkink, Steve. Telephone conversation with author, 20 February 2015.

Strutt, David. Interview by author, Des Moines, Iowa, 15 August 2014. Correspondence with author, 9, 19 February 2015. Telephone conversation with author, 17 February 2015.

Taggart, Peter. Interview by author, West Des Moines, Iowa, 8 September 2014. Correspondence with author, 5 February 2015.

Thurston, Stan. Interview by author, Des Moines, Iowa, 6 October 2014. Telephone conversation with author, 9 February 2015. Correspondence with author, 20 February 2015.

Urban, Tom. Interview by author, Des Moines, Iowa, 11 September 2014.

Weitz, Ann. Telephone conversation with author, 4 March 2013.

Weitz, Robert. Telephone conversation with author, 24 April 2014.

Weitz, Edwin. Telephone conversation with author, 5 December 2013.

Weitz, Emily. Interview by author, West Des Moines, Iowa, 20 March 2014.

Weitz, Fred. Interviews by author, Des Moines, Iowa, 20 March, 18 April, 11 November 2013; 15 January, 20 March, 15 May, 29 September, 18 December 2014; 30 January, 13 February 2015. Correspondence with author, 9 July, 4, 8 December 2014; 9 February 2015. Telephone conversation with author, 5 February 2015.

Weitz, Stevenson. Interview by author, West Des Moines, Iowa, 27 March 2014. Correspondence with author, 9 July 2014.

NOTES

Introduction

1. *Des Moines Register*, 17 February 1985.

2. For list of oldest companies in Des Moines, see *Des Moines Register*, 11 August 2013.

3. Quotation is also from *Des Moines Register*, 11 August 2013.

4. For quotation, see Debra Rubin et al., "The Test of Time," *Engineering News-Record*, 29 March 2004, 36.

5. See Weitz Company, 1975 Consolidated Statement of Earnings and "The Weitz Company: The Vision to Build 150 Years," (2005), 10–11, 30, both in Weitz Company Papers, private collection held by the Weitz Company, Des Moines, Iowa. See also *Des Moines Register*, 27 September 1995.

Chapter 1

1. Immigration numbers are from Bruce Levine, *The Spirit of 1848: German Immigrants, Labor Conflict, and the Coming of the Civil War* (Urbana and Chicago: University of Illinois Press, 1992), 2.

2. On Karl Weitz and his family, see Ann Weitz, "Charles Weitz," unpublished, undated typescript, 1; and Greta Weitz Brown, "Weitz," unpublished typescript, 1977, Fred Weitz Papers, private papers held by Fred Weitz, Des Moines, IA [hereafter cited as Weitz Papers]. Greta Brown was a grandchild of Karl Weitz. As part of her family history project, Brown had a number of her grandfather's writings translated from German to English. For education, see Jonathan Sperber, *The European Revolutions, 1848-1851* (Cambridge: Cambridge University Press, 2005), 33–34. On changing economic conditions, see Levine, *Spirit of 1848*, 19–20, 28–29.

3. On a *Wanderbuch* and the tradition of journeymen wandering about the countryside in search of additional training and work, see Karl Weitz's *Wanderbuch* (and English translation), in Weitz Family Papers, box 1, folder 4, State Historical Society of Iowa [hereafter cited as Weitz Family Papers]; Brown, "Weitz," 12–14; "The Wanderbuch of Wilibald Koch," at http://www.peterspioneers.com/wanderbuch.htm, accessed on 13 April 2013; and Henry Mayhew, *German Life and Manners as seen in Saxony at*

the Present Day (London: W. H. Allen, 1864), 413–16. For the French version of the same process, see "Campagnonnage," entry in the "Encyclopedia of 1848 Revolutions," http://www.ohio.edu/chastain/ac/companon.htm, accessed on 13 April 2013.

4. Sperber, *European Revolutions*, 12–19.

5. For the declining conditions for journeymen, see Levine, *Spirit of 1848*, 16–34.

6. For Karl's journey, see Weitz *Wanderbuch*, 2, 7–14, Weitz Family Papers.

7. Ibid., 14–23.

8. For the revolution in Paris, see Jill Harsin, *Barricades: The War of the Streets in Revolutionary Paris, 1830 to 1848* (New York: Palgrave, 2002); and Roger Gould, *Insurgent Identities: Class, Community, and Protest in Paris from 1848 to the Commune* (Chicago: University of Chicago Press, 1995).

9. On Karl being assigned to the light cavalry, see entry in Weitz *Wanderbuch*, section titled "The following is my own biography," 23, Weitz Family Papers. For events in Prussia and smaller German states, see Sperber, *European Revolutions*, x.

10. Jerome Blum, *In the Beginning: The Advent of the Modern Age* (New York: Charles Scribner's Sons, 1994), 293–94. See also Sabine Freitag, *Friedrich Hecker: Two Lives for Liberty*, trans. by Steven Rowan (Saint Louis, MO: Saint Louis Mercantile Library, 2006), 89–125. Karl wrote of going to Baden to quiet the revolution that he noted, "was caused by the gentlemen Hecker and Struve." See Weitz *Wanderbuch*, section titled, "The following is my own biography," 24, Weitz Family Papers.

11. Charles Dahlinger, *The German Revolution of 1849: Being an Account of the Final Struggle, in Baden for the Maintenance of Germany's First National Representative Government* (New York and London: G. P. Putnam's Sons, 1903), 187–214. For Karl being shot and his recovery, see Weitz *Wanderbuch*, "The following is my own biography," 25, Weitz Family Papers.

12. Such immigrant guidebooks included, for example, Francis Joseph Grund, *Manual and Guide for Emigrants to the United States of America* (Stuttgart: J. G. Cotta'scher, 1843), Francis J. Reason, *Handbook and Guide for Emigrants to the United States* (Stuttgart and Tübingen, Gotta, 1843); and August Rauschenbusch, *Some Instructions for Emigrants to the Western United States of North America and Travel Photos* (Elberfeld and Iserlohn: Julius Baedeker, 1848).

13. For the importance of travel guides, see Kathleen Conzen, *Immigrant Milwaukee, 1836-1860: Accommodation and Community in a Frontier City* (Cambridge and London: Harvard University Press, 1976), 35–36; and Mischa Honeck, *We are the Revolutionists: German-speaking Immigrants and the American Abolitionists after 1848* (Athens and London: University of Georgia Press, 2011), 17–18. For more on these guidebooks and quotation, see Levine, *Spirit of 1848*, 53–54.

14. For Karl's slight limp, see Greta Weitz Brown, interview by the Des Moines Oral History Project, Des Moines Public Library, 20 January 1976. On Karl's decision to leave Germany, see Weitz *Wanderbuch*, 25, Weitz Family Papers.

15. On the emigration in general, see Mack Walker, *Germany and the Emigration, 1816-1885* (Cambridge, MA: Harvard University Press, 1964). See also Roger

Daniels, *Coming to America: A History of Immigration and Ethnicity in American Life* (New York: Harper Collins, 1990), 146–149; Frederick Luebke, *Germans in the New World: Essays in the History of Immigration* (Urbana and Chicago, University of Illinois Press, 1990), 161–62; and Conzen, *Immigrant Milwaukee*, 27–28.

16. For motivations to emigrate, see Conzen, *Immigrant Milwaukee*, 22–33; and Luebke, *Germans*, 161. Quotation is from Daniels, *Coming to America*, 148. On skilled Germans, see Daniels, *Coming to America*, 150.

17. On the Weitz family weaving business closing and Christian deciding to travel to America, see Brown, "Weitz," 25. Oddly, Karl does not mention Christian in his brief statement about coming to American that he included in his *Wanderbuch*, but reference to both of them making the journey together can be found in Johnson Brigham, *Des Moines: The Pioneer of Municipal Progress and Reform of the Middle West with The History of Polk County, Iowa* (Chicago: S. J. Clarke, 1911), 2: 1051; Lorenzo F. Andrews, *Pioneers of Polk County, Iowa and Reminiscences of the Early Days* (Des Moines, IA: Baker-Trisler, 1908), 1: 263; and *The History of Polk County, Iowa: Containing a History of the County, its Cities, Towns, & Biographical Sketches of its Citizens* (Des Moines, IA: Union Historical Co., 1880), 881.

18. *Wanderbuch, Coming to America*, 149. For more on different passport regulations, see http://www.landesarchivbw.de/highlight.php?hl_link=http://www.auswander-erbw.de/sixcms/detail.php?template=a_artikel&id=6615&id2=&sprache=en&q=dutch, accessed on 1 May 2013.

19. On German settlements and the German triangle, see Daniels, *Coming to America*, 149–50.

20. For Germans in Ohio, see Hubert G. H. Wilhelm, "Germans in Ohio," in Allen G. Nobel, ed., *To Build a New Land* (Baltimore and London: Johns Hopkins University Press, 1992), 60–78. Journalist, author, and state librarian for Iowa Johnson Brigham claimed that Karl became fluent in French and English; see Brigham, *Des Moines: The Pioneer of Progress*, 2: 1051.

21. Wilhelm, "Germans in Iowa," 63–64. Population for Ashland from *U.S. Census, 1850: A Statistical View of Each of the States and Territories* (Washington: Robert Armstrong, Public Printer, 1853), 819.

22. See naturalization papers of Charles Weitz, Weitz Family Papers, box 1, folder 5. The 1850 US Census listed the two brothers as Charles and Christian Whites rather than Weitz and identified them as cabinetmakers; see *U.S. Census, 1850, Ashland, Ohio*: Roll: M432_658, 436B [database online], Ancestry.com, Provo, UT.

23. Columbus population from *U.S. Census, 1850: A Statistical View of the States*, 827. On Karl's work, see translation and transcription of Charles Weitz's first workbook, 1852–1856, 3, Fred Weitz Papers, private collection held by Fred Weitz, Des Moines, Iowa [hereafter cited as Fred Weitz Papers].

24. For information and quotation about German Village, see German Village Society's webpage, germanvillage.com, accessed on 3 May 2013.

25. On Helena Kinnel, see *Des Moines Register*, 9 July 1924; 21 May 1929; and Brown, "Weitz," 75–80. For Karl and Helena's wedding, see Charles Weitz's blue leather record book, 8; Weitz Company Papers, private collection held by the Weitz Company, Des Moines, Iowa [hereafter referred to as Weitz Company Papers]; and marriage certificate of Charles Weitz and Helena Kinnel, 3 July 1854, Fred Weitz Papers. The couple was married in Columbus in the Evangelical Lutheran Church, actually called the German English Evangelical Lutheran Church, which had broken away from Saint Paul's United Lutheran Reformed Church in 1847. When Karl and Helena married, the German English Evangelical Lutheran Church was holding services in a building it rented from the German Independent Protestant Church near Mound and Third Streets on the city's south side. The church erected its own building just down Third Street at the corner of Fulton Street in 1856. It was renamed Trinity Evangelical Lutheran Church and continues to operate today. For more information on the church, see William Alexander Taylor, *Centennial History of Columbus and Franklin County, Ohio* (Chicago: S. J. Clarke, 1909), 2: 191; and *Directory of the City of Columbus for the years 1850-51* (Columbus, OH: E. Glover and William Henderson, 1850), 90.

26. On Des Moines being renamed and the state capital's relocation, see Orin Dahl, *Des Moines: Capital City* (Tulsa, OK: Continental Heritage, 1978), 33–35. For Karl's decision to move, see Andrews, *Pioneers of Polk County*, 1: 263; and *The History of Polk County*, 881. Quotation is from *Portrait and Biographical Album of Polk County, Iowa* (Chicago: Lake City Publishing, 1890), 487. On Christian living with Karl and Helena, see translation and transcription of Charles Weitz's first workbook, 1852–1856, 3, Fred Weitz Papers; and for Karl's comment on making the trip to Des Moines, see Weitz blue record book, 3, Weitz Company Papers.

27. On journey, see Brown, "Weitz," 61; *Portrait and Biographical Album*, 487; and Brigham, *Des Moines: The Pioneer of Progress*, 2: 1051–52. Karl's quotation from Charles Weitz blue record book, 3, Weitz Company Papers.

Chapter 2

1. Tacitus Hussey, *Beginnings: Reminiscences of Early Des Moines* (Des Moines, IA: American Lithographing and Printing, 1919), 194. On Charles's difficulty finding a job in Des Moines, see *Portrait and Biographical Album of Polk County, Iowa* (Chicago: Lake City Publishing, 1890), 487. For background history of Des Moines, see Ilda Hammer, *The Book of Des Moines* (Des Moines, IA: Board of Education, 1947), 53–67; Orin Dahl, *Des Moines: Capital City* (Tulsa, OK: Continental Heritage, 1978), 27–33; and Will Porter, *Annals of Polk County, Iowa and City of Des Moines* (Des Moines, IA: George A. Miller Printing, 1898), 171.

2. Hammer, *Book of Des Moines*, 42–54.

3. Ibid., 69; and Porter, *Annals of Polk County*, 173–74; Hussey, *Beginnings*, 64.

4. Porter, *Annals of Polk County*, 186–87; Hammer, *Book of Des Moines*, 69; and David Wiggins, *The Rise of the Allens: Two Soldiers and the Master of Terrace Hill* (Mount Horeb, WI: Historical-Midwest Books, 2002), 210.

5. H. B. Turrill, *Historical Reminiscences of the City of Des Moines* (Des Moines, IA: Redhead and Dawson, 1857), 104–105.

6. On boarding with Esterling, see translation and transcription of Charles Weitz's first workbook, 1852–1856, 4, Fred Weitz Papers, private collection held by Fred Weitz, Des Moines, Iowa [hereafter cited as Fred Weitz Papers]. See also Charles Weitz obituary, *Des Moines*, 10 November 1906; and *Portrait and Biographical Album of Polk County, Iowa* (Chicago: Lake City Publishing, 1890), 487. For more on F. M. Hubbell, see William Friedricks, *Investing in Iowa: The Life and Times of F. M. Hubbell* (Des Moines, IA: Iowan Books, 2007).

7. For Ashby's estimate of Germans in Des Moines, see Ann Weitz, "Charles Weitz," 8, unpublished typescript, Fred Weitz Papers. On buying from Grimmel and paying with work, see translation and transcription of Charles Weitz's first workbook, 1852–1856, 4, Fred Weitz Papers; and Charles Weitz Ledger, 1855–1858, Weitz Company Papers.

8. See translation and transcription of Charles Weitz's first time book, 7, Fred Weitz Papers; Lorenzo F. Andrews, *Pioneers of Polk County, Iowa and Reminiscences of the Early Days* (Des Moines, IA: Baker-Trisler, 1908), 1: 265; Weitz, "Charles Weitz," 8; and Greta Weitz Brown, "Weitz," unpublished typescript, 1977, 83, in Weitz Company Papers, private collection held by the Weitz Company, Des Moines, Iowa [hereafter cited as Weitz Company Papers].

9. Charles Weitz Account Book, 1856–March 1857 in Weitz Company Papers; and translation and transcription of Charles Weitz's first time book, 5–9, Fred Weitz Papers.

10. On establishing the Catholic church in Des Moines, see Andrews, *Pioneers of Polk County*, 1: 39; Turrill, *Historical Reminiscences*, 94; and Porter, *Annals of Polk County*, 750–51. For Charles building the church, see Charles Weitz Account Book, 1856–March 1857, Weitz Company Papers.

11. On the English Lutheran Church (Saint John's), see Porter, *Annals of Polk County*, 762; Turrill, *Historical Reminiscences*, 92–93; and *Portrait and Biographical Album of Polk County*, 464–65; Andrews, *Pioneers of Polk County*, 1: 266; and Saint John's Evangelical Lutheran Church's website, http://stjohnsdsm.org/history/, accessed on 1 July 2013.

12. Turrill, *Historical Reminiscences*, 96–98; and J. M. Dixon, *Centennial History of Polk County, Iowa* (Des Moines, IA: State Register, Printer, 1876), 205–08. Iowa Central College never got off the ground, and the building was taken over by the Baptists in the 1860s, who opened it as Des Moines University. It eventually merged with Highland Park College, another Des Moines institution, and Central College in Pella. Central College continued in Pella, but the colleges in Des Moines combined into Des Moines University. The Des Moines school closed in 1929.

13. For more on German Lutheran Church, see Porter, *Annals of Polk County*, 761–62 Background on Des Moines Lodge 25 of the IOOF can be found in

Dixon, *Centennial History*, 225–26. On Charles joining the lodge, see unmarked newspaper clipping, 6 October 1906, scrapbook, excerpts, and clippings, Weitz Company Papers.

14. Quotation is from Dahl, *Des Moines*, 35. See Johnson Brigham, *Des Moines: The Pioneer of Municipal Progress and Reform of the Middle West with The History of Polk County, Iowa* (Chicago: S. J. Clarke, 1911), 1: 174–76, 178; Porter, *Annals of Polk County*, 174–75; John E. Briggs, "The Removal of the Capital City from Iowa City to Des Moines," *Iowa Journal of History and Politics* 14 (January 1916), 56–95; and Andrews, *Pioneers of Polk County*, 266.

15. Brigham, *Des Moines*; statement by Turrill is from Hammer, *Book of Des Moines*, 69.

16. For Porter quotation, see Porter, *Annals of Polk County*, 191; Larson's quotation from John Lauritz Larson, *Bonds of Enterprise: John Murray Forbes and Western Development in America's Railroad Age* expanded edition (Iowa City: University of Iowa Press, 2001), 70; for more on the Savery House, see Wiggins, *Rise of the Allens*, 367–68.

17. Youngerman hired Charles on 29 September 1859; see Charles Weitz Record Book, 1858–59, Weitz Company Papers. For short biography on Youngerman, see *Portrait and Biographical Album*, 745–46.

18. Charles Weitz Record Book, 1858–59, Weitz Company Papers. On the need for fencing, see Hammer, *Book of Des Moines*, 75–76.

19. See Charles Weitz, Account Book, 1855; Charles Weitz, Workman's Weekly Pocket Time Book, 1856–1865; and Charles Weitz Record Book, 1858–59, all in Weitz Company Papers.

20. Charles's worth as recorded in the 1860 census is taken from Weitz, "Weitz," 58. For the 1860 worth of Lampson Sherman, Jefferson Scott Polk, Hoyt Sherman, and Benjamin F. Allen, see William M. Ferraro, "Representing a Layered Community: James, Lampson P. and Hoyt Sherman and the Development of Des Moines, 1850-1900," *The Annals of Iowa* 57 (Summer 1998), 252, 257, 260, and 262; and for F. M. Hubbell's worth, see Population Schedule of the Eighth Census of the United States, 1860, Iowa, Microfilm roll 339, p. 697.

21. Hammer, *Book of Des Moines*, 83; Porter, *Annals of Polk County*, 205; and Weitz Ledger 1855–1867 and large Weitz journal 1861–66, Fred Weitz Papers.

22. Ibid. Compared to carpenters working in Des Moines in 1866, there were, for instance, three architects, sixty-eight attorneys, nine barbers, thirty-seven blacksmiths, six brewers, twenty-one butchers, and thirty-five grocers, six lumber dealers, twenty-seven physicians, thirty plasterers, nineteen real estate dealers, and seven stonecutters. For these numbers and the rest of the occupational breakdown in 1866 Des Moines, see *Des Moines City Directory and Business Guide, 1866-1867* (Des Moines, IA: Mills & Co., 1866), 149–158.

23. Leland Sage, *History of Iowa* (Ames: Iowa State University Press, 1974), 153–54; and Dorothy Schwieder, *Iowa: The Middle Land* (Ames: Iowa State University Press, 1996), 73–75.

24. Barbara Beving Long, *Des Moines and Polk County: Flag on the Prairie* (Northridge, CA: Windsor Publications, 1988), 38–39; Hammer, *Book of Des Moines*, 83; and Brigham, *Des Moines*, 185–87.

25. For reference to Charles drilling recruits, see Andrews, *Pioneers of Polk County*, 266.

26. For *Register* quote, see *Iowa State Register*, 3 May 1863; and for German American service in the war, see Bruce Levine, *The Spirit of 1848: German Immigrants, Labor Conflict, and the Coming of the Civil War* (Urbana and Chicago: University of Illinois Press, 1992), 256.

27. For background and governor's call for militia units, see *Iowa State Register*, 23, 24 August; 1, 11, 13 September 1864. For organizing of German unit, see *Iowa State Register*, 10 September 1864, "Muster Roll" and framed description of unit organization, 10 September 1864, Fred Weitz Papers.

28. For contemporary accounts, see *Iowa State Register*, 14–18 October 1864. See also Brigham, *Des Moines*, 227, and http://dailyiowegian.com/correspondents/ x519476822/Confederate-raid-into-Davis-County, accessed on 17 July 2013.

29. *Iowa State Register*, 7 September 1864; William Friedricks, *Covering Iowa: The History of the Des Moines Register and Tribune Company, 1849-1985* (Ames: Iowa State University Press, 2000), 22–23.

30. Dahl, *Des Moines*, 46–47; and Friedricks, *Investing in Iowa*, 30, 35–37.

31. *Iowa State Register*, 3 November 1867.

32. See large Weitz journals, 1865–66 and 1867–68, Weitz Company Papers.

33. Weitz Ledger, 1861–66, Weitz Company Papers.

34. Large Weitz journal, 1865–66; Weitz memorandum book, 1865–66; and large Weitz journal, 1867–68, all in Weitz Company Papers.

35. Ibid.

36. Large Weitz journal, 1865–66; Weitz memorandum book, 1865–66; and large Weitz journal 1869–75, all in Weitz Company Papers. See also *Bushnell's Des Moines Residence and Business 1874-75* (Des Moines, IA: Bushnell Publishers, 1874), 18.

37. For more on founding of Jonathan Lodge and first quotation, see Andrews, *Pioneers of Polk County*, 267. Second quotation is from *Iowa State Register*, 15 June 1866.

38. Brown, "Weitz," 95–98, 101, 103; and Weitz, "Charles Weitz," 12–13.

39. Quotation from Weitz, "Charles Weitz," 17.

40. Dixon, *Centennial History*, 203–04; and *Iowa State Register*, 20 September, 3 December 1868.

41. *Iowa State Register*, 26 March, 13 October 1869; *Evening Statesman*, 20 January, 10 August 1869; and *Bushnell's Residence and Business Directory of Des Moines, Iowa, 1871* (Des Moines, IA: Carter, Hussey, and Curl, 1871), 33.

42. For general information on the Turners, see Henry Metzner, *History of the American Turners*, 4th rev. ed. (Louisville, KY: National Council of the American Turners,

1989). On the Turners in Des Moines, see *Iowa State Register*, 27 April, 5 May, 2 October, 3 November 1867; 30 September 1868. On Charles doing work for Turners, see Ann Weitz, "Charles Weitz," 17. For 1872 "Turnerfest," see *Iowa State Register*, 25 April, 5, 29 May, 2, 5–7, 9 June 1872. For story of Charles helping with festival and being given honorary membership, see Charles Weitz to his relatives in Schotten, 1 December 1872, translated in Brown, "Weitz," 37.

43. *Iowa State Register*, 14 August 1867; Weitz Ledger, 1861–66, and large Weitz journal, 1867–68, Weitz Company Papers.

44. *Des Moines City Directory and Business Guide*, 1869 (Des Moines, IA: Mills & Co., 1869), xxxii.

45. Census information for Hubbell, Polk, Allen, and the Sherman brothers from Ferraro, "Representing a Layered Community," 261; the census information on Charles is from Brown, "Weitz," 58.

Chapter 3

1. Quotation from translated version of letter, included in Greta Weitz Brown, "Weitz," unpublished typescript, 1977, 36, Fred Weitz Papers, private collection held by Fred Weitz, Des Moines, Iowa [hereafter cited as Fred Weitz Papers].

2. For population numbers, see http://www.iowadatacenter.org/archive/2011/02/city-pop.pdf, accessed on 10 September 2013. Quotation about Des Moines becoming a great manufacturing center from *Bushnell's Des Moines Directory, 1884-85* (Des Moines: Iowa Directory and Gazetteer Co., 1884), 27; and for information on railroads into Des Moines, see Barbara Beving Long, *Des Moines and Polk County: Flag on the Prairie* (Northridge, CA: Windsor Publications, 1988), 29.

3. For more on Charles's building activity in 1871–72, see large Weitz journal, 1869–75, Weitz Company Papers, privately held by the Weitz Company, Des Moines, Iowa [hereafter cited as Weitz Company Papers].

4. For coal mining in Des Moines in general, see Long, *Des Moines*, 53–56; more on Wesley Redhead and his interest in Des Moines coal can be found in Johnson Brigham, *Des Moines: The Pioneer of Municipal Progress and Reform of the Middle West with The History of Polk County, Iowa* (Chicago: S. J. Clarke, 1911), 2: 908–12; and for Charles's venture into coal, see Weitz Record Book 1869–87, Weitz Company Papers.

5. Charles Weitz Record Book, 1876–77, Weitz Company Papers.

6. Charles Weitz Record Book, 1872–73, Weitz Company Papers.

7. Ann Weitz, "Charles Weitz," 23–24, unpublished typescript, Fred Weitz Papers; see also *Bushnell's Des Moines Directory, 1874-75*, (Des Moines, IA: Bushnell & Co., 1874), 169; and for significant contractors ten years later, see *Bushnell's Des Moines Directory, 1884-85* (Des Moines, IA: Iowa Directory and Gazetteer Co., 1884), 557, 559.

8. Charles Weitz memorandum book, 1877–79, Weitz Company Papers.

9. On Charles's bidding in general, see Charles Weitz memo book, 1877–79; Charles Weitz memo book, 1879–80; and large Charles Weitz journal, 1879–83, all in Weitz Company Papers. For joint bid with Youngerman, see Charles Weitz memo book, 1879–80.

10. On John Woods, see large Charles Weitz journal, 1879–83, Weitz Company Papers; and *Bushnell's Des Moines Directory, 1888* (Des Moines, IA: Des Moines Directory Co., 1888), 701.

11. On Hawthorne and Garfield schools, see Charles Weitz memo books, 1877–79, 1880–81, 1881–85, Weitz Company Papers; and on Rawson School, see Charles Weitz memo book, 1883 84, Weitz Company Papers.

12. Robert Denny, "Bicentennial Reflections: The History of Des Moines Public Schools, 1846-1876," 16–17 on http://www.dmschools.org/wp-content/uploads/2011/10/dmpshistory.pdf, accessed on 3 October 2013; and Weitz v. Independent District of Des Moines, *Northwestern Reporter*, 42, (May 4–August 10, 1889), 577–78.

13. Ibid. See also Weitz v. Independent District of Des Moines, *Northwestern Reporter*, 44, (January 25–April 26, 1890), 696–97; and "Cases at Law and in Equity Determined by the Supreme Court of the State of Iowa," January 17, 1893–May 11, 1893 (Columbus, MO: E. W. Stephens, 1895), 81–86. See also *Iowa State Register*, 2 June 1889; 8 February 1890.

14. References to Charles's reserved personality are in "Resolution of the Board of Directors of the German Savings Bank," 27 November 1906, Weitz large scrapbook, Fred Weitz Papers; Charles's obituary, *Des Moines Capital*, 10 November 1906; Brigham, *Des Moines*, 2: 1051–52; Lorenzo F. Andrews, *Pioneers of Polk County, Iowa and Reminiscences of the Early Days* (Des Moines, IA: Baker-Trisler, 1908), 1: 263–28; and *Portrait and Biographical Album of Polk County, Iowa* (Chicago: Lake City Publishing, 1890), 487–88.

15. On formation of this Knights of Pythias lodge and its early growth, see J. M. Dixon, *Centennial History of Polk County, Iowa* (Des Moines, IA: State Register, Printer, 1876), 234.

16. Unmarked clipping and translation in Charles Weitz blue record book, Weitz Company Papers.

17. First quotation from Brigham, *Des Moines*, 1: 288. More information about refinery from *Bushnell's Des Moines City Directory, 1881* (Des Moines, IA: J. P. Bushnell, 1881), 73. Details on Charles's dealings with refinery and stockholders are from Charles Weitz memo book, 1879–80, Weitz Company Papers.

18. Earle Ross, "The First Iowa State Fair," *The Palimpsest* (July 1954), 270–279; Earle Ross, "The Pioneer Period," *The Palimpsest* (July 1954), 280–292; and Mary Kay Shanley, *Our State Fair: Iowa's Blue Ribbon Story* (Des Moines, IA: Blue Ribbon Foundation, 2000), 15–22.

19. Shanley, *Our State Fair: Iowa's Blue Ribbon Story*, 30–31, 35; Earle Ross, "The Fair in Transition," *The Palimpsest* (July 1954), 293–305; Brigham, *Des Moines*, 1: 287, 303; Ilda Hammer, *The Book of Des Moines* (Des Moines, IA: Board of Education, 1944), 90–91; and William Friedricks, *Investing in Iowa: The Life and Times of F. M. Hubbell* (Des Moines, IA: Iowan Books, 2007), 121.

20. Charles Weitz memo book, 1887; and Charles Weitz, McCormick Harvesting Machine Company paid invoice, March 1887, Weitz Company Papers. For others erecting exhibition halls at the fairgrounds, see *Iowa State Register*, 14 May 1886.

21. For population, see http://www.iowadatacenter.org/archive/2011/02/citypop.pdf, accessed on 10 September 2013. On board of trade, see Brigham, *Des Moines*, 1: 267, 292. For quotation about improvements, see *Iowa State Register*, 9 May 1886.

22. *Iowa State Register* quoted in Brigham, *Des Moines*, 1: 292. On the construction of the state capitol, see *Iowa Official Register, 1898* (Des Moines, IA: F. R. Conaway, State Printer, 1898), v–xxxi.

23. On bidding for the city hall job, see Charles Weitz memo book, 1881–85 and Charles Weitz large journal, 1879–83, Weitz Company Papers. On Garrety getting the contract, see *Iowa State Register*, 25 May, 2 June 1882. For inadequacy of jail, see Brigham, *Des Moines*, 1: 295–96; and for Charles's work on the jail, see Charles Weitz memo book, 1885–86, Weitz Company Papers.

24. Quotations are from *Iowa State Register*, 31 May 1882.

25. For *Register*'s support of Charles's and Mrs. Mattes's plans for the street, see *Iowa State Register*, 25 December 1882. On the building, see Brigham, *Des Moines*, 1: 296, 301; and Will Porter, *Annals of Polk County, Iowa and the City of Des Moines Iowa* (Des Moines, IA: George A. Miller, 1898), 475. See also Charles Weitz memo book, 1883–84, Weitz Company Papers.

26. Orin Dahl, *Des Moines: Capital City* (Tulsa, OK: Continental Heritage Inc., 1978), 61.

27. *Iowa State Register*, 25 June 1884; Charles Weitz memo books, 1879–80, 1881–85; and Charles Weitz Record Book, 1886–87, all in Weitz Company Papers.

28. Charles Weitz memo books, 1883–84, 1884–85, and 1888–89; and bill for work on Des Moines Saddlery Building, 20 January 1888, Weitz Company Papers. See also Weitz, "Charles Weitz," 37, Fred Weitz Papers.

29. On move, see Weitz, "Weitz," 35; and *Des Moines Register*, 13 November 1996. For printed announcement of move, see Weitz large scrapbook, Fred Weitz Papers.

30. Charles Weitz memo books, 1884–85, 1885–86; Charles Weitz Record Book, 1886–87; and Charles Weitz Ledger, 1890–91, Weitz Company Papers

31. Ibid. See also Friedricks, *Investing in Iowa*, 48–51; Porter, *Annals of Polk County*, 855–57; Brigham, *Des Moines*, 2: 7–8.

32. Brigham, *Des Moines*: 1: 530, Bushnell's *Des Moines Directory, 1884*, 30; and Charles Weitz memo book, 1883–84, Weitz Company Papers.

33. Charles Weitz memo book, 1884–85, Weitz Company Papers.

34. On library association board, see Brigham, *Des Moines*, 1: 586–87; and Weitz, "Charles Weitz," 40. For statement about Des Moines being a Republican city, see *Iowa State Register*, 27 February 1886; for election and results, see *Iowa State Register*, 28 February, 2 March 1886. For the national context, see Jon Teaford, *The Unheralded Triumph: City Government in America, 1870-1900* (Baltimore, MD: Johns Hopkins University Press, 1984).

35. Quotation from Porter, *Annals of Polk County*, 402. See also Hammer, *Book of Des Moines*, 76–78.

36. Brigham, *Des Moines*, 1: 305, 311, *Des Moines Register*, 12 March 1997; and Andrews, *Pioneers of Polk County*, 1: 267.

37. Report is quoted from *Iowa State Register*, 5 May 1889. For initial discussions of asphalt, see Brigham, *Des Moines*, 1: 328; and Hammer, *Book of Des Moines*, 78.

38. For the waterworks and its relationship with the city of Des Moines, see Charles Sing Denman, "History of the Des Moines Water Works, 1871-1919," typescript, Des Moines Water Works Papers, private collection held by the Des Moines Water Works, Des Moines, IA; and Friedricks, *Investing in Iowa*, 93–97.

39. Ibid. For the aldermen's meeting with Hubbell, see F. M. Hubbell Diary, 18 February 1889, F. M. Hubbell Papers, State Historical Society of Iowa, Des Moines.

40. Brigham, *Des Moines*, 1: 314, 318; Porter, *Annals*, 491; Dahl, *Des Moines: Capital City*, 63; Hammer, *Book of Des Moines*, 87–88; City Council of Des Moines, "Updated Information Requested by the City Development Committee For: Voluntary Annexation of Proposed Annexation Areas to the City of Des Moines, Iowa, A98-03," 13 July 2005, https://www.dmgov.org/NewsDocuments/InvoluntaryAnnexationPetition.pdf, accessed on 1 October 2013; and David Elbert, *Celebrating 125 Years: Standing on the Shoulders of Giants*, (Des Moines, IA: Business Publications Corp., 2013), 31–2.

41. For 1884 charges and quote, see *New York Times*, 27 June 1884.

42. Brigham, *Des Moines*, 1: 300. On the charges against Charles and his colleagues, see the *New York Times*, 23 May 1890; *Omaha Daily Bee*, 1 October 1890; and the *Iowa State Register*, 4–6 December 1890.

43. On Drady's acquittal, see Brigham, 1: 321; and on Kavanagh's rejection of the demurrer and quotation, see *Iowa State Register*, 5 December 1890.

44. *Iowa State Register*, 6 December 1890.

45. For decision and first quotation, see *Iowa State Register*, 6 December 1890. On refunding the money, see Porter, *Annals of Polk County*, 402. Even as the case faded into the background, it eventually became part of the narrative that led progressive Des Moines mayor and city councilman John MacVicar and other like-minded reformers to lobby for a commission form of government in place of the ward-based city council. In 1907, local voters adopted such a system, which called for all councilmen to be elected at large. Widely referred to as the "Des Moines Plan," it was modeled after a similar structure first developed in Galveston, Texas, in 1901. On MacVicar, see Patrice Beam, "John MacVicar," in David Hudson, Marvin Bergman,

and Loren Horton, eds., *The Biographical Dictionary of Iowa* (Iowa City: University of Iowa Press, 2009), 333–34; and on the Des Moines Plan, see Dahl, *Des Moines: Capital City*, 65, 85, 87.

Chapter 4

1. Johnson Brigham, *Des Moines: The Pioneer of Municipal Progress and Reform of the Middle West with The History of Polk County, Iowa* (Chicago: S. J. Clarke, 1911), 1: 317–412; Orin Dahl, *Des Moines: Capital City* (Tulsa, OK: Continental Heritage, 1978), 53–90.

2. On the Industrial Home for the Blind in Iowa, see Peggy Chong, "The History of the Industrial Home for the Blind of Iowa," on the Iowa Department for the Blind website, http://www.iowablindhistory.org/blindhistory/employment–industrial–home–blind, accessed on 25 October 2013.

3. Ibid. See also Charles Weitz large memo book, 1890–91, Weitz Company Papers, private collection held by the Weitz Company, Des Moines, Iowa [hereafter cited as Weitz Company Papers].

4. See Orchard Place website, http://www.orchardplace.org/index.php/about/history, accessed on 26 October 2013; and Charles Weitz, large memo book 1890–91, Weitz Company Papers.

5. On Cottage Hospital, see Fred Weitz Record Book, 1892–93, Weitz Company Papers; Ann Weitz, "Charles Weitz," 43, unpublished typescript, Fred Weitz Papers, private collection held by Fred Weitz, Des Moines, Iowa [hereafter cited as Fred Weitz Papers]; and biographical entry on Annice Baldwin Tracy in http://www.kinyon.com/iowa/iawomen1914/00572tracy.htm, accessed on 28 October 2013. Cottage Hospital evidently went out of business in 1899, the year it was last listed in the city directory; see *R. L. Polk & Co.'s Des Moines City Directory, 1899* (Des Moines, IA: R. L. Polk, 1899), 237. For other work, see Fred Weitz Record Book 1892–93, and Charles Weitz workbook, 1891–93, Weitz Company Papers. On the Homestead Building, see *Iowa State Register*, 19, 21 March 1893; and "Homestead Building," National Register of Historic Places Nomination Form, 77–06995, July 1981, State Historic Preservation Office, Des Moines, IA.

6. See Charles Weitz Record Book, 1869–87, and Charles Weitz workbook, 1891–93, Weitz Company Papers, Weitz, "Charles Weitz," 39, Fred Weitz Papers; *Des Moines Tribune*, 23 November 1935; and *R. L. Polk & Co.'s Des Moines City Directory, 1894* (Des Moines, IA: R. L. Polk, 1894), 552.

7. See *Polk's City Directory, 1894*, 552; Greta Weitz Brown, "Weitz," unpublished typescript, 1977, 95–103, Fred Weitz Papers; *Des Moines Tribune*, 23 November 1935; and Sara M. Baldwin, ed., *Who's Who in Des Moines, 1929: Biographical Sketches of Men and Women of Achievement* (Louisville, KY: Robert M. Baldwin, 1929), 268.

8. See Michael McGerr, *A Fierce Discontent: The Rise and Fall of the Progressive Movement in America* (Oxford and New York: Oxford University Press, 2003), 7; Edward

Chase Kirkland, *Dream and Thought in the Business Community, 1860-1900* (Ithaca, NY: Cornell University Press, 1956), 31–2; and William Friedricks, *Investing in Iowa: The Life of F. M. Hubbell* (Des Moines, IA: Iowan Books, 2007), 63–4.

9. For information on the transaction, the home, the china cabinet, and quotation, see Brown, "Weitz," 63–5. See also Weitz, "Charles Weitz," 41; and *Des Moines Register*, 12 March 1997.

10. On renaming the company, see *The Vision to Build 150 Years* (2005), a sesquicentennial history developed by the Weitz Company, 7, Weitz Company Papers. On the bank's founding and capitalization, see *Northwestern Reporter*, 165, December 14, 1917–February 1, 1918 (Saint Paul, MN: West Publishing, 1918), 808. For more on the bank and Charles's association with it, see Lorenzo F. Andrews, *Pioneers of Polk County, Iowa and Reminiscences of the Early Days* (Des Moines, IA: Baker-Trisler, 1908), 2: 353; "Resolution of the Board of Directors of the German Savings Bank," 27 November 1906, large Weitz scrapbook, Weitz Company Papers; *R. L. Polk & Co.'s Des Moines City Directory, 1894* (Des Moines, IA: R. L. Polk, 1894), 182; *Des Moines City Directory, 1897*, 262; *Des Moines City Directory, 1899*, 325; *Des Moines City Directory, 1902*, 304; *Des Moines City Directory, 1904*, 399; and *Des Moines City Directory, 1906*, 404.

11. On the reform school, see Douglas M. Wertsch, *The Girls' Reform School of Iowa, 1865-1899* (Lewiston, NY: Edwin Mellin Press, 1997). On job and Fritz serving as manager, see two envelopes of cancelled checks, box 4, folder 1, Weitz Company Inc. Papers, State Historical Society of Iowa Des Moines [hereafter cited as Weitz Company Inc. Papers]. On Fritz's first listing as a foreman, see *R. L. Polk & Co.'s Des Moines City Directory, 1894* (Des Moines, IA: R. L. Polk, 1895), 605. For context on treating the mentally ill in Iowa, see Bryan Justin Riddle, "Treatment, Warehousing, and Dispersion: Mt. Pleasant Insane Asylum, 1844-1980 (master's thesis, Iowa State University, 2010); and on Weitz Company building the Polk County Asylum for the Insane, see various invoices and receipts for work on the facility, box 4, folder 2, Weitz Company Inc. Papers.

12. The Cowles home was built in 1909 and the Herring home in 1910. For the Weitz brothers erecting them, see Ann Weitz notes of interview with Heinrich Weitz, n.d., Fred Weitz Papers.

13. On Fred's house, see Weitz, "Charles Weitz," 47; Fred Weitz, interview by author, Des Moines, Iowa, 13 April 2013; *Des Moines Tribune*, 26 November 1957; unmarked clipping on Fred's house on Forty-Second Street, box 1, folder 3, Weitz Family Papers, State Historical Society of Iowa, Des Moines [hereafter cited as Weitz Family Papers]; unmarked clipping, Charles Godfrey Jr. Papers, private collection held by Charles Godfrey Jr., Lathrop Village, Michigan; and *R. L. Polk & Co.'s Des Moines City Directory, 1899* (Des Moines, IA: R. L. Polk, 1899), 737. For very brief announcement of wedding, see *Des Moines Leader*, 4, 6 September 1898.

14. For Des Moines Saddlery job, see *Des Moines Leader*, 5 May 1899. For background on Younkers, see William Temple, *The Younker Story* (1970); *Younkers Grows Up with Iowa* (1939); and Becki Plunkett, "Lipman Younker, Samuel Younker, and Marcus Younker," in David Hudson, Marvin Bergman, and Loren Horton, eds., *The Biographical Dictionary of Iowa* (Iowa City: University of Iowa Press, 2009), 576–78.

15. For the 1899 project, see Dahl, *Des Moines: Capital City*, 236–37; unmarked clipping, Younkers Inc. scrapbook, box OS1-10, Younkers Inc. Papers, State Historical Society of Iowa, Des Moines; *Des Moines Leader*, 4, 11 April, 9 November 1899; and the *Iowa Capital*, 8 April 1899.

16. *Des Moines Leader*, 9 November 1899.

17. See "Notes on Century Lumber," in file of papers from Heinrich Weitz's apartment, 14 September 1981, Weitz Warehouse Collection, box 0715-01, Weitz Company Papers. Century Lumber first appears in the city directory in 1901, see *R. L. Polk & Co.'s Des Moines City Directory, 1901* (Des Moines, IA: R. L. Polk, 1901), 221. Watt had joined German Savings Bank as the cashier in 1899, see *Polk's Des Moines City Directory, 1899*, 325, 733.

18. On Charles suffering from a "nervous condition," see *Des Moines Tribune*, 10 November 1906; on trip to Florida, see Weitz, "Charles Weitz," 41, Fred Weitz Papers; Weitz family photographs taken in Florida, 1902–3, photos 4–6, box 2, folder 1, Weitz Family Papers; and for a reference to Charles in Saint Andrews Bay, Florida, *Des Moines Leader*, 16 February 1902. For background on "nervous conditions," see Megan Burke, Rebecca Fribush, and Peter Sterns, "Nervous Breakdown in 20th-Century American Culture," *Journal of Social History* 33 (Spring 2000), 565–584. On Charles's transfer of the company to his sons, see "Bill of Sale," 5 December 1902; large Charles Weitz scrapbook, Weitz Company Papers.

19. See "Bill of Sale," 5 December 1902; "Last Will and Testament of Charles Weitz," 12 December 1902; "Articles of Co-Partnership" (agreement between Charlie, Fred, and Edward), 1 May 1903, all in large Charles Weitz scrapbook, Weitz Company Papers. The management change at Century Lumber is reflected in the 1903 city directory, which listed Charlie as president, Watt and Wood remained vice president and secretary respectively, and Fred Weitz was listed as treasurer, see *R. L. Polk & Co.'s Des Moines City Directory, 1903* (Des Moines, IA: R. L. Polk, 1903), 233.

20. On Charlie and Fred and their different personalities, see Fred Weitz, interviews, 18 April, 11 November 2013; and Elizabeth Johnson, interview by author, Des Moines, Iowa, 3 September 2013. Quotations are from *Des Moines Tribune*, 18 February 1935.

21. For move on the City Beautiful Movement in Des Moines and the Des Moines Riverfront Civic Center district, see James Jacobsen, "The City Beautiful Movement and City Planning in Des Moines, Iowa, 1892-1938," National Register of Historic Places, Multiple Property Documentation Form, 7 July 1988, http://pdfhost.focus. nps.gov/docs/NRHP/Text/64500184.pdf, accessed on 18 November 2013.

22. Ibid.

23. On Weitz bid and Capital City Brick and Pipe getting the job, see *Des Moines Leader*, 6 June 1899. For Zeller quotation and more on building, see *Des Moines Register*, 9 October 2011; and on Weitz finishing library building, see unmarked clipping, large Weitz scrapbook, Weitz Company Papers.

24. For general background on the Iowa State Fairgrounds and its buildings, see Thomas Leslie, *Iowa State Fair: Country Comes to Town* (Princeton, NJ: Princeton

Architectural Press, 2007). For specifics on the buildings, see "Iowa State Fair and Exposition Grounds Historic District," National Register of Historic Places Nomination Form, 77-06995, 5 January 1987, State Historic Preservation Office, Des Moines, IA. Quotation about roof from Iowa State Fair Blue Ribbon Foundation website, http://www.blueribbonfoundation.org/renovations/live-stock-pavilion, accessed on 15 November 2013. For details of winning bids for Livestock Pavilion, Agriculture Building, horse barn, and powerhouse, see *Iowa Yearbook of Agriculture, 1902* (Des Moines, IA: Iowa State Printer, 1903), 151; *Iowa Yearbook of Agriculture, 1904*, 132–33; and *Iowa Yearbook of Agriculture, 1907*, 205.

25. Brown, "Weitz," 67–68.

26. For quotation about passing on company, see "Bill of Sale," 5 December 1902, large Charles Weitz scrapbook.

27. On Charles's death and quotation, see *Des Moines Register*, 11 November 1906; see also *Des Moines Capital*, 10 November 1906.

28. See *Des Moines Register*, 11 August 2013.

29. For background on the fort and bringing it to Des Moines, see David Elbert, *Celebrating 125 Years: Standing on the Shoulders of Giants*, (Des Moines, IA: Business Publications Corp., 2013) 13; Brigham, *Des Moines*, 1: 600–02; Friedricks, *Investing in Iowa*, 120; and Jerome Greene and Louis Anderson, "Fort Des Moines Historic Complex, Des Moines," Polk County, Iowa: Historic American Buildings Survey (HABS) No. IA-121 (Denver: National Park Service), 3–6. For initial contracts, see *Des Moines Register and Leader*, 23 October 1902; and on the Atkinson brothers getting contracts, see *Des Moines Register and Leader*, 26 July 1903.

30. See *Waterloo Daily Courier*, 9 February 1905.

31. For trustees, see "Last Will and Testament of Charles Weitz," 12 December 1902; for purchasing land, see unmarked clipping, 9 January 1908; and for completed building and quotation about elevator, see unmarked clipping, 27 March 1909, all in large Charles Weitz scrapbook. See also Brown, "Weitz, 92–94. On being first high-rise apartment building west of the Mississippi River, see *Omaha World-Herald*, 8 July 1996.

32. See Fred Weitz to Alice Weitz, 4 February 1932, Fred Weitz Papers.

33. On architects, see Virgil Stanford Jr., "Municipal Building (Des Moines City Hall)," typescript, 1981, prepared for Historic American Buildings Survey, National Park Service, US Department of the Interior, Washington, DC, 3–5, HABS no. IA-152. Quotes on interior are from Stanford, "Municipal Building," 2.

34. On bidding and awarding of contract, see *Des Moines Register and Leader*, 2, 16 December 1909; and *Des Moines Tribune*, 31 December 1909.

35. Unmarked clippings, large Charles Weitz scrapbook. Zeller quotation is from John Zeller, "From the Real to the Ideal; Images of Des Moines in the Progressive Era," http://www.lib.drake.edu/heritage/odm/article.html, accessed on 18 November 20013.

36. On the building and quotation, see unmarking clipping, 31 July 1910; see also Century Lumber Company, announcement of move into new building, 20 July 1910, both in large Charles Weitz scrapbook.

Chapter 5

1. James Pierce to William Harding, 13 June 1917, large Weitz scrapbook, Weitz Company Papers, private collection held by the Weitz Company, Des Moines, Iowa [hereafter cited as Weitz Company Papers].

2. For Heinrich Weitz's view of his father, see Ed Weitz, telephone conversation with author, 5 December 2013.

3. On Alice Weitz and her various activities, see *Des Moines Tribune*, 26 November 1957; the *Daily Iowa Capital*, 3 May 1899; *Des Moines Leader*, 2 October 1901, 9 February, 22 May, 8 June 1902; *Cedar Falls Gazette*, 30 September 1904; and *Iowa City Press-Citizen*, 27 October 1917.

4. For more on the family's Christmas Eve party, see Fred Weitz, interview by author, Des Moines, Iowa, 18 April 2013; Phil Brown, interview by author, Des Moines, Iowa, 2 May 2013; Charles Godfrey Jr., telephone conversation with author, 16 November 2013; and Ed Weitz, telephone conversation. See also taped interview from 1949 Weitz party, Charles Godfrey Jr. Papers, private collection held by Charles Godfrey Jr., Lathrup Village, Michigan [hereafter cited as Charles Godfrey Jr. Papers].

5. Heinrich Weitz's views were recounted by Ed Weitz, telephone conversation. See also Fred Weitz to Alice Weitz, 4 February 1932; and Ann Weitz, "Charles Weitz," 53, 70, unpublished typescript, both in Fred Weitz Papers, private collection held by Fred Weitz, Des Moines, Iowa [hereafter cited as Fred Weitz Papers].

6. Unmarked clipping, folder 3 (Alice Weitz clippings), box 1, Weitz Family Papers, State Historical Society of Iowa, Des Moines, Iowa. See also Alice Weitz to Ella Wilson (her mother), 1, 6, 8, 12, 17, 27 March, 5, 13, 16, April 1911, Fred Weitz Papers; and Ed Weitz, telephone conversation.

7. Greta Weitz Brown, "Weitz," 26–27, Fred Weitz Papers.

8. Unmarked clipping, 4 July 1911, Weitz scrapbook 3, Weitz Company Papers.

9. For background on the Hubbell Building, see William Friedricks, *Investing in Iowa: The Life and Times of F. M. Hubbell* (Des Moines: Iowan Books, 2007), 102–3; and *Des Moines Register and Leader*, 21 January 1912. On the building's completion and Weitz advertisement, see *Des Moines Register and Leader*, 27 April 1913.

10. For background on Crane in Des Moines, see *The Valve World* 8 (December 1916), 423.

11. Ibid., 423, 425. On first use of the steam shovel, see *Des Moines Register*, 17 July 1955. For Kresge Building, see unmarked clipping, 8 September 1910, large Weitz scrapbook, and Weitz, "Charles Weitz," 54.

12. On 1915 building season, see *Des Moines Register and Leader*, 12 June 1915; on population surpassing 100,000, see *Des Moines Register and Leader*, 28 April 1915. For more on the better economy, the Seventh Street Viaduct, and Grand Avenue bridge, see Orin Dahl, *Des Moines: Capital City* (Tulsa, OK: Continental Heritage, 1978), 101.

13. On jobs and connection that led to post office work, see Weitz, "Charles Weitz," 54, 69–70. See also *American Contractor*, 9 January 1915, 49, and 27 March 1915, 77A.

14. On post office jobs, see *American Contractor*, 20 November 1915, 73; 2 June 1917, 2; 14 June 1917, 62; 23 June 1917, 64; 4 November 1916, 38; 12 March 1918, 60; and 30 March 1918, 56; *Engineering and Contracting*, 19 July 1916, 34; and 8 November 1916, 30; and "List of Current Jobs, 8-1917," in large Weitz scrapbook. For examples of contracts the company did not win, see *American Contractor*, 1 January 1916, 81; and 5 February 1916, 94.

15. On State Savings Bank in Lamoni, see *American Contractor*, 28 April 1917; and for Valley National Bank Building, "List of Current Jobs, 8-1917," in large Weitz scrapbook, and *American Contractor*, 18 March 1916, 24.

16. See "List of Current Jobs, 8-1917; and unmarked clipping, 6 August 1911, in large Weitz scrapbook; and *American Contractor*, 20 May 1916, 83; 3 June 1916, 49; 4 November 1916, 38; 19 May 1917, 78. See also *Engineering and Contracting*, 11 October 1916, 28. On Charles's and Edward's homes, see Fred Weitz, interview by author, Des Moines, Iowa, 18 April 2013.

17. See *American Contractor*, 2 December 1916, 106; unmarked clippings on Camp Dodge, Weitz scrapbook 3; and *Des Moines Register*, 17 June 1917. See also *Engineering and Contracting*, 15 August 1917, 144.

18. "Report of F. W. Weitz Pertaining to the Building of Camp Dodge Cantonment," Weitz Company Papers; *Des Moines Tribune*, 13 December 1922; and *Des Moines Capital*, 13 February 1923.

19. See "Report of F. W. Weitz," and Fred Emory Haynes, "Social Work at Camp Dodge," *Iowa Journal of History and Politics*, 16 (October 1918), 471. On letting of contract to Weitz and Bolton quote, see unmarked clippings, Weitz scrapbook 3, Weitz Company.

20. Quotation from Haynes, "Social Work at Camp Dodge," 471.

21. Fred Weitz quoted from *Des Moines Tribune*, 12 October 1917.

22. For details of Camp Dodge construction, see Mary Jones and Michael Vogt, *Camp Dodge* (Charleston, SC: Arcadia Publishing, 2009), 19–38; and David Snook, "The Building of Camp Dodge: History of the Iowa National Guard," on Iowa National Guard website, Page Content http://www.iowanationalguard.com/History/History/Pages/Building-Camp-Dodge.aspx, accessed on 3 January 2014.

23. Quotation from Snook, "Building of Camp Dodge," Iowa National Guard website. For quotation from "Time is Precious" placard, see *The Contractor*, 4 January 1918, 31.

24. For more on the anti-German sentiment, see Frederick Luebke, *Bonds of Loyalty: German-Americans and World War I* (DeKalb, IL: Northern Illinois University Press, 1974). For quotation on 100 percent American campaign, see James Roark et al. *The American Promise: A Compact History*, vol. 2, 4th ed. (Boston and New York: Bedford St. Martin's, 2010), 553. On the Babel Proclamation, see Nancy Derr, "The Babel Proclamation," *Palimpsest* 60 (July/August 1979), 99–115; and Stephen Frese, "Divided by a Common Language: The Babel Proclamation and Its Influence in Iowa History," *History Teacher* 39 (November 2005), 59–88.

25. Phil Brown, interview by author, Des Moines, Iowa, 2 May 2013. On picnic and fireworks at Fred's house, see unmarked clipping, Charles Godfrey Jr. Papers. For Alice and *Prairie Gold*, see *Iowa City Press-Citizen* 5, 27 October 1917.

26. First quotation from *The American Contractor*, 25 August 1917, 20; second quotation from I. P. Shelby to Charles Weitz' Sons, 21 January 1919, in Weitz scrapbook 3, Weitz Company Papers; and on meeting deadlines, see Mary Jones and Michael Vogt, *Camp Dodge* (Charleston, SC: Arcadia Publishing, 2009), 21.

27. *Des Moines Capital*, 13 February 1923; *Des Moines Tribune*, 13 February 1923; and *Des Moines News*, 13 February 1923. See also J. E. Tusant & Son v. Charles Weitz Sons et al., *Northwestern Reporter* 191 (Iowa 1923), 884–90.

28. Ibid. On the district judge's ruling, see *Des Moines Daily News*, 11 June 1921.

29. *Des Moines Capital*, 4 December 1922.

30. For cantonment lawsuits, see *New York Times*, 25 November, 5 December 1922; *American Contractor*, 9 December 1922, 20–21; and for Fred's quotations, see the *Des Moines Capital*, 5 December 1922; and the *Des Moines Tribune*, 4 December 1922.

31. *Des Moines Tribune*, 5 December 1922.

32. On Harry Daugherty, see James Giglio, *H.M. Daugherty and the Politics of Expediency* (Kent, OH: Kent State University Press, 1978).

33. Quotation is from *Des Moines Tribune-Capital*, 17 June 1927; see also *Des Moines Tribune-Capital*, 14 June 1927.

34. *Des Moines Tribune*, 25 January 1918; and *Des Moines Register*, 27 January 1918.

35. *Des Moines Register*, 17 July 1955; Ann Weitz notes of interview with Heinrich Weitz, n.d., Fred Weitz Papers.

36. On Century's purchase of Peoples Lumber Company, see *Lumber World Review*, 25 June 1913, 45; for quotation on its warehouse, see *Polk's Des Moines City Directory, 1914*, 1642; and for more on Century Lumber, its facilities, and its use of advertising, see "Advertising Basis for Successful Lumber Business," *American Builder*, January 1922, 70–71.

37. On Carl and Harold working at Century Lumber, see *Polk's Des Moines City Directory, 1915* (Des Moines, IA: R. L. Polk, 1915), 1210, and *Polk's Des Moines City Directory, 1921*, 1316. On Brockett, see *Des Moines Register*, 18 February 1933; *Des Moines Tribune*, 21 February 1933; and various unmarked newspaper clippings,

Weitz scrapbooks 1, 2, and 3, Weitz Company Papers. On Century's purchase of Peoples Lumber Company, see *Lumber World Review*, 25 June 1913, 45; for quotation on its warehouse, see *Polk's Des Moines City Directory, 1914*, 1642; and for more on Century Lumber, its facilities, and its use of advertising, see "Advertising Basis for Successful Lumber Business," *American Builder*, January 1922, 70–71.

38. Heinrich observing end of war celebrations, see Ann Weitz notes of interview with Heinrich Weitz, n.d., Fred Weitz Papers; for description of downtown Des Moines during the celebrations, see *Des Moines Register*, 11, 12, 1918. For postwar inflation and the strikes of 1919, see Lynn Dumenil, *The Modern Temper, American Culture and Society in the 1920s* (New York: Hill and Wang, 1995), 219–220; and David Kennedy, *Over Here: The First World War and American Society* (New York and Oxford: Oxford University Press, 1980), 243–295.

39. For the strike in Des Moines, see *Des Moines Register*, 23 March; 1, 2, 3, 7 April; and 25 May 1919.

40. *Des Moines Register*, 25 May 1919.

41. *Des Moines Capital*, 13 July 1919; 29 February 1920; *American Contractor*, 2 August 1919, 79; 20 September 1919, 60E; 13 December 1919, 57; and *Iowa City Press-Citizen*, 10 February 1921.

42. See Craig McCue, *West Des Moines and Valley Junction* (Charleston, SC: Arcadia Publishing, 2009), 56; Michael Swanger, "Beloved Ballroom," *West Des Moines Living*, January 1912, 5–9; and Fred Weitz, interview by author, Indianola, Iowa, 15 January 2014.

43. See *Des Moines Capital*, 2 December 1920; *American Contractor*, 8 July 1922, 32; and Weitz, "Charles Weitz," 67–68.

44. "Concrete Plant That Cuts Labor Costs," *Concrete*, April 1919, 163.

45. Weitz, "Charles Weitz," 68.

46. See Charles Weitz' Sons v. United States Fidelity & Guaranty Co., *Northwestern Reporter*, 219 (Iowa 1928), 411–415.

47. Ibid; see also *Des Moines Register*, 9 May 1928.

48. See *American Contractor*, 22 January 1921, 52; and Weitz, "Weitz," 67, 73–4.

49. Des Moines Women's Club Roster 127 (2012–13), 9; Des Moines Women's Club website, http://www.fredtruck.com/dmwc/styled-2/styled-4/index.html, and Hoyt Sherman Place website, http://www.hoytsherman.org/index.php?option=com_content&view=article&id=18&Itemid=79, both accessed on 3 February 2013.

50. On fire, see *Des Moines Capital*, 11 March 1922. Century Lumber advertisement ran the following day, *Des Moines Capital*, 12 March 1922. For company finances, see Weitz v. US Fidelity, 412.

51. See *American Contractor*, 21 January 1922, 84; 19 August 1922, 54A; Weitz notes of interview with Heinrich Weitz; *Des Moines Register*, 11 October 1925; *Des Moines Tribune*, 18 February 1935; list of early Weitz building projects, Weitz Company Papers; and Robert Denny, "Bicentennial Reflections: The History of Des Moines

Public Schools, 1846-1876," 119, 134 on http://www.dmschools.org/wp-content/uploads/2011/10/dmpshistory.pdf, accessed on 3 October 2013.

52. For firms that continued operating through the period, see Rudy Weitz, "Pioneer Building Industry in Polk County," a paper presented to the Pioneer Club, Des Moines, Iowa, 6 September 1969, 17–19, in possession of author. For companies that went out of business, see *Polk's Des Moines City Directory, 1923* (Des Moines, IA: R. L. Polk, 1923), 1833; *Des Moines City Directory, 1924*, 884; *Des Moines City Directory, 1927*, 1818; *Des Moines City Directory, 1928*, 1767; *Des Moines City Directory, 1926*, 1873; *Des Moines City Directory, 1927*, 1818; *Des Moines City Directory, 1928*, 1765; and *Des Moines City Directory, 1929*, 1682.

53. See Fred Weitz to Alice Weitz, 4 February 1932, Fred Weitz Papers.

54. Ibid. On creation of new subsidiary, see Weitz, "Charles Weitz," 76; *Polk's Des Moines City Directory, 1930* (Des Moines, IA: R.L. Polk, 1930), 997; *Polk's Des Moines City Directory, 1931*, 102, 975. On its incorporation, see Iowa Secretary of State web page, http://sos.iowa.gov/search/business/(S(h2kjj3ay-cf44gn55azdg5ze3))/summary.aspx?c=ZR-OQO5UqGRISPTuThrEJ-8ksnk-ll05-vjJe_x1rQ-81, as well as Missouri Secretary of State web page, https://www.sos.mo.gov/BusinessEntity/soskb/Corp.asp?464087, both accessed on 27 January 2014. See also "State of Missouri, Certificate and License" for the Weitz Company, 14 January 1929, Weitz Company Inc., minutes, stock certificates, trade names binder, Weitz Company Papers; and "Wolf and Company Comments," Weitz warehouse collection, box 0714-01, Weitz Company Papers.

55. See Helena Weitz obituary in *Des Moines Register*, 21 May 1929.

56. For list of post offices built by Weitz and the building of the temple, see Weitz, "Weitz," 73–4, 78. On Tulsa federal building, see unmarked clipping, 30 October 1930, Weitz scrapbook 1, Weitz Company Papers.

57. Weitz, "Weitz," 75–6. The Weitz Company got out of the furnace business in January 1931, when it sold its oil burners, equipment, machinery, and tools to Carbon Coal Company in Des Moines. See minutes of the "Regular Meeting Board of Directors," 19 January 1931, Weitz Company Papers.

58. For story of Pampa post office, see *Pampa* (Texas) *Daily News*, 2, 3 March 1933; and *Colorado* (Texas) *Citizen*, 9 March 1933. On federal building in Helena, Montana, see *Helena Daily Independent*, 2 December 1932; 6 February, 25 March, 26 June 1933.

59. On the beginning of the reorganized company, see "Wolf and Company Comments," Weitz warehouse collection, box 0714-01, Weitz Company Papers; and minutes of "Special Meeting of Stockholders," 8, 18 February 1933, Weitz Company Papers. On company officers, see *Polk's Des Moines City Directory, 1934* (Des Moines, IA: R. L. Polk, 1934), 786. The separation of ownership appears clear in the city directories. In the 1933 edition, Charles Weitz is listed as the Weitz' Sons vice president and Edward Weitz as its secretary, but that was the last time they were mentioned with the Weitz construction concern; see *Polk's Des Moines City Directory, 1933*, 827. Fred, however, remained listed as a vice president of Century Lumber until his death. See also "Minutes of Meetings of Weitz Brothers

Trust," 12 November 1935, Weitz warehouse collection, box 0714-01, Weitz Company Papers.

60. The Weitz Company failed to get post office jobs in Mason City and Waverly, Iowa, and in Neosho, Missouri. See *Mason City Globe Gazette*, 10 August 1933; *Daily Capital News* (Jefferson City, Missouri), 29 August 1934; and the *Waterloo Courier*, 6 February 1935. See also Fred Weitz to Alice Weitz, 4 February 1932, Fred Weitz Papers. On Fred's stroke and death, see *Des Moines Tribune*, 18 February 1935.

Chapter 6

1. Hy-Vee's story is told in Kathleen Gilbert, *The History of Hy-Vee: 75 Years of "A Helpful Smile"* (Phoenix, Arizona: Heritage Publishers, 2004). For Ruan, see William Friedricks, *In for the Long Haul: The Life of John Ruan* (Ames: Iowa State Press, 2003).

2. See Rudolph Weitz, "Pioneer Building Industry in Polk County," a paper presented to the Pioneer Club, 6 September 1969, in possession of author; and Joseph Frazier Wall, *Policies and People: The First Hundred Years of The Bankers Life, Des Moines, Iowa* (Englewood Cliffs, NJ: Prentice-Hall, 1979), 91.

3. On the postwar boom and the 1950s, see Lizabeth Cohen, *A Consumers' Republic: The Politics of Mass Consumption in Postwar America* (New York: Vintage Books, 2004); David Halberstam, *The Fifties* (New York: Fawcett Columbine, 1993); J. Ronald Oakley, *God's Country: America in the Fifties* (New York: Dembner Books, 1986); and William O'Neill, *American High: The Years of Confidence* (New York: Free Press, 1986). For quotation and more on the period, see John Diggins, *The Proud Decades: America in War and Peace, 1941-1960* (New York and London: W. W. Norton, 1988), 178.

4. *Des Moines Register*, 11 December 1955; *Polk's Des Moines City Directory, 1934* (Des Moines, IA: R. L. Polk, 1934), 786; *Polk's Des Moines City Directory, 1935*, 849; James C. Ehrhardt and Steven J. Sweeney, *Iowa National Bank Notes* (Okoboji, IA: William R. Higgins Jr. Foundation, 2006), 56; unmarked clipping, Weitz scrapbook 1, Weitz Company Papers, private collection held by the Weitz Company, Des Moines, Iowa [hereafter cited as Weitz Company Papers]; and *Altoona* (Iowa) *Herald*, 17 May 1934.

5. For staff in 1934, see *Polk's Des Moines City Directory, 1934* (Des Moines, IA: R. L. Polk, 1934), 786; and on Cleo Anderson, see *Weitz Surveyor* 1 (August 1950), 2. This was an in-house newsletter published by the Weitz Company, Weitz Company Papers. For cutting back on office space and saving on heating costs, see Cleo Anderson to Ann Weitz, 20 July 1982, Weitz warehouse collection, box 0714-01, Weitz Company Papers; and for quotation, see minutes of the "Regular Meeting of the Board of Directors," 27 January 1934, Weitz Company Papers. On profits, see Ann Weitz, "Charles Weitz," 77, unpublished typescript, in Fred Weitz Papers, private collection held by Fred Weitz, Des Moines, Iowa [hereafter cited as Fred Weitz Papers].

6. See Fred Weitz, interviews by author, Des Moines, Iowa, 18 April, 11 November 2013; Phil Brown, interview by author, Des Moines, Iowa, 2 May 2013; Edwin Weitz, telephone conversation with author, 5 December 2013; and *Des Moines Register*, 11 December 1955.

7. Fred Weitz, interview, 18 April 2013; Phil Brown, interview; unmarked clipping, Weitz scrapbook 1, Weitz Company Papers; and Sarah Stevenson Weitz, "Family History," 36, unpublished typed manuscript edited by Steve Weitz, 2008, Fred Weitz Papers.

8. Unmarked clippings, Weitz scrapbook 1, Weitz Company Papers; and Weitz, "Family History," 34–36.

9. Weitz, "Family History," 36.

10. Ibid. See also *Des Moines Register*, 11 December 1955; *Polk's Des Moines City Directory, 1927* (Des Moines, IA: R. L. Polk, 1927), 1384; *Polk's Des Moines City Directory, 1931*, 974; *Polk's Des Moines City Directory, 1933*, 827; and Fred Weitz, correspondence with author, 26 February 2014.

11. Fred Weitz, interview, 11 November 2013; and Steve Weitz, interview by author, West Des Moines, Iowa, 27 March 2014.

12. On Heinrich, see Edwin Weitz, telephone conversation with author, 5 December 2013 and correspondence with author, 17 April 2014; Fred Weitz, interviews; *Des Moines Register*, 16 July 1930, 17 July 1955; *Helena* (Montana) *Daily*, 26 June 1933; *Polk's Des Moines City Directory, 1932* (Des Moines, IA: R. L. Polk, 1932), 915, *Polk's Des Moines City Directory, 1936*, 896; and Ann Weitz notes of interview with Heinrich Weitz, n.d., Fred Weitz Papers.

13. Ibid.

14. The Weitz Company built post offices in Algona and Leon, Iowa, in 1936, and post offices in Sigourney, Iowa, and Rushville and White Hall, Illinois, in 1937. On the West Des Moines school project, see Terri Fredrickson and Alda Post, *West Des Moines: From Railroads to Crossroads, 1893-1993* (West Des Moines, IA: West Des Moines Centennial Inc., 1993), 82. On PWA, see Jason Scott Smith, *Building New Deal Liberalism: The Political Economy of Public Works, 1933-1956* (Cambridge: Cambridge University Press, 2006); and for Phenix Elementary being converted into apartments, see *Des Moines Register*, 16 January 2015.

15. See website, http://www.houstondeco.org/1930s/appraisers.html, accessed on 30 December 2014; and Fred Weitz, interview, 11 November 2013.

16. For building permits, see US Bureau of the Census, *Statistical Abstract of the United States, 1939*, 866. Weitz built a Des Moines home at 4415 Greenwood Drive for physician Dennis Kelly in 1935 and a home at 18 Thirty-Fourth Street for Flora Dunlop in 1936, see Ann Weitz notes of interview with Heinrich Weitz, *Polk's Des Moines City Directory, 1941* (Des Moines, IA: R. L. Polk, 1941), 240, 449. For all-electric homes during the 1930s, see Philip Santo, *Inspections and Reports on Dwellings: Assessing Age*, 2nd ed. (Hoboken, NJ: Taylor & Francis, 2013), 166; and *New York Times*, 20 December 1931; 29 May 1938. In advertisements, local utilities

such as the Iowa Electric Light and Power Company or the Muscatine Municipal Electric Plant stressed the benefits of all-electric homes in Iowa, see *Baynard News*, 10 March 1938; or the *Muscatine Journal and News-Tribune*, 3 July 1935. This "all-electric home" still stands today at 3420 Saint Johns Road in Des Moines.

17. See Weitz workbook 9, Weitz Company Papers, Weitz, "Weitz," 78; Wall, *Policies and People*, 91–100; and unmarked clippings, on Hills Department Store being built, 1 March, 9 April, 14, 23 May 1939, in Weitz scrapbook, 1935–45, Weitz warehouse collection, box 0715-01, Weitz Company Papers.

18. Weitz, "Weitz," 78, and Wall, *Policies and People*, 91–100; and *Des Moines Register*, 11 July 1938.

19. On the federal budget, see James Roark et al. *The American Promise: A Compact History*, vol. 2, 4th ed. (Boston and New York: Bedford-St. Martin's, 2010), 633; unemployment figures from *Historical Statistics of the United States, Colonial Times to 1970* (Washington, DC: Bureau of the Census, 1975), 135; and employment numbers from David Horowitz and Peter Carroll, *On the Edge: The U.S. Since 1941*, 2nd ed. (Belmont, CA: West/Wadsworth, 1998), 27. Works on the home front during World War II include John Blum, *V was for Victory* (New York: Harcourt, Brace Jovanovich, 1976); Geoffrey Perrett, *Days of Sadness, Years of Triumph: The American People, 1939-1945* (New York: Coward, McCann and Geoghegan, 1979); and Richard Polenberg, *War and Society: The United States, 1941-1945* (Philadelphia: Lippincott, 1972).

20. See Dorothy Schwieder, *Iowa: The Middle Land* (Ames: Iowa State University Press, 1996), 281–82; and Leland Sage, *A History of Iowa* (Ames: Iowa State University Press, 1974), 316–318.

21. *Des Moines Register*, 12 June, 3 July 1941; *Des Moines Tribune*, 7 July 1941; and Lisa Ossian, *The Home Fronts of Iowa, 1939-1945* (Columbia and London: University of Missouri Press, 2009), 63–64.

22. *Ames* (Iowa) *Daily Tribune*, 18 July 1941; *Des Moines Register*, 18 July 1941; and Weitz, "Weitz," 80.

23. *Des Moines Tribune*, 18, 26 July 1941; and *Des Moines Register*, 18, 23, 30 July 1941.

24. *Des Moines Tribune*, 8 July, 2, 5 August, 17 October 1941; *Des Moines Register*, 30, 31 July, 5 August, 7 September 1941, 17 October, 28 November 1941; *Iowa City Press-Citizen*, 13 September 1941; and Weitz, "Weitz," 84–85.

25. *Des Moines Register*, 14 December 1941; 4 March 1942. Quotation is from Weitz Company report, quoted in Weitz, "Weitz," 86–87.

26. For information on the Gillette Tire Company in Eau Claire and U. S. Rubber's acquisition of it, see Wisconsin Historical Society website on digital collection of Uniroyal records, http://digicoll.library.wisc.edu/cgi/f/findaid/findaid-idx?c=wiarchives;cc=wiarchives;view=text;rgn=main;didno=uw-whs-ec00cb, accessed on 23 March 2014.

27. Ibid.; see also Rudy Weitz's Eau Claire Ordnance Plant daily diary, Weitz Company Papers; and *Mason City Globe-Gazette*, 28 May 1942. For work in Muscatine, see

Muscatine Journal and News-Tribune, 24 November, 30 December 1943; Grain Processing Corporation website, http://www.grainprocessing.com/corporate-info/history.html, and Kent Corporation website, http://www.kentww.com/history/, both accessed on 21 March 2014. For Clinton job, see Weitz Production Record Book; for Firestone job, see Weitz Production Record Book and unmarked clippings, 17 September, 12 November, and 12 December 1944 in Weitz warehouse scrapbook, Weitz Company Papers.

28. Nebraska Historical Society website, description of Cornhusker Ordnance Plant, http://nebraskahistory.org/lib-arch/research/manuscripts/business/cornord.htm, accessed on 22 March 2014; *Lincoln* (Nebraska) *Star*, 13 August 1944; *Nebraska State Journal*, 5, 29 August 1944; and "Historic Properties Report: Cornhusker Army Ammunition Plant, Grand Island, Nebraska," (August 1984), 13–32, http://www.dtic.mil/dtic/tr/fulltext/u2/a175830.pdf, accessed on 22 March 2014.

29. *Mason City Globe-Gazette*, 13 August 1942; John S. Nollen, Grinnell College (Iowa City: State Historical Society of Iowa, 1953), 127–128; Weitz Company Production Record Book, 1941–1952, Weitz Company Papers.

30. *Iowa State Daily*, 27 March 2001; Ossian, *Home Fronts*, 88–89; Schwieder, *Iowa: The Middle Land*, 285; and Weitz workbooks, 3, 4, 8, 9, 10–14, 20, 21, 22–27, Weitz Company Papers.

31. *Weitz Surveyor* 4 (August 1955), 1. See *Polk's Des Moines City Directory, 1943* (Des Moines, IA: R. L. Polk, 1943), 125, 684. See "Grant of Possession," 17 February 1934 agreement between Weitz Realty Company and Bankers Life, which took possession of the Weitz Building in exchange for the remainder of the mortgage being forgiven, Weitz Company Papers. Century Lumber was reincorporated in 1940 as Century Lumber Company Inc. It remained operated by Ed Weitz, an uncle of Rudy's and the descendants of Charles, as well as another uncle. However, other family members, including Rudy and his three siblings, Heinrich, Greta Brown, and Elsa Rose Godfrey, all held shares. Although details remain unclear, the lumber company was liquidated in 1952. For information, see "Notes on Century Lumber," in file of papers from Heinrich Weitz's apartment, 14 September 1981, Weitz warehouse collection, box 0715-01, Weitz Company Papers, and Orin Dahl, *Des Moines: Capital City* (Tulsa, OK: Continental Heritage, 1978), 233.

32. See unmarked clipping, 27 July 1943, in Weitz scrapbook, 1935–45, Weitz warehouse collection, box 0715-01, Weitz Company Papers; "Look to Weitz for the Latest," reprinted from *The Central Contractor* (December 1948); Weitz, "Weitz," 90; *Weitz Surveyor* 4 (December 1955), 1; and *Des Moines Register*, 27 May 1974.

33. See Fred Weitz, interview, 18 April 2013; and Iowa Secretary of State web page, http://sos.iowa.gov/search/business/(S(hkwunb45ylt3xo554llzckvz))/summary.aspx?c=KhWTsN2E_wk5OaqtuhRN4PaMJDrkrj3xWhJFjsHl4pA1, accessed on 24 March 2014.

34. See Weitz, "Family History," 37; and Fred Weitz, interview, 11 November 2013.

35. Ibid. For quotation and more on changes family experienced, see also Fred Weitz, interview, 20 March 2013.

36. James T. Patterson, *Grand Expectations: The United States, 1945-1974* (Oxford and New York: Oxford University Press, 1996), 61.

37. Weitz Production Record Book.

38. On inflation, labor, and postwar strikes, see Patterson, *Grand Expectations*, 39–60; Cohen, *Consumers' Republic*, 107–9; and Diggins, *Proud Decades*, 98–102. For standoff between the CIO and the Weitz Company, see *Des Moines Register*, 22 January, 8 February 1946.

39. Weitz Production Record Book; Ossian, *Home Fronts*, 72; Ilda Hammer, *The Book of Des Moines* (Des Moines, IA: Board of Education, 1944), 144; and Dahl, *Des Moines*, 135.

40. For housing shortage, veterans staying at Fort Des Moines, and housing starts, see William Friedricks, *The Real Deal: The Life of Bill Knapp* (Des Moines, IA: Business Publications Corporation, 2013), 41–42. For Des Moines population growth, see http://www.statelibraryofiowa.org/datacenter/archive/2011/02/citypop.pdf, accessed on 4 April 2014; and for more on the GI Bill, see Cohen, *Consumers' Republic*, 137–146.

41. See Harry K. Schwartz, "Sin and Section 608," *Harvard Crimson*, 27 April 1954.

42. On garden apartments and the Colonial Village complex, see Virginia Historic Landmarks Commission, "National Register of Historic Places Inventory/Nomination: Monroe Courts Historic District," May 1980, http://www.dhr.virginia.gov/registers/Counties/Arlington/000-0013_Colonial_Village_1980_Final_Nomination.pdf, accessed on 4 April 2014; and http://www.arlingtonva.us/departments/CPHD/ons/hp/file77259.pdf, accessed on 6 April 2014. On Rudy using FHA financing, see Fred Weitz, interviews, 20 March 2013, 20 March 2014.

43. See *Weitz Surveyor* 1 (May 1950), 4 and 1 (August 1950), 4.

44. Ibid. See also Weitz, "Weitz," 93; Charles Godfrey Jr., telephone conversation with author, 12 November 2013; and Fred Weitz, interview, 20 March 2013.

45. Edward Ayers et al., *American Passages: A History of the United States* (Fort Worth, TX: Harcourt Brace, 2000), 932; Jenny Barker Devine, "Loyal and Forever True: Student Life at Iowa State University," in Dorothy Schwieder and Gretchen Van Houten, eds., *Tradition and Transformation: A Sesquicentennial History of Iowa State University* (Ames: Iowa State University Press, 2007), 160; and Cohen, *Consumers' Republic*, 139–40.

46. Stephanie Porter, Grinnell College Special Collections, correspondence with author, 7 April 2014; Nollen, *Grinnell College*, 211, 216–17; and Weitz, "Weitz," 92.

47. *Weitz Surveyor* 7 (May 1958), 1; 7 (November 1958), 2. For more on the library and quote about it being built on a nonprofit basis, see Henry Alden, "Grinnell College's Burling Library," 460, http:// www.ideals.illinois.edu/bitstream/handle/2142/37371/crl_22_06_457_opt.pdf?sequence=2, accessed on 13 April 2014.

48. *Weitz Surveyor* 1 (August 1950), 1–2; 2 (May 1951), 1–2; 3 (July 1952); 1; Stow Persons, *The University of Iowa in The Twentieth Century: An Institutional History* (Iowa City: University of Iowa Press, 1990), 159–164; and Weitz Production

Record Book. For more on Drake's buildings, see http://buildingamoderncampus. com/dorms.html and http://buildingmoderncampus.com/hubbell.html, both accessed on 15 April 2014.

49. *Council Bluffs* (Iowa) *Nonpareil*, 7 April 1949; *Weitz Surveyor* 1 (October 1950), 1; 1 (December 1950), 1; 3 (July 1952), 2; 3 (December 1952), 1–2; 4 (August 1955), 1; and 5 (February 1956), 2.

50. For more on firms' moving to professional management, see works of Alfred Chandler Jr., *Strategy and Structure: Chapters in the History of the American Industrial Enterprise* (Cambridge, MA: MIT Press, 1962); and *The Visible Hand: The Managerial Revolution in American Business* (Cambridge, MA: Belknap Press, 1977).

51. "The Weitz Company, Inc." *Architecture and Design* 8 (March 1949), n.p.; and "Look to Weitz For the Latest."

52. Ibid. For a general background on tilt-up construction, see Richard Crompton, "Tilt-up Construction," (master's thesis, University of Florida, 1992), on the Internet Archive, https://archive.org/stream/tiltupconstructi00crom/tiltupconstructi00crom_djvu.txt, accessed on 29 April 2014.

53. On Luthe Hardware and the Merchant Transfer warehouse, see "The Weitz Company, Inc." *Architecture and Design* 8 (March 1949), n.p.; and "Look to Weitz For the Latest."

54. "Look to Weitz for the Latest"; see also "Many Iowa Industries 'Housed' by Weitz," *Iowa Business and Industry*, October 1951, 6; and "The Weitz Company, Inc."

55. *Des Moines Register*, 22 January 1946, 24 July 1949; Weitz Production Record Book; "Look to Weitz for the Latest"; and *Cityview*, 21 June 2012.

56. *Weitz Surveyor* 1 (October 1950), 4; 2 (March 1951), 2; 3 (December 1952), 1, 4; "The Weitz Company, Inc."; and Weitz Production Record Book.

57. *Des Moines Register*, 13 May 1992; *Weitz Surveyor* 2 (March 1951), 1; and Weitz Production Record Book.

58. Ibid. Various contractor websites explain the distinctions between tilt-up and precast concrete, see, for example, http://ajwengineering.com/construction-engineers/concrete-construction/tilt-up-concrete-works/, accessed on 29 April 2014.

59. See *Business Record*, 10 May 2013; http://www.dmtechhs.com/dmths.htm, accessed on 23 April 2014; *Des Moines Register*, 7, 14, 15 October 1951; 13 May 1992; *Iowa City Press-Citizen*, 13 September, 13 October 1951; *Mount Pleasant* (Iowa) *News*, 2 April 1952; *Esterville* (Iowa) *Daily News*, 6 May 1952; *Weitz Surveyor* 5 (November 1956), 1; 2 (March 1951), 1; 6 (May 1957), 1; and 7 (May 1958), 2. The Solar plant in Des Moines was closed in 1959; today the building is home to CDS Global Co., a magazine fulfillment company.

60. *Iowa City Press-Citizen*, 3 November 1951; and *Carroll* (Iowa) *Daily Times Herald*, 1 December 1951.

61. *Des Moines Register*, 13 June 1971; 7 January 1973; *Weitz Surveyor* 3 (September 1952), 2; 3 (December 1952), 2; 5 (September 1956), 1; and Weitz Production Record Book.

62. On appointment, see *Mount Pleasant News*, 3 December 1953.

63. For quotation, see *Des Moines Tribune*, 7 April 1955. More on Rudy's appointment is from Fred Weitz, correspondence with author, 24 April 2014.

64. See Edwin Weitz, telephone conversation; Bob Weitz, telephone conversation with author, 24 April 2014; Steve Weitz, interview; and Fred Weitz, interviews, 18 April 2013; 20 March 2014.

65. Steve Weitz, interview; Fred Weitz, interviews, 18 April 2013; 20 March 2014.

Chapter 7

1. On oldest business, see *Des Moines Register*, 11 December 1955. On celebration, see the invitation to Weitz Company 100th Anniversary Dinner, 3 December 1954, in Weitz 1950s scrapbook, Weitz Company Papers, private collection held by the Weitz Company, Des Moines, Iowa [hereafter cited as Weitz Company Papers].

2. Example of advertisement taken from Weitz Company ad featuring Cherry-Burrell Corporation, *Des Moines Register*, 31 July 1955. For other company advertisements that ran during the 1955 anniversary year from such publications as the *Des Moines Register*, *Wallace Farmer*, *Iowan* magazine, and *Iowa Business and Industry*, see Weitz 1950s scrapbook, Weitz Company Papers.

3. For first quote, see *Weitz Surveyor* 4 (August 1955), 1. For Fred Weitz quote, see *Des Moines Tribune*, 1 December 1980.

4. See "The Men Who Run Weitz Company," *Mid-West Contractor*, 20 January 1960, 54.

5. Quotation from Sarah Stevenson Weitz, "Family History," unpublished manuscript edited by Stevenson Weitz, 2008, 39, Fred Weitz Papers, private collection held by Fred Weitz, West Des Moines, Iowa [hereafter cited as Fred Weitz Papers]. See also *Des Moines Tribune*, 7 April 1955.

6. For "odds and ends" quote and information on Heinrich, see Fred Weitz, interview by author, Des Moines, Iowa, 11 November 2013.

7. For Des Moines and suburban population growth, see http://www.statelibraryofiowa.org/datacenter/archive/2011/02/citypop.pdf, accessed on 27 May 2014. From 1950 to 1960, Ankeny grew from 1,229 to 2,964; West Des Moines, from 5,615 to 11,949; Urbandale, from 1,777 to 5,821; and Windsor Heights, from 1,414 to 4,715.

8. See *100 Years and Counting: EMC Insurance Companies* (Cedar Rapids, IA: WDG Publishing and Employers Mutual Casualty Co., 2011), 100–101, 180–83; Traci Larsen, correspondence with author, 5 March 2014; *Weitz Surveyor* 4 (August 1955), 2; 4 (October 1955), 3; and *Building*, a later Weitz in-house publication, 29 August 1969, 4.

9. *Weitz Surveyor* 4 (August 1955), 2; 5 (September 1956), 1; 6 (November 1957), 1; 7 (November 1958), 1, 4; and Weitz Company completed projects notebook, 1956–1962, Weitz Company Papers; and *Des Moines Register*, 4 December 1965.

10. See *Weitz Surveyor* 4 (December 1955), 1; 7 (February 1958), 2, 3; 7 (May 1958), 3; 7 (August 1958), 3; *Des Moines Tribune*, 5 September 1957; *Des Moines Register*, 7 February 1957, 18 February 1958; US Army Corps of Engineers, Rock Island District web page, http://www.mvr.usace.army.mil/Missions/Recreation/Coralville Lake/AboutUs.aspx, accessed on 30 May 2014; *Burlington* (Iowa) *Hawk-Eye Gazette*, 20 September 1959.

11. On Eisenhower's New Look policy and its context within the Cold War, see John Lewis Gaddis, *Strategies for Containment: A Critical Appraisal of American National Security Policy during the Cold War*, rev. ed. (Oxford and New York: Oxford University Press, 2005), 125–196.

12. *Weitz Surveyor* 5 (February 1956), 1; 6 (February 1957), 1; 6 (August 1957), 1; 7 (August 1958), 1; and Weitz Company completed projects notebook, 1956–1962, Weitz Company Papers.

13. "Men Who Run Weitz Company," 21.

14. *Carroll Daily Times Herald*, 27 October 1954; Midwest Concrete Industries pamphlet, n.d., Weitz Company Papers; Rudy Weitz Journal, 6, 8, 9 February 1956, Fred Weitz Papers; and Fred Weitz, interviews, 18 April, 11 November 2013.

15. Emily Weitz, interview by author, West Des Moines, Iowa, 20 March 2014; Fred Weitz, interview, 20 March 2014; Sarah Weitz, "Family History," 39.

16. Rudy Weitz Journal, 27 June 1956; 15 April 1957; Fred Weitz, interview, 20 March 2013; and Fred Weitz, correspondence with author, 17 June 2014.

17. Ibid.

18. See Rudy Weitz Journal, 9, 11, 16, January, 10 May 1956; 29 April, 14, 17 May, 24 July 1957. For quotation, see journal entry on 19 January 1962. See also "Articles of Incorporation of Carson Construction Company," 22 May 1957; and "Minutes of Special Meeting of Board of Directors of Carson Construction Company," 28 September 1962, all in Fred Weitz Papers; Ann Weitz, "Weitz," 94; Fred Weitz, interview, 11 November 2013; and Edwin Weitz, telephone conversation with author, 5 December 2013; and *Weitz Surveyor* 5 (February 1956), 4.

19. Robert Weitz, telephone conversation with author, 24 April 2014; and Stevenson Weitz, interview by author, West Des Moines, Iowa, 27 March 2014.

20. Stevenson Weitz, interview.

21. Ibid.

22. Fred Weitz, interview, 20 March 2013; Stevenson Weitz, interview.

23. For first quotation, see Rudy Weitz Journal, 9 February 1956; on purchase, see Rudy Weitz Journal, 28 March 1956; and for second quotation, see Rudy Weitz Journal, 8 May 1956.

24. For quote, see Fred Weitz, interview, 11 November 2013. See also Rudy Weitz Journal, 7 July 1956.

25. Rudy Weitz Journal, 2, 4, 5 December 1956; 11, 15 January, 31 July, 27 August 1957; *Des Moines Register*, 27 November, 6 December 1956; *Des Moines Tribune*, 7 December 1956; and *Weitz Surveyor* 6 (February 1957), 4; 6 (August 1957), 1.

26. Fred Weitz, interview, 11 November 2013; Rudy Weitz Journal, 10 January, 25 February, 23 April, 24 June 1957; *Mason City Globe Gazette*, 28 June 1957; and Weitz Company completed projects notebook, 1956–1962, Weitz Company Papers.

27. Rudy Weitz Journal, 29 October 1957; 24, 27 February, 28 June, 19 December 1958; 10 January, 12 February, 21, 25 May 1959.

28. Rudy Weitz Journal, 11, 22 January, 9, 11 March, 6, 15 May, 21 June, 29 September, 18, 24 October, 1960.

29. Rudy Weitz Journal, 6, 9 October 1958; and *The Register-News* (Mount Vernon, Illinois) 4 October 1956.

30. See Rudy Weitz Journal, 13, 17 October, 5, 14, 17, 18 November, 8, 19, 30 December 1958; 7 January 1959.

31. *Kansas City Star*, 13 December 1959.

32. Rudy Weitz Journal, 4 January, 11, 12, 16, 18 February, 14, 18, 21, 23, 24, 27 May, 2, 14 June, 13 July 1960.

33. Rudy Weitz Journal, 11, 12 April, 3, 18, 21, 23, 27 May, 2, 5, 7 June, 17, 19 August, 5 September, 14 October 1960; and Bill Bontrager, interview by author, Cumming, Iowa, 6 May 2014.

34. See US Department of State, Office of Historian web page, https://history.state.gov/milestones/1961-1968/pl-480, accessed on 26 June 2014.

35. William J. Burns, *Economic Aid and American Foreign Policy Toward Egypt, 1955-1981* (Albany: State University of New York Press, 1985), 119.

36. *Kansas City Star*, 16 February 1962; 19 May 1963; Bill Bontrager, interview; and Fred Weitz, interviews, 18 April, 11 November 2013.

37. Fred Weitz, interviews, 18 April, 11 November 2013; 20 March 2014. For discussion of Fred's possible move to Kansas City and Downing quotations, see Rudy Weitz Journal, 28 April, 1 June 1961.

38. On Fred being "fed up," see Fred Weitz, interview, 18 April 2013; on Leonard Howell retiring, see Rudy Weitz Journal, 1 December 1961; and for last two quotes, see Rudy Weitz Journal, 8 September 1961; and 8 February 1962.

39. For Rudy's quote, see Rudy Weitz Journal, 25 January 1962; on alternatives and Fred's duties and new job, see Rudy Weitz Journal, 20 February, 15, 21 March 1962. See also Fred Weitz, interview, 18 April 2013; 20 March 2014.

40. Weitz Company completed projects notebook, 1963–1971.

41. Ibid. See also *Building* (February 1973), 4 (in-house newsletter published by the Weitz Company), Weitz Company Papers; and *Des Moines Register*, 26 September 1971; 17 September 1972; 18 February 2001; 8 May 2005.

42. Rudy Weitz Journal, 5, 11, 16 July, 3 August 1966; "Minutes of Special Meeting of the Board of Directors of the Weitz Company," 14 January 1972, Weitz Company Papers; Fred Weitz, interview, 29 September 2014; and Donald Brown, interview by author, West Des Moines, Iowa, 13 May 2014.

43. On the history of CCRCs, see Howard E. Winklevoss and Alwyn V. Powell, *Continuing Care Retirement Communities: An Empirical, Financial, and Legal Analysis* (Homewood, IL: Richard D. Irwin Inc.), 6–11; and Ronald J. Angel and Jacqueline L. Angel, *Who Will Care for Us? Aging and Long-Term Care in Multicultural America* (New York and London: New York University Press), 118–19.

44. Sara Barker, "Kenneth Berg's Plan for Self-Financing by the Elderly," *Star Magazine, Kansas City Star*, 1 June 1975, 6–10; and Rudy Weitz Journal, 16 April 1962.

45. See Larry Laird, telephone conversation with author, 1 August 2014; Barker, "Kenneth Berg's Plan," 7; Kenneth P. Berg, *Affordable Retirement Living* (Lee's Summit, MO: Senior Power Press, 1975), 87–94; and Rudy Weitz Journal, 16, 25 April 1962.

46. Fred Weitz, "Speech at Life Care Services 40th Anniversary, 2011," transcript in possession of author; and Fred Weitz, interview, 20 March 2013; and Rudy Weitz Journal, 16, 25 April 1962.

47. Ibid. See also Rudy Weitz Journal, 14, 18 June, 28 November, 6 December 1962; 6 April, 7 July, 7 October 1963; 2 August 1965; and 11 December 1967.

48. Rudy Weitz Journal, 28 May, 1 June, 14 July 1964; 12 December 1966; Weitz Company completed projects notebook, 1963–1971, Weitz Company Papers; and "Life Care Services Project History," Fred Weitz Papers. On Hart, see *Des Moines Register*, 13 June 1965; and Fred Weitz, interview, 15 May 2014.

49. Ibid. See also Weitz, "Speech at Life Care Services," and Berg, *Affordable Retirement*, 103–118.

50. For general background, see Jean-Jacques Dethier and Kathy Funk, "The Language of Food PL 480 in Egypt," on Middle East Research and Information Project web page, http://www.merip.org/mer/mer145/language-food, accessed on 7 July 2014. For cancellation of project, see *New York Times*, 1 April 1966.

51. Visit from CIA officer is recounted in Rudy Weitz Journal, 27 September 1965.

52. Rudy Weitz Journal, 7 June 1966; Fred Weitz, interviews, 18 April, 11 November 2013; Bill Bontrager, interview; Barnard and Burk and Weitz-Hettelsater, "Proposal for Design and Construction of Proposed Grain Elevator, Co-operative Group, New Orleans," 25 March 1966, Weitz Company Papers; and Ann Weitz, notes, chapter 12, Weitz warehouse collection, box 0714-01, Weitz Company Papers.

53. See Ann Weitz, notes, chapter 12; and Rudy Weitz Journal, 29, 30 July, 15, 28 October 1968; 29 March, 30 April, 8, 13, 22, 26 29, May, 12, 18 June, 3, 8, 11 July 1969.

54. *Des Moines Register*, 27 May 1974.

55. See Rudy Weitz Journals, 1970–71.

56. Fred Weitz, interview, 15 May 2014; Bill Bontrager, interview.

57. Black & Veatch International, "Final Report for Guyana Rice Modernization Project, Guyana Rice Board, Georgetown Guyana," USAID loan no. 504-L-008, from website, http://pdf.usaid.gov/pdf_docs/pdkaf207.pdf, accessed on 7 July 2014; and Rudy Weitz Journal, 5 April 1968; 28 September 1972; and purchase agreement 17 November 1972 between the Weitz Company and Weitz-Hettelsater Corporation, Weitz Company Papers.

58. Rudy Weitz Journal, 5 July, 23 September, 27 October, 12 December 1966.

59. Julia Gentleman, telephone conversation with author, 6 June 2014; Fred Weitz, interview, 11 November 2013; Rudy Weitz Journal, 16 October, 18 November 1971; "MCI: Midwest Concrete Industries" brochure.

60. For Fred's thinking about expanding the company's interest in the retirement home business and quote, see *Des Moines Register*, 7 December 1987. See also Fred Weitz, interviews, 20 March 2013; 20 March 2014; and Weitz, "Speech at Life Care Services."

61. Fred Weitz, interview, 30 January 2015; Larry Laird, telephone conversation; and Weitz, "Speech at Life Care Services."

62. Weitz, "Speech at Life Care Services;" Ann Weitz, notes, chapter 12; "Life Care Services Project History."

63. Ibid. See also Fred Weitz, correspondence with author, 8 July 2014. For sale of Wakonda Village and University Terrace, see Rudy Weitz Journal, 29 November 1961; and 20 January 1964.

64. Fred Weitz, correspondence with author, 10 July 2014; and Stevenson Weitz, interview. Quotation from Stevenson Weitz, correspondence with author, 9 July 2014.

65. *Building* (February 1973), 1–2. See also Rudy Weitz Journal, 12 January 1973; and *Des Moines Register*, 27 May 1974.

66. For editorial, see *Des Moines Tribune*, 29 May 1974.

Chapter 8

1. Fred's reference to the company as opportunist from *Business Record*, 29 April 1985. On Cohen purchase increasing business by more than half, see *The Denver Post*, 30 July 1986.

2. Quotation from Fred Weitz, correspondence with author, 9 February 2015. On stock purchase plan and purpose, see Fred Weitz to members of the board of directors of the Weitz Corporation, 29 July 1983, Weitz Corporation Minute Book, 1983–1991, LCS Papers, private collection held by LCS Companies, Des Moines, Iowa [hereafter cited as LCS Papers].

3. For Fred's first quotation on his father, see Gregory Goaley, "Frederick W. Weitz II: The Weitz Corporation," *Des Moines Area Business Magazine*, March 1989, 18. For Jack Hall's impression of Rudy and Fred's second quotation, see Jack Hall,

telephone conversation, 30 July 2014. See also Glenn DeStigter, interviews with author, Des Moines, Iowa, 12 March 2013; 30 July 2014; and Jerry Gosselink, telephone conversation, 4 September 2014.

4. Quotations from *Des Moines Tribune*, 1 December 1980.

5. Ibid. On Fred's wry sense of humor, see David Strutt, interview by author, Des Moines, Iowa, 15 August 2014.

6. Webb quote from *Des Moines Tribune*, 1 December 1980. On Fred's Clint Eastwood stare, see Goaley, "Frederick W. Weitz," 18.

7. Fred's description of himself from *Des Moines Tribune*, 1 December 1980.

8. Minutes of Organizational Meeting of Weitz Brothers Inc., 21 March 1975, Fred Weitz Papers, private collection held by Fred Weitz, West Des Moines, Iowa [hereafter cited as Fred Weitz Papers]. Steve Weitz began attending Weitz Company board meetings on a more regular basis in 1973 and became a board member in 1974, see Weitz Company Inc., book 3, Weitz Company Papers, private collection held by the Weitz Company, Des Moines, Iowa [hereafter cited as Weitz Company Papers].

9. For Swab resignation and Urban and Mazie joining board, see Minutes of Board of Directors Meeting of Weitz Brothers Inc., 20 November 1976, Fred Weitz Papers. Heinrich Weitz died on 28 August 1981 and was not replaced on the board until Fred Hubbell was invited to join in 1987, see meeting minutes, 14 November 1981; and Marilyn Wilson to Roscoe Paulson, 23 December 1987, both in Fred Weitz Papers.

10. On renaming the corporation, see Articles of Amendment to the Articles of Incorporation of Weitz Brothers Inc., 11 March 1983, Fred Weitz Papers. Fred's first quotation from Minutes of Meeting of Board of Directors of Weitz Company Inc., 2 November 1974; Fred's second quotation about 1975 from *Building*, an in-house Weitz publication, January 1976, 1, both from Weitz Company Papers. On Hart resigning, see special meeting minutes, Weitz Company, 12 June 1972, Weitz Company Papers. For creation of Vulcan, see Jack Hall, telephone conversation; Glenn DeStigter, interviews with author, Des Moines, Iowa, 12 March 2013; and 30 July 2014; Fred Weitz, interview by author, Des Moines, Iowa, 11 November 2013; and meeting minutes, Weitz Company, 2 November 1974, Weitz Company Papers.

11. For Hall quote, see Hall, telephone conversation; and on Vulcan projects, see *Building*, January 1976, 3; and *The Builder*, January 1979, 6–7; this was another Weitz publication, Weitz Company Papers. See also Glenn DeStigter, interviews with author, Des Moines, Iowa, 12 March 2013; 30 July 2014.

12. On Oggero being named marketing director, see Minutes of Meeting of Board of Directors of Weitz Company, 2 August 1975, Weitz Company Papers; *Des Moines Register*, 7 September 1975; and *Building*, January 1976, 2. For more on Oggero, see Hall, telephone conversation; and David Strutt, interview. On creation of *The Builder*, see *Building*, January 1976, 1.

13. *The Builder* (June 1976), 4; (January 1979), 2–3.

14. For Bill Knapp quote and the downtown turnaround, see William Friedricks, *The Real Deal: The Life of Bill Knapp* (Des Moines, IA: Business Publications Corporation, 2013), 104–5. For more on downtown's revival, see William Friedricks, *In for the Long Haul: The Life and Times of John Ruan* (Ames, IA: Iowa State Press, 2003), 132–33; Orin Dahl, *Des Moines: Capital City* (Tulsa, OK: Continental Heritage, 1978), 182–83; and Robert Houser, "Some Significant Dates in History of Des Moines," Robert Houser Papers, private collection held by author, West Des Moines, Iowa [hereafter cited as Houser Papers].

15. On details of building the Ruan Center, see Friedricks, *In for the Long Haul*, 118–23, 146–47.

16. Ibid. For putting up IBM Building, see *Des Moines Register*, 11 June 1972. On new Weitz office space, see *Des Moines Tribune*, 8 September 1975; Minutes of Meeting of Board of Directors, Weitz Company, 2 November 1974; 8 February, 2 August, 1 November 1975, Weitz Company Papers; Minutes of Meeting of Board of Directors, Weitz Corporation, 21 November 1987, Life Care Services Papers; and Fred Weitz, interview, 29 September 2014.

17. Friedricks, *In for the Long Haul*, 132–33; William Friedricks, *Covering Iowa: The History of the Des Moines Register and Tribune Company, 1849-1985* (Ames: Iowa State University Press, 2000), 193–94; and *Des Moines Register*, 11 November 1975.

18. On Fred's various board positions, see, for example, *Des Moines Register*, 1 April, 20 December 1970; 10 January 1971; 8 December 1972; 2 February 1975; for Valley Bank service, see *Des Moines Register*, 1 April 1970. For Rudy's comment about Grinnell, see Rudy Weitz Journal, 13 May 1969, Fred Weitz Papers.

19. On Rudy and Fred being the third father-son team to serve as president of the chamber, see David Elbert, *Celebrating 125 Years: Standing on the Shoulders of Giants* (Des Moines, IA: Business Publications Corporation, 2013), 177. The other father-son duos to serve as president of the chamber included the Kaufmanns and the Hubbells. B. F. Kaufmann was president of its forerunner, the Commercial Exchange, in 1890, and B. F. Kaufmann Jr. served as president in 1917; James W. Hubbell was president in 1934 and his son, James W. Hubbell Jr., was president in 1972. For quotations and Fred's time as president, see *Des Moines Tribune*, 1 December 1980.

20. Des Moines Development Corporation mission statement and typescript history, Houser Papers; *Des Moines Tribune*, 9 March 1982: and *Des Moines Register*, 1 September 1985.

21. Friedricks, *In for the Long Haul*, 148–49; and *Des Moines Register*, 25 March, 2 June, 27 July 1981.

22. See Friedricks, *Real Deal*, 114–15. Fred's quote about doing the project at cost from *Des Moines Register*, 10 September 1981.

23. For construction volume, see Minutes of Special Meeting of Board of Directors of Weitz Company, 27 October 1973, Weitz Company Papers.

24. Larry Laird, telephone conversation with author, 1 August 1914; Fred Weitz, interview, 20 March 2013; Kenneth Berg, *Senior Power: New Life for You* (Lee's Summit,

MO: Senior Power Publishing, 1976), vii–viii; and Minutes of Special Meeting of Board of Directors, Weitz Company, 27 October 1973; 1 November 1975, Weitz Company Papers.

25. Minutes of Special Meeting of Board of Directors of Weitz Brothers Inc., 8 May 1976; meeting minutes, Weitz Brothers Inc., 7 August 1976; and synopsis of Berg deal, all in Fred Weitz Papers.

26. Berg died in a car accident in 2007. For more on the accident and Berg's legal problems, see *Kansas City Star*, 13 March 1983; 14 June 2007; and "Hearing before the Special Committee on Aging," United States Senate, Ninety-Eighth Congress, First Session, Washington, DC, 25 May 1983, 47, 49–52, 62–64, 87–91, 154–168, http://www.aging.senate.gov/imo/media/doc/publications/5251983.pdf, accessed on 20 January 2015.

27. For trademarking term "life-care," see LCS symposium booklet, 1993; on concept and first quotation, see "Life Care Services Corporation" brochure, n.d.; and for second quotation and more on life-care concept, see "Retirement: The Life-Care Concept, An Overview," n.d., all in Fred Weitz Papers.

28. Larry Laird, telephone conversation, 1 August 2014; Fred Weitz, interview, 29 September 2014; and Fred Weitz, "Speech at Life Care Service 40th Anniversary, 2011," transcript in possession of author.

29. For LCS projects, see "Life Care Services Project History," Fred Weitz Papers. On hiring Stan Thurston, see Weitz, "Speech at Life Care Services"; and *Des Moines Register*, 16 March 1987.

30. Weitz, "Speech at Life Care Services"; and Fred Weitz, interview, 20 March 2013.

31. Ibid. See also Jerry Gosselink, telephone conversation with author, 4 September 2014; and Peter Taggart, interview by author, West Des Moines, Iowa, 8 September 2014.

32. Weitz, "Speech at Life Care Services"; and clipping of article, L. Call Dickinson Jr., "Turning 25 and Going Strong," *LCRC Seasons* (Spring 2001), Fred Weitz Papers.

33. Ibid.; and Fred Weitz, interview, 20 March 2014.

34. For Fred's recollection, see *Des Moines Register*, 7 December 1987; and for more on Gully incident, see *Daily Herald* (Chicago, Illinois) 1, 13 December 1977.

35. Larry Laird, telephone conversation, 1 August 2014; and Minutes of Meeting of Board of Directors of Weitz Brothers Inc., 13 August 1977; 11 November 1978, Fred Weitz Papers.

36. Weitz, "Speech at Life Care Services"; Larry Laird, telephone conversation, 1 August 2014; and correspondence with author, 1 August 2014.

37. For Fred's quotation and more on moving into Sunbelt, see *Des Moines Register*, 17 February 1985. On establishing the branch offices, see Jack Hall, telephone conversation; Jerry Gosselink, telephone conversation; Peter Taggart, interview; meeting minutes, Weitz Brothers Inc., 14 November 1981, Fred Weitz Papers; and *Business Record*, 29 April 1985.

38. Fred's idea of acting like a local contractor is from *Des Moines Register*, 17 February 1985. That the Tempe office developed a good reputation and that business was slower at Palm Beach office is from *Business Record*, 29 April 1985. For projects, see *The Builder* (January 1982), 4, 8.

39. For powerhouse quote, see *Des Moines Register*, 8 May 2005. Employee numbers from *Des Moines Tribune*, 1 December 1980.

40. For piece of the action quote and more of stock purchase plan, see Fred Weitz to members of the board of directors of the Weitz Corporation, 29 July 1983, Life Care Services Papers. See also Fred Weitz, interview, 29 September 2014.

41. See Weitz Company Inc. Stockholder Buy-Sell Agreement, 1 April 1977 by and between Weitz Brothers Inc. and Jack Hall, Michael Carlstrom, Glenn DeStigter, Jerry Gosselink, Richard Oggero, and B. Roscoe Paulson; Life Care Services Corporation Stockholder Buy-Sell Agreement, 1 November 1977 by and between Weitz Brothers Inc. and Larry Laird; for Bontrager being offered stock, see minutes of informal meeting of board of directors of Weitz Brothers Inc.; 1 November 1977; and Life Care Services Corporation Stockholder Buy-Sell Agreement, 1 April 1979 by and between Weitz Brothers Inc. and Phil Roberts, Stan Thurston, and H. B. Kedney, all in Fred Weitz Papers.

42. See Fred Weitz, interview, 20 March 2014; and Emily Weitz, interview by author, West Des Moines, Iowa, 20 March 2014.

43. See Fred Weitz, interview, 29 September 2014; and *Des Moines Register*, 17 February 1985; 28 March 1993.

44. Economic numbers are from Friedricks, *Real Deal*, 150. Fred quote from *Des Moines Register*, 17 February 1985; and Weitz business volume and rankings from *Des Moines Register*, 17 February 1985; and *Engineering News-Record*, 22 April 1982, 91.

45. Peter Taggart, interview; and Minutes of Board of Directors Meeting of Weitz Brothers Inc., 23 May, 14 November 1981; 11 June 1982.

46. *Des Moines Register*, 24 April 1983. *The Builder* (June 1981), 2–4.

47. On Hub Tower and Kaleidoscope Mall, see *Des Moines Register*, 1 September 1985. On Drake neighborhood development, see Friedricks, *Real Deal*, 160–162; and Barbara Beving Long, *Des Moines and Polk County: Flag on the Prairie* (Northridge, CA: Windsor Publications, 1988), 119; and Glenn DeStigter, correspondence with author, 4 October, 2014.

48. *Business Record*, 17 December 1984.

49. For background of track, see *Des Moines Register*, 21 December 1986, 26 February 1989; and *Des Moines Skywalker*, 22–28 February 1989. For more on Wilkey devoting time to track project, see Fred Weitz, interview, 6 December 2011.

50. On the appearance of a conflict of interest and Fred quote, see *Business Record*, August 6–12, 1990.

51. For contract and quote from Clarke and comment about Crowley, see *Des Moines Register*, 6 March 1987.

52. Larry Laird, telephone conversation, 1 August 2014; *Des Moines Register*, 16 March 1987; Minutes of Meeting of Board of Directors of the Weitz Corporation, 21 February 1987, LCS Papers.

53. For facilities built and dates, see "Life Care Services Project History," Fred Weitz Papers; for operations becoming more important than development, see Larry Laird, telephone conversations, 1, 5 August 2014.

54. On Boston office, see David Strutt, interview; Glenn DeStigter, interview, 30 July 2014; Fred Weitz, interview, 20 March, 11 November 2013; and Chuck Floyd, telephone conversation with author, 16 October 2014. For more on Boston and Fred's quotes, see *Business Record*, 6–12 August 1990; and for getting contracts in Portsmouth, see http://www.answers.com/topic/the-weitz-company-inc.

55. Stan Thurston, interview by author, Des Moines, Iowa, 6 October 2014; Ed Kenny, interview by author, Des Moines, Iowa, 24 November 2014; and Fred Weitz, interview, 30 January 2015.

56. Ibid.; see also Fred Weitz, interview, 29 September 2014; Fred Weitz, telephone conversation with author, 5 February 2015; Ed Kenny, correspondence with author, 3 February 2015; Stan Thurston, telephone conversation with author, 9 February 2015; David Strutt, interview; and "Life Care Services Project History," Fred Weitz Papers.

57. Fred Weitz, interview, 29 September 2014; David Strutt, interview; Glenn DeStigter, interview, 30 July 2014; and *Des Moines Register*, 25 August 1986.

58. Fred Weitz, interview, 29 March 2014; David Strutt, interview. For quotation, see *Des Moines Register*, 25 August 1986. On purchase, see also *Denver Post*, 11 August 1986; and *Des Moines Register*, 20 August 1986. For *Engineering News-Record* ranking, see *Des Moines Register*, 30, 18 May 1987; and for story about *Die Hard* film and building, see *Des Moines Register*, 29 July 1988.

59. David Strutt, interview; Fred Weitz, interview, 29 September 2014; and Glenn DeStigter, interview, 12 March 2013.

60. Fred's quotations from Goaley, "Frederick W. Weitz II," 18. On ESOP, see Strutt, interview; Fred Weitz, interview, 29 September 2014.

61. Quotation from *Des Moines Register*, 1 September 1985. See also Fred Weitz, correspondence with author, 9 February 2015.

62. For Wilkey leaving Weitz and quotations, see *Des Moines Register*, 16 January 1990.

63. Quotation and more on Wilkey resigning is from Fred Weitz, interview, 29 September 2014; see also Glenn DeStigter, interview, 30 July 2014; Stan Thurston, interview; David Strutt, interview; Peter Taggart, interview; and Jerry Gosselink, telephone conversation.

64. *Des Moines Register*, 14 January 1990. For previous "Powers That Be" rankings, see *Des Moines Register*, 3, 10, 17 October 1976.

65. *Des Moines Register*, 14 January 1990.

66. *Business Record*, 6–12 August 1990.

67. See *Des Moines Register*, 28 March 1993; Fred Weitz, interview, 29 September 2014; Glenn DeStigter, interview, 30 July 2014; and David Strutt, interview.

68. *Des Moines Register*, 28 March 1993.

Epilogue

1. Fred Weitz's first quotation from *Des Moines Register*, 28 March 1993; second quotation, *Des Moines Register*, 8 May 2005; Weitz Company revenue figures from and on LCS, see *Des Moines Register*, 17 August 2004.

2. *Des Moines Register*, 15 June 1991; 29 August 1999; 18 February 2001; and "Life Care Services Corporation: History of an Industrial Leader," fall 1993, LCS file, Fred Weitz Papers, private collection held by Fred Weitz, Des Moines, Iowa.

3. Robert Bachman, telephone conversation with author, 30 October 2014; and Fred Weitz, interview by author, Des Moines, Iowa, 29 September 2014.

4. Ibid. See also Weitz Corporation, Board of Directors Meeting Minutes, 5 March 1994, Life Care Services Papers, private collection held by Life Care Services, Des Moines, Iowa [hereafter cited as LCS Papers]; and David Strutt, interview by author, Des Moines, Iowa, 15 August 2014.

5. James Brandl, telephone conversation with author, 31 October 2014. For more on the split-off of the information technology group, see "Information Booklet for the Weitz Corporation Split-Off and Plans of Reorganization," 5, Weitz Company Papers, private collection held by the Weitz Company, Des Moines, Iowa [hereafter cited as the Weitz Company Papers]; *Des Moines Register*, 5 June 2000; Fred Weitz, interview, 29 September 2014; and David Strutt, interview.

6. James Brandl, telephone conversation.

7. Ibid.

8. Ibid. See also Steve Sikkink, telephone conversation with author, 20 February 2015; Weitz Corporation, Board of Directors Meeting Minutes, 5 March 1994, LCS Papers; and *Des Moines Register*, 29 October 2011.

9. See Alliance Technologies website, https://www.alliancetechnologies.net/company/history, accessed on 23 December 2014.

10. See Dave Strutt, correspondence with author, 9, 19 February 2015; Dave Strutt, interview; Weitz Corporation, Board of Directors Meeting Minutes, 28 January 1995, LCS Papers; Fred Weitz, interview, 29 September 2014; Fred Weitz, correspondence with author, 8, 9 December 2014; Stan Thurston, interview by author, Des Moines, Iowa, 6 October 2014; "Information Booklet for Weitz Corporation Split-Off," 2, 5–6, 9–10, 19–23, Weitz Company Papers; and Lisa Grieve, telephone conversation with author, 23 February 2015.

11. Fred Weitz, interview, 29 September 2014; Jerry Gosselink, telephone conversation with author, 4 September 2014; and Stan Thurston, interview.

12. David Strutt, interview. See also Tom Urban, interview by author, Des Moines, Iowa, 11 September 2014; and Fred Weitz, interviews, 29 September 2014; 13 February 2015.

13. For Hy-Vee partnership and quotation, see *Des Moines Register*, 27 September 1995; and 31 January 2000. For more on partnership and its dissolution, see http://www. hy-vee.com/company/press-room/press-releases/hy-vee-acquires-total-stake-hy-vee-weitz-construction.aspx, and http://www.weitz.com/project/hy-vee/, both accessed on 2 December 2014.

14. *Des Moines Register*, 15 November 1993; 22 November 2003; 9 January 2004; and 8 May 2005.

15. David Strutt, telephone conversation with author, 17 February 2015; and "Weitz Senior Living," brochure, n.d., Weitz Company Papers.

16. *Des Moines Register*, 12 December 1998; and 8 February 2001; "Weitz Golf," brochure, n.d., Weitz Company Papers; and Weitz web page, http://www.weitz. com/project_category/commercial/golf/, accessed on 4 December 2014.

17. *Des Moines Register*, 8 February 2001; 5 April 2006; and *Business Record*, 4 December 2010. See also Weitz web page, http://www.weitz.com/about/affiliates/ watts-constructors, accessed on 26 December 2014; "Weitz Summary Annual Report, 2001," 7, Weitz Company Papers; and Glenn DeStigter, interview by author, Des Moines, Iowa, 5 December 2014.

18. "The Weitz Company: The Vision to Build 150 Years," 20–21, Weitz Company Papers; Weitz web page, http://www.weitz.com/project_category/commercial/, accessed on 27 December 2014.

19. Tricia McClain, correspondence with author, 1 December 2014; Joan Hinners, correspondence with author, 4 December 2014; Fred Weitz, correspondence with author, 18 December 2014; Lisa Grieve, telephone conversation and correspondence with author, 24 February 2015; and Linda Birocci, correspondence with author, 23 February 2015. In addition to the Weitz Building, Essex Meadows Inc. also sold the River Hills theater complex to LCS. A year later, both were purchased by the county and torn down for construction of the Iowa Events Center.

20. David Strutt, telephone conversation.

21. Stan Thurston, interview, Ed Kenny, interview by author, Des Moines, Iowa, 24 November 2014; and Fred Weitz, correspondence with author, 8, 9 December 2014.

22. Ed Kenny, interview; and *ASHA 50: American Seniors Housing Association 2014*, 4, 6, LCS Papers.

23. Glenn DeStigter, interview, 5 December 2014; "The Weitz Company: The Vision to Build 150 Years," 30; Weitz Company v. Craig P. Damos, no. LALC127577, at 5 (Iowa District Court, 13 June 2013) (findings of fact, conclusions of law, and judgment entry); and *Des Moines Register*, 5 April 2006; 16 December 2007; and "The Weitz Company Proxy Statement for Special Meeting of Shareholders to be held November 28, 2012", 55, Glenn DeStigter Papers, private collection held by Glenn DeStigter, Ankeny, Iowa [hereafter cited as DeStigter Papers].

24. Weitz Co. v. Damos, 4; Leonard Martling, interview by author, Des Moines, Iowa, 11 December 2014; DeStigter, interview, 5 December 2014; and "The Weitz Company Proxy Statement for Special Meeting, 55, DeStigter Papers.

25. Weitz Co. v. Damos, 3–4; DeStigter, interview, 5 December 2014; and "The Weitz Company Proxy Statement for Special Meeting," 55, DeStigter Papers.

26. "The Weitz Company Proxy Statement for Special Meeting," 55, DeStigter Papers. Quotation from *Business Record*, 15 February 2013.

27. On Damos being forced out, see *Cityview*, 27 October 2011; *Business Record*, 15February 2013; and *Business Record* online 29 April 2013, http://www.businessrecord.com/Content/Default/1Click/Article/Weitz-countersues-Craig-Damos/-3/248/57829, accessed on 20 January 2015. For Martling's immediate actions as CEO and status of the company, see Leonard Martling, interview; Weitz Co. v. Damos, 6; and "The Weitz Company Proxy Statement for Special Meeting," 55, DeStigter Papers.

28. Leonard Martling, interview; Glenn DeStigter, interview, 5 December 2014; Weitz Co. v. Damos, 6; and *Des Moines Register*, 21 July, 9 September 2012.

29. Weitz Co. v. Damos, 5; *Wall Street Journal*, 5 September 2012; *Des Moines Register*, 6, 11 2012; and Leonard Martling, interview. Martling quote from *Des Moines Register*, 9 September 2012.

30. *Business Record*, 15 February 2013. For more on Trillium Woods deal, see Glenn DeStigter, interview, 5 December 2014; and Ed Kenny, interview. In an issue that ultimately became related to the sale, former CEO Craig Damos had sued the Weitz Company in September 2011, claiming the company paid him less than he deserved under an agreement to repurchase his stock over a five-year period. The stock had been valued at $214 a share in 2009, shortly before Damos resigned, but declined in value in each of the succeeding years. These valuations were done annually by an independent firm, but Damos argued he should be paid $214 per share for his entire block of stock. The court held in favor of the company, saying that the stock payments based on the annual valuations were proper. Damos also claimed that the OCI purchase altered the agreement and asked that his payments be accelerated because of the acquisition. The court also ruled against Damos on that issue. Damos appealed and is awaiting a ruling from the appellate court. Lastly, when OCI bought Weitz, Damos was the only shareholder to refuse the stock purchase price of $75 per share and challenged the method of valuation. In the spring of 2014, the court again found in favor of the company, stating that the actually stock value was less than the amount established by Weitz. Damos appealed and is awaiting a ruling from the appellate court. For more, see David Strutt, correspondence with author, 20 January 2015, and telephone conversation; *Cityview*, 27 October 2011; *Business Record*, 15 February 2013; and *Business Record* online 29 April 2013, http://www.businessrecord.com/Content/Default/1Click/Article/Weitz-countersues-Craig-Damos/-3/248/57829, accessed on 20 January 2015; and Weitz Co. v. Damos.

31. Thomas Schleifer, "Consolidation's Consequences in Construction Services," 5 May 2014, from the ENR.com web page, http://enr.construction.com/opinions/viewpoint/2014/0505-consolidation8217s-consequences-in-construction-services.

asp, accessed on 23 December 2014; *Evansville Courier & Press*, 29 December 2011; http://www.bloomberg.com/apps/news?pid=newsarchive&sid=aBcmCCH2R930; and http://texas.construction.com/texas_construction_news/2010/0101_SpawMaxwell.asp, both accessed on 4 January 2015.

32. Fred's quotation from *Des Moines Register*, 18 September 2013. See also Fred Weitz, interviews, 29 September, 18 December 2014; David Strutt, interview, 15 August 2014.

33. Tousley quote from *Business Record*, 15 February 2013; and for Strutt's quote and views, see David Strutt, interview. See also Leonard Martling, interview; and Leonard Martling business card, in possession of author.

INDEX

Italic page references indicate photographs.

INDEX